ICAS 2019

The Fifteenth International Conference on Autonomic and Autonomous Systems

June 2 - 6, 2019

Athens, Greece

ICAS 2019 Editors

Irina Topalova, FaGEEIM, Technical University Sofia, Bulgaria
Paolo Paoletti, School of Engineering, University of Liverpool, UK

Printed from e-media with permission by:

Curran Associates, Inc.
57 Morehouse Lane
Red Hook, NY 12571

proceedings.com

Some format issues inherent in the e-media version may also appear in this print version.

Printed by Curran Associates, Inc. (2019)

International Academy, Research, and Industry Association (IARIA)
412 Derby Way
Wilmington, DE 19810

Phone: (408) 893-6407
Fax: (408) 527-6351

petre@iaria.org

Additional copies of this publication are available from:

Curran Associates, Inc.
57 Morehouse Lane
Red Hook, NY 12571 USA
Phone: 845-758-0400
Fax: 845-758-2633
Email: curran@proceedings.com
Web: www.proceedings.com

Table of Contents

Manned-Aircraft-Leader, Unmanned-Aircraft-Follower Teaming Architecture 1
Mohammad Sadraey

Evaluating LTL Formulas for On-Board Unmanned Vehicle Health Monitoring 9
Michael Poteat and Yiannis Papelis

Dynamic, Model-based Reconfiguration for Flexible Robotic Assembly Lines 15
Niki Kousi, Christos Gkournelos, Sotiris Aivaliotis, George Michalos, and Sotiris Makris

A Robust Polyurethane Depositing System for Deployment on Disaster Scenario Robotics 21
Alec Burns, Sebastiano Fichera, and Paolo Paoletti

DART Project: A High Precision UAV Prototype Exploiting On-board Visual Sensing 27
Michele Basso, Luca Bigazzi, and Giacomo Innocenti

A Navigational System for Quadcopter Remote Inspection of Offshore Substations 32
Elisabeth Welburn, Hassan Hakim Khalili, Ananya Gupta, Joaquin Carrasco, and Simon Watson

Towards a Methodology to Test UAVs in Hazardous Environments 38
Vincent Page, Matt Webster, Michael Fisher, and Mike Jump

Design of Autonomous Systems for Cybersecurity Threat Detection Using Deep Learning 46
Strahil Sokolov

Transfer Learning Approach for Autonomous Agents in Collective Games 51
Vanya Markova and Ventseslav Shopov

Deep Learning with Evolutionary Strategies for Building Autonomus Agents Beahviour 55
Ventseslav Shopov and Vanya Markova

Adaptive Control of Traffic Congestion with Neuro-Fuzzy based Weighted Random Early Detection 59
Irina Topalova and Pavlinka Radoyska

Organic Self-Adaptable Real-Time Applications 65
Lial Khaluf and Franz-Josef Rammig

Funnel Control for a Class of High-Order Nonlinear Systems 72
Yong-Hua Liu and Chun-Yi Su

Software Architectural Style for Autonomic Cloud Computing 75

Zakarya Alzamil

ICAS 2019

Forward

The Fifteenth International Conference on Autonomic and Autonomous Systems (ICAS 2019), held between June 02, 2019 to June 06, 2019 - Athens, Greece, was a multi-track event covering related topics on theory and practice on systems automation, autonomous systems and autonomic computing.

The main tracks referred to the general concepts of systems automation, and methodologies and techniques for designing, implementing and deploying autonomous systems. The next tracks developed around design and deployment of context-aware networks, services and applications, and the design and management of self-behavioral networks and services. We also considered monitoring, control, and management of autonomous self-aware and context-aware systems and topics dedicated to specific autonomous entities, namely, satellite systems, nomadic code systems, mobile networks, and robots. It has been recognized that modeling (in all forms this activity is known) is the fundamental for autonomous subsystems, as both managed and management entities must communicate and understand each other. Small-scale and large-scale virtualization and model-driven architecture, as well as management challenges in such architectures are considered. Autonomic features and autonomy requires a fundamental theory behind and solid control mechanisms. These topics gave credit to specific advanced practical and theoretical aspects that allow subsystem to expose complex behavior. We aimed to expose specific advancements on theory and tool in supporting advanced autonomous systems. Domain case studies (policy, mobility, survivability, privacy, etc.) and specific technology (wireless, wireline, optical, e-commerce, banking, etc.) case studies were targeted. A special track on mobile environments was indented to cover examples and aspects from mobile systems, networks, codes, and robotics.

Pervasive services and mobile computing are emerging as the next computing paradigm in which infrastructure and services are seamlessly available anywhere, anytime, and in any format. This move to a mobile and pervasive environment raises new opportunities and demands on the underlying systems. In particular, they need to be adaptive, self-adaptive, and context-aware. Adaptive and self-management context-aware systems are difficult to create, they must be able to understand context information and dynamically change their behavior at runtime according to the context. Context information can include the user location, his preferences, his activities, the environmental conditions and the availability of computing and communication resources. Dynamic reconfiguration of the context-aware systems can generate inconsistencies as well as integrity problems, and combinatorial explosion of possible variants of these systems with a high degree of variability can introduce great complexity.

Traditionally, user interface design is a knowledge-intensive task complying with specific domains, yet being user friendly. Besides operational requirements, design recommendations refer to standards of the application domain or corporate guidelines.

Commonly, there is a set of general user interface guidelines; the challenge is due to a need for cross-team expertise. Required knowledge differs from one application domain to another, and the core knowledge is subject to constant changes and to individual perception and skills.

Passive approaches allow designers to initiate the search for information in a knowledge database to make accessible the design information for designers during the design process. Active approaches, e.g., constraints and critics, have been also developed and tested. These mechanisms deliver information (critics) or restrict the design space (constraints) actively, according to the rules and guidelines. Active and passive approaches are usually combined to capture a useful user interface design.

We welcomed academic, research and industry contributions. The conference had the following tracks:

- UNMANNED: Driver-less cars and unmanned vehicles
- Technologies for Real Robotic Autonomy
- Application of Neural Networks in Intelligent Autonomous Systems
- Autonomic computing and self-adaptability

We take here the opportunity to warmly thank all the members of the ICAS 2019 technical program committee, as well as all the reviewers. The creation of such a high quality conference program would not have been possible without their involvement. We also kindly thank all the authors who dedicated much of their time and effort to contribute to ICAS 2019. We truly believe that, thanks to all these efforts, the final conference program consisted of top quality contributions.

We also thank the members of the ICAS 2019 organizing committee for their help in handling the logistics and for their work that made this professional meeting a success.

We hope that ICAS 2019 was a successful international forum for the exchange of ideas and results between academia and industry and to promote further progress in the area of autonomic and autonomous systems. We also hope that Athens, Greece provided a pleasant environment during the conference and everyone saved some time to enjoy the historic charm of the city.

ICAS 2019 Chairs

ICAS Steering Committee

Satoshi Kurihara, University of Electro-Communications, Japan
Ljubo Vlacic, Griffith University, Australia
Roy Sterritt, Ulster University, UK
Mark J. Balas, Embry-Riddle Aeronautical University, USA
Elisabetta Di Nitto, Politecnico di Milano, Italy
Radu Calinescu, University of York, UK
Karsten Böhm, Fachhochschule Kufstein, Austria
Richard Anthony, University of Greenwich, UK
Jacques Malenfant, Sorbonne Université | LIP6 Lab, France
Wladyslaw Homenda, Warsaw University of Technology, Poland
Albert M. K. Cheng, University of Houston, USA

ICAS Industry/Research Advisory Committee

Loris Penserini, Informatica e Società Digitale - IES, Italy
Stefanos Vrochidis, Centre for Research and Technology Hellas - Thermi-Thessaloniki, Greece
Tsuyoshi Ide, IBM T. J. Watson Research Center, USA
Petr Skobelev, Knowledge Genesis Group / Samara Technical University, Russia
Rajat Mehrotra, Intelligent Automation Inc., USA
Andreas Kercek, Lakeside Labs GmbH, Austria
Claudius Stern, biozoom services GmbH - Kassel | FOM University of Applied Sciences - Essen, Germany

ICAS 2019
Committee

ICAS Steering Committee

Satoshi Kurihara, University of Electro-Communications, Japan
Ljubo Vlacic, Griffith University, Australia
Roy Sterritt, Ulster University, UK
Mark J. Balas, Embry-Riddle Aeronautical University, USA
Elisabetta Di Nitto, Politecnico di Milano, Italy
Radu Calinescu, University of York, UK
Karsten Böhm, Fachhochschule Kufstein, Austria
Richard Anthony, University of Greenwich, UK
Jacques Malenfant, Sorbonne Université | LIP6 Lab, France
Wladyslaw Homenda, Warsaw University of Technology, Poland
Albert M. K. Cheng, University of Houston, USA

ICAS Industry/Research Advisory Committee

Loris Penserini, Informatica e Società Digitale - IES, Italy
Stefanos Vrochidis, Centre for Research and Technology Hellas - Thermi-Thessaloniki, Greece
Tsuyoshi Ide, IBM T. J. Watson Research Center, USA
Petr Skobelev, Knowledge Genesis Group / Samara Technical University, Russia
Rajat Mehrotra, Intelligent Automation Inc., USA
Andreas Kercek, Lakeside Labs GmbH, Austria
Claudius Stern, biozoom services GmbH - Kassel | FOM University of Applied Sciences - Essen, Germany

ICAS 2019 Technical Program Committee

Sherif Abdelwahed, Mississippi State University, USA
Lounis Adouane, POLYTECH'Clermont-Ferrand, France
Jose Aguilar, Universidad de Los Andes, Venezuela
Ignacio Alpiste, University of the West of Scotland, UK
Alba Amato, Institute for High-Performance Computing and Networking (ICAR), Napoli, Italy
Razvan Andonie, Central Washington University, USA
Richard Anthony, University of Greenwich, UK
Markus Bader, Technische Universität Wien, Austria
Mark J. Balas, Embry-Riddle Aeronautical University, USA
Stefania Bandini, RCAST - Research Center for Advanced Science & Technology | The University of Tokyo Komaba Campus, Japan
Giovanni Beltrame, Ecole Polytechnique de Montreal, Canada / University of Tübingen, Germany
Julita Bermejo-Alonso, Universidad Politécnica de Madrid (UPM), Spain
Karsten Böhm, Fachhochschule Kufstein, Austria

Radu Calinescu, University of York, UK
Paolo Campegiani, University of Roma Tor Vergata, Italy
Valérie Camps, Paul Sabatier University - IRIT, Toulouse, France
José Manuel Castro Torres, University Fernando Pessoa / LIACC - Artificial Intelligence and Computer Science Laboratory / ISUS - Intelligent Sensing and Ubiquitous Systems, Portugal
Albert M. K. Cheng, University of Houston, USA
Feng Chu, University of Evry, France
Siobhan Clarke, Trinity College Dublin, Ireland
Rem Collier, University College Dublin, Ireland
Stéphanie Combettes, University Paul Sabatier of Toulouse, IRIT Lab, France
Emilio Cruciani, Gran Sasso Science Institute, Italy
Prithviraj (Raj) Dasgupta, University of Nebraska, USA
Giovanni De Magistris, IBM Research AI, Tokyo, Japan
Angel P. del Pobil, Jaume I University, Spain
Elisabetta Di Nitto, Politecnico di Milano, Italy
Sotirios Diamantas, Tarleton State University (Texas A&M), Stephenville, USA
Akif Durdu, Selcuk University, Turkey
Larbi Esmahi, Athabasca University, Canada
Anna Esposito, Seconda Università di Napoli & IIASS, Italy
Thaddeus Eze, University of Chester, UK
Luis Fernando Orleans, Universidade Federal Rural do Rio de Janeiro, Brazil
Hugo Ferreira, INESC TEC / Porto Polytechnic Institute, Portugal
Seyedshams Feyzabadi, Intuitive Surgical Inc., USA
Maurizio Fiasché, Politecnico di Milano, Italy
Manuel Filipe Santos, Universidade do Minho | Research Centre Algoritmi, Portugal
Paolo Fiorini, University of Verona, Italy
Ziny Flikop, Scientist, USA
Stefano Franchi, University of Texas A&M, USA
Matjaz Gams, Jozef Stefan Institute, Slovenia
Fabio Gasparetti, ROMA TRE University, Italy
Marie-Pierre Gleizes, University Paul Sabatier of Toulouse | IRIT, France
Fatemeh Golpayegani, Trinity College Dublin, Ireland
Teodor Lucian Grigorie, Military Technical Academy "Ferdinand I" in Bucharest, Romania
William Grosky, University of Michigan-Dearborn, USA
Jordi Guitart, Universitat Politècnica de Catalunya (UPC), Spain
Maki K. Habib, The American University in Cairo, Egypt
Fei Han, Colorado School of Mines, USA
Cédric Herpson, University Pierre and Marie Curie (UPMC) | LIP6, Paris, France
Gerold Hoelzl, University of Passau, Germany
Wladyslaw Homenda, Warsaw University of Technology, Poland
Wei-Chiang Hong, Jiangsu Normal University, China
Marc-Philippe Huget, Polytech Annecy-Chambery-LISTIC | University of Savoie, France
Jinho Hwang, IBM T.J. Watson Research Center, USA
Tsuyoshi Ide, IBM T. J. Watson Research Center, USA

Konstantinos Ioannidis, Information Technologies Institute - Centre for Research and Technology Hellas, Thessaloniki, Greece
Luis Iribarne, University of Almería, Spain
Reza Javanmard, University of Science and Technology of Mazandaran, Iran
Michael Jenkin, York University, Canada
Richard Jiang, Northumbria University, UK
Kevin Jones, University of Plymouth, UK
Paulo Jorge Sequeira Goncalves, Instituto Politecnico de Castelo Branco, Portugal
Imed Kacem, Université de Lorraine, France
Bilal Kartal, Borealis AI, Edmonton, Alberta, Canada
Alexey M. Kashevnik, St. Petersburg Institute for Informatics and Automation of the Russian Academy of Sciences (SPIIRAS), Russia
Andreas Kercek, Lakeside Labs GmbH, Austria
Pete Khooshabeh, US Army Research Laboratory, USA
Won-jong Kim, Texas A&M University, USA
Ah-Lian Kor, Leeds Beckett University, UK
Timo Korthals, Universität Bielefeld, Germany
Igor Kotenko, St. Petersburg Institute for Informatics and Automation of the Russian Academy of Sciences (SPIIRAS), Russia
Satoshi Kurihara, University of Electro-Communications, Japan
Ouiddad Labbani-Igbida, XLIM CNRS UMR 7252 Institute | ENSIL-ENSCI Engineering School | University of Limoges, France
Diego Latella, Consiglio Nazionale delle Ricerche - Istituto di Scienza e Tecnologie dell'informazione "A. Faedo", Pisa, Italy
Jannik Laval, University of Lyon | DISP Lab, France
Jinoh Lee, Istituto Italiano di Tecnologia (IIT), Italy
Alessandro Leone, National Research Council of Italy | Institute for Microelectronics and Microsystems, Lecce, Italy
Jiaoyang Li, University of Southern California, USA
Noel Lopes, Polytechnic of Guarda, Portugal
Marin Lujak, IMT Lille Douai, France
José Machado, University of Minho, Portugal
Prabhat Mahanti, University of New Brunswick, Canada
Jacques Malenfant, Sorbonne Université | LIP6 Lab, France
Pushparaj Mani Pathak, Indian Institute of Technology, Roorkee, India
Dinesh Manocha, University of North Carolina at Chapel Hill, USA
Jerusa Marchi, Universidade Federal de Santa Catarina, Brazil
Leandro Soriano Marcolino, Lancaster University, UK
Konrad Andrzej Markowski, Warsaw University of Technology, Poland
Goreti Marreiros, Polytechnic of Porto, Portugal
Rajat Mehrotra, Intelligent Automation Inc., USA
René Meier, Lucerne University of Applied Sciences and Arts, Switzerland
Marcio Mendonça, Universidade Tecnológica Federal do Paraná, Brazil
Yasser F. O. Mohammad, KDDI Laboratories, Japan / Assiut University, Egypt

Masayuki Murata, Osaka University Suita, Japan
Adnan Abou Nabout, Bergische Universität Wuppertal, Germany
Kai Nagel, TU Berlin, Germany
Nicol Naidoo, University of KwaZulu-Natal, South Africa
Roberto Nardone, University of Naples Federico II, Italy
Nathalia Nascimento, Catholic University of Rio de Janeiro (PUC-Rio), Brazil
Chrystopher Nehaniv, University of Waterloo, Canada
António J. R. Neves, University of Aveiro, Portugal
Rafael Oliveira Vasconcelos, University Tiradentes (UNIT), Brazil
Flavio Oquendo, IRISA - University of South Brittany, France
Paolo Paoletti, University of Liverpool, UK
Eros Pasero, Politecnico of Turin, Italy / Tongji University, Shanghai, China
Loris Penserini, Informatica e Società Digitale - IES, Italy
Johan Philips, University of Leuven (KU Leuven), Belgium
Francesco Pierri, Universita` degli Studi della Basilicata, Italy
Agostino Poggi, DII - University of Parma, Italy
José Ragot, Université de Lorraine, France
Sazalinsyah Razali, Universiti Teknikal Malaysia Melaka (UTeM), Malaysia
Douglas Rodrigues, University of Sao Paulo (USP), Brazil
Spandan Roy, Indian Institute of Technology Delhi, India
Fariba Sadri, Imperial College London, UK
Lakhdar Sais, CRIL - CNRS, University of Artois, France
Jagannathan Sarangapani, Missouri University of Science and Technology, USA
Jurek Z. Sasiadek, Carleton University, Canada
Alain Servel, Independent Consultant, France
Madhavan Shanmugavel, Monash University Malaysia Campus, Malaysia
Pietro Siciliano, Institute for Microelectronics and Microsystems IMM-CNR, Italy
Fábio Silva, University of Minho, Portugal
Maria Silvia Pini, University of Padova, Italy
Edoardo Sinibaldi, Istituto Italiano di Tecnologia (IIT), Italy
David Sislak, Czech Technical University in Prague, Czech Republic
Petr Skobelev, Knowledge Genesis Group / Samara Technical University, Russia
Antonino Staiano, University of Naples, Parthenope, Italy
Bernd Steinbach, University of Mining and Technology, Freiberg, Germany
Claudius Stern, biozoom services GmbH - Kassel | FOM University of Applied Sciences - Essen, Germany
Roy Sterritt, Ulster University, UK
Chun-Yi Su, Concordia University, Montreal, Canada
Ryszard Tadeusiewicz, AGH University of Science and Technology, Poland
Brahim Tamadazte, FEMTO-ST Institute / CNRS, France
Giorgio Terracina, Università della Calabria, Italy
Guy Theraulaz, Université Paul Sabatier, Toulouse, France
Emanuele Tonucci, IES - Informatica e Società Digitale, Italy
Irina Topalova, Technical University Sofia, Bulgaria

Ali Emre Turgut, Middle East Technical University (METU), Turkey
Paulo Urbano, Universidade de Lisboa, Portugal
Egon L. van den Broek, Utrecht University, The Netherlands
Pierluigi Vellucci, Università di Roma "La Sapienza", Italy
Ramon Vilanova i Arbos, Escola d'Enginyeria - UAB, Spain
Ljubo Vlacic, Griffith University, Australia
Stefanos Vrochidis, Centre for Research and Technology Hellas - Thermi-Thessaloniki, Greece
Yin-Tien Wang, Tamkang University, Taiwan
Zijian Wang, Stanford University, USA
Stephan Weiss, Alpen-Adria Universität Klagenfurt, Austria
Yu Weiwei, Northwestern Polytechnical University, China
Chenxia Wu, Nuro.ai, USA
Wenjun Xu, National University of Singapore, Singapore
Reuven Yagel, Azrieli - Jerusalem College of Engineering, Israel
Linda Yang, University of Portsmouth, UK
Wuu Yang, National Chiao-Tung University, Taiwan
Xin-She Yang, Middlesex University, UK
Mingyi Zhang, Huawei US R&D Research Center, USA
Minghui Zheng, University at Buffalo, USA
Saman Zonouz, Rutgers University, USA

Manned-Aircraft-Leader, Unmanned-Aircraft-Follower Teaming Architecture

Mohammad H. Sadraey
Southern New Hampshire University
Manchester, NH 03106, USA
Email: m.sadraey@snhu.edu

Abstract - **Unmanned Aerial Vehicles (UAVs), due to their remarkable development, relatively low cost, and low risk to human are a prime candidate for the teaming with manned aircraft in performing complex missions. There are various challenges and techniques for manned-unmanned aircraft collaboration. This paper introduces the concept of manned-unmanned aircraft teaming, as well as teaming architecture. The technical requirements for a manned-aircraft-leader, unmanned-aircraft-follower teaming are discussed. In addition, the teaming formulation, teaming laws, and sense-and-avoid system are developed. A particular teaming law and a guidance algorithm for a manned-aircraft-leader, unmanned-aircraft-follower teaming architecture are developed. At the end, the success of the teaming architecture and performance of the sense-and-avoid and guidance systems are examined through various flight simulations.**

Keywords - Manned-Unmanned Teaming; Unmanned Aerial Vehicle; and Sense-And-Avoid.

I. INTRODUCTION

Today's aircraft inventory includes a diverse mix of manned and unmanned systems. Unmanned aerial vehicles are a prime candidate for the teaming with manned aircraft in performing complex/dangerous missions. Unmanned aircraft systems are subject to regulation by the Federal Aviation Administration (FAA) to ensure safety of flight, and safety of people and property on the ground. Incidents involving unauthorized and unsafe use of small, remote-controlled aircraft have risen [16] dramatically. One of the main goals for the manned-unmanned teaming is to provide flexible and safe flight operations. Teaming a UAV system with manned systems will offer advantages to both.

To achieve the full potential of unmanned systems at an affordable cost, efforts must be conducted to implement technologies and evolve tactics, techniques and procedures that improve the teaming of unmanned systems with the manned aircraft. An efficient teaming will create an environment such that both parties operate within their limits, while generating an unachievable goal by one party. The functions of a UAV in a team with manned aircraft depend in nature on the different UAV configurations and their characteristics.

A literature survey has reflected that various technical documents have investigated many aspects of manned-unmanned teaming. Unmanned vehicle systems are being introduced into Army systems to extend manned capabilities and act as “force multipliers” [1]. Jameson et al. [2] have presented the collaborative autonomy for manned/unmanned teams. The researchers in [3] have explored the expansion of the envelope of unmanned aircraft systems operational employment for manned-unmanned teaming. Accuracy assessment of professional grade unmanned systems for high precision airborne mapping is investigated in [4]. Clough et al. [5] have presented a perspective on the autonomous control challenges for UAVs from a researcher's point of view. Autonomous vehicle technologies for small fixed-wing UAVs have been discussed in [6]. There is a number of consequences for UAV design requirements especially on UAV modeling and simulation, some of which have been investigated in [7]. The augmentations, motivations, and directions for aeronautics applications of man–machine integration design and analysis system have been explored in [8].

The researchers in [9] developed new methodologies and quantitative measurements for evaluating human-robot team performance to achieve effective coordination between teams of humans and unmanned vehicles. Significant challenges facing a successful teaming are presented in the next section. A team of a manned aircraft and an UAV in a flight mission is a complex system [10] and requires the approach of multidisciplinary systems engineering. Fundamentals of manned-unmanned aircraft teaming are presented in [17].

In the literature survey, we did not find any publication that fully develops the manned-aircraft-leader, unmanned-aircraft-follower teaming architecture. There is a number on-going research projects by National Aeronautics and Space Administration (NASA) in this area employing various manned aircraft and UAVs. The major contributions of this paper are to provide a model for decision making within the realms of guidance, sense-and-avoid and teaming, as well as to provide a teaming formulation and a teaming law.

The rest of the paper is structured as follows. In Section II, teaming problem formulation including three categories of teaming is presented. The line of sight guidance law to guide the UAV is developed in Section III. The UAV in turning flight has a couple of constraints and limits, these constraints and limits are introduced in Section IV. Collision avoidance is a primary concern in full integration of UAVs with manned aircraft; Section V presents the sense-and-avoid problem. Section VI introduces the manned-aircraft-leader, unmanned-aircraft-follower teaming law. Finally, the success of the teaming architecture and performance of the sense-and-avoid and guidance systems are examined via flight simulations in Section VII. We conclude the paper in in Section VIII.

II. TEAMING PROBLEM FORMULATION

Formulation of manned-unmanned teaming problem basically requires mathematical modeling of UAV flight dynamics, human decision making process, and communication between human and autopilot. Fig. 1 demonstrates the functional block diagram of a teaming flight operation. In principle, there are two independent decision makers: 1. Autopilot for UAV, and 2. Human pilot for the manned aircraft. Moreover, there are two separate trajectories, and two feedbacks. The teaming law creates command for both manned and unmanned aircraft. There is one group of input (mission parameters) and two outputs (i.e., trajectories). Both trajectories are fed back to the same point for comparison with the mission input. Any difference will create an error signal for the teaming law block. The teaming law will generate two signals: one for the pilot of maned aircraft, and one for the autopilot of the UAV.

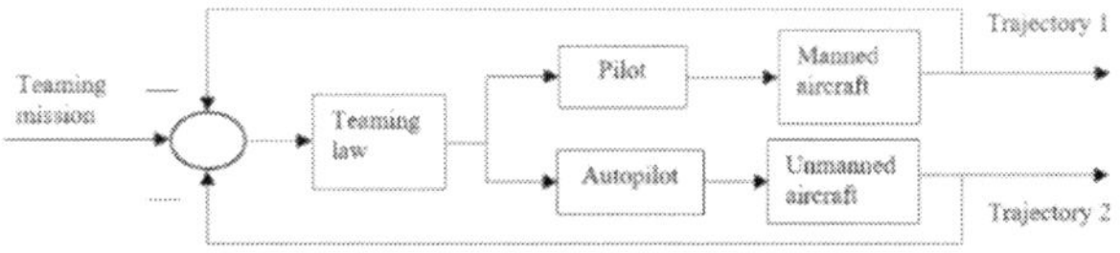

Figure 1. Functional block diagram of a teaming flight operation

Fig. 1 contains information concerning dynamic behavior, but it does not include any information on the physical construction of the team. Each team member has a unique trajectory which is controlled by its controller (one by a pilot, and one by an autopilot). Both UAV and manned aircraft provide a feedback to another team member. The teaming law governs the relationship between team members in conducting a flight team mission. The Guidance, Navigation and Control (GNC) of the UAV is within the autopilot, while the pilot will guide and control the manned aircraft.

The mathematical model of aircraft/UAV (dynamics model), and autopilot have been provided by [12]. In general, there are three categories of teaming, each governed by a distinct law: 1. UAV-leader, manned-aircraft-follower; 2. manned-aircraft-leader, UAV-follower; and 3. mixed leader-follower. This paper is primarily focusing on category 2.

Each teaming case has a number of advantages and disadvantages, and is suited for specific applications and flight missions. For instance, the teaming category 1 (i.e., UAV-leader, manned-aircraft-follower), is appropriate for a flight mission where the operation involves some hazards to human. Two examples for teaming category 1 are: 1. Observing a volcano, 2. Monitoring a target in the enemy zone for a military mission. In such a mission, the UAV takes the lead and the manned aircraft will follow suit. If any hazard arises, the UAV will be the first to face and handle it. This category will guarantee the safety of human plot in the manned aircraft. A pictorial representation of the functions performed by each team member in the category 2 is illustrated in Fig. 2.

The UAV flight parameters are measured by both UAV avionics and manned aircraft measurement devices. Thus, the manned aircraft has two feedbacks; one from the UAV, and one from its own flight. The UAV will fly to accomplish the trajectory as the leader, while the manned aircraft will be guided and controlled based on the teaming law. However, the teaming category 2 is appropriate for a flight mission where the UAV acts as a reserve and no hazard is involved to human pilot. The teaming law for this category may be based on various techniques and guidance laws.

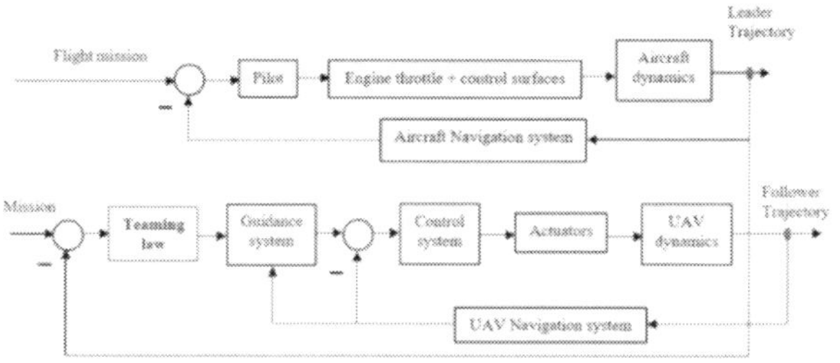

Figure 2. Manned-aircraft-leader, UAV-follower teaming block diagram

In the second category, the manned aircraft flight parameters are measured by both UAV avionics and manned aircraft measurement devices, as well as the pilot's eyes. Thus, the UAV has two feedbacks; one from the manned-aircraft-leader and one from its own flight. The manned aircraft (human pilot) will fly to accomplish the mission trajectory as the leader, while the UAV will be guided and controlled based on the teaming law. The pilot decision making process could be independent from the teaming law, as he/she plays the role of the leader. The mathematical formulations of control systems, guidance systems, and navigation systems are presented by many books and papers including [12].

III. GUIDANCE LAW

The UAV must employ a guidance law to follow the manned aircraft. Guidance is defined as the process of producing a trajectory based on what is received from the command subsystem and the feedback from the navigation system. The guidance subsystem produces the desired states which go to the control subsystem. The output of the guidance subsystem is sent to the control subsystem; based on the guidance law. The control system implements this command through actuators driving control surfaces such as the elevator, aileron, and rudder. Navigation system is mainly responsible for measuring the flight variables including the aircraft's angles, the rate of change of the angles, and the body axis accelerations. The guidance system compares the location of the aircraft with the pre-determined reference trajectory, and modifies the autopilot commands to drive the error to zero. The guidance subsystem often produces an acceleration command. Thus, the guidance subsystem makes the necessary correction to keep the vehicle on course by sending the proper signal to the control system of an autopilot.

The guidance system may be based on categories; for this teaming formation, the Line-Of-Sight (LOS) seems a good fit which satisfies the teaming requirements. The basic principle in LOS guidance law is to guide the UAV on a LOS course in an attempt to keep it on a line joining the target and the ground station (tracking line). For a teaming of two, the line of sight is defined as the line joining the follower UAV and the leader UAV. In addition, the leader UAV is following a moving ground target. For this law, the target-tracking radar acquires the target shortly after take-off and then guides the UAV into the beam of the target-tracking radar. For the guidance command, the actual distance from the tracking line to the UAV is required.

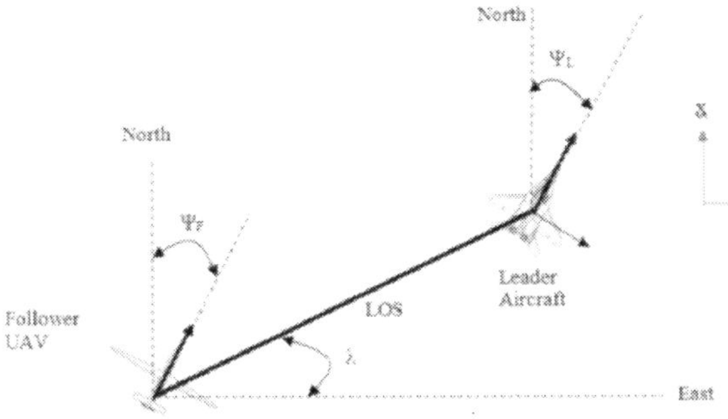

Figure 3. Line-Of-Sight (Top view)

An imaginary line between the follower-UAV to the leader UAV is referred to as line-of-sight. The line of sight angle (λ) is determined by forming a right triangle, when putting follower UAV and target, each at a corner. Then, the hypotenuse is along the line of sight. The line of sight angle is calculated by trigonometry from Fig. 3 as:

$$\lambda = tan^{-1}\left(\frac{y_T - y_U}{x_T - x_U}\right) \tag{1}$$

where x_T and x_U represent the distance between target and UAV to a reference line along x-axis, and y_T and y_U represent the distance between target and UAV to a reference line along y-axis. If the reference is selected to be at the UAV location, both y_U and x_U will be zero. The instantaneous distance between UAV and the target will be:

$$D_{TU} = \sqrt{(y_T - y_U)^2 + (x_T - x_U)^2} \tag{2}$$

The closing velocity (V_c) - the negative rate of change of separation between UAV and target - is obtained [11] by:

$$V_c = \frac{-\left(V_{TUx}(x_T - x_U) + V_{TUy}(y_T - y_U)\right)}{D_{TU}} \tag{3}$$

where V_{TUx} and V_{TUy} are components of the relative velocity and are given by

$$V_{TUx} = \dot{x}_T - \dot{x}_U \tag{4}$$

$$V_{TUy} = \dot{y}_T - \dot{y}_U \tag{5}$$

The instantaneous line-of-sight rate is computed by taking the derivative of the equation 1, which leads to:

$$\dot{\lambda} = \frac{V_{TUy}(x_T - x_U) - V_{TUx}(y_T - y_U)}{D_{TU}^2} \tag{6}$$

In the line-of-sight guidance law, the velocity of the follower UAV (V_n) perpendicular to the LOS should be equal to the LOS rate at that point. It is assumed that the LOS value is available from the use of onboard sensors (e.g., radar).

$$V_n = D_{TU}\dot{\lambda} \tag{7}$$

where $\dot{\lambda}$ is the rate of change of the line of sight angle, and D_{TU} denotes the distance between the follower UAV and the target or leader UAV. Moreover, V_n is velocity of the follower UAV perpendicular to the LOS. Hence, the guidance command is perpendicular to the line of sight. The guidance system output in xy plane (V_C) may be readily converted to a sideslip angle (β) command to control system. There is a relationship between this speed (i.e., in y-direction) and sideslip angle as:

$$\beta = \frac{V_n}{V_{oU}} \tag{8}$$

where V_{oU} is the initial UAV airspeed. So, the follower UAV is guided so as to remain on the commanded LOS. As soon as the follower UAV is reached to the commanded circle around the target and stabilized, the guidance system will be activated to guide the aircraft such that to keep a constant line-of-sight angle. The LOS variables are available in both manned and unmanned aircraft from the use of onboard vision sensors. The guidance equations derived for the xy plane. However, similar governing equations are derived and used in xz plane.

IV. Maneuverability Constraints

One of the basic maneuvers to make a flight smooth, and to correct the line of sight, is to turn around to follow the leader UAV. A turning flight has a couple of constraints, including: 1. Maximum turn rate (ω_{max}), 2. Minimum turn radius (R_{min}), 3. Maximum load factor (n_{max}), 4. Minimum and maximum airspeed (V_{min}, V_{max}), 5. Maximum bank angle (ϕ_{max}). The following set of equations governs the relation between parameters of a turning flight. The load factor is a function of bank angle. The maximum allowable bank angle is limited by the load factor:

$$\phi_{max} = \cos^{-1}\left(\frac{1}{n_{max}}\right) \tag{9}$$

The turn radius (R) and turn rate (ω) are functions of airspeed (V), and load factor (n):

$$R = \frac{V^2}{g\sqrt{n^2 - 1}} \tag{10}$$

$$\omega = \frac{g\sqrt{n^2 - 1}}{V} \tag{11}$$

The stall speed during a turn is a function of bank angle:

$$V_{s_t} = \sqrt{\frac{2mg}{\rho S C_{L_{max}} \cos(\phi)}} \tag{12}$$

where S denotes the wing area, m the UAV mass, ρ the air density, and C_{Lmax} the UAV maximum lift coefficient.
When the theoretical airspeed corresponding to the minimum turn is less than the stall speed, the UAV has to turn with the corner speed (V^*):

$$V^* = \left[\frac{2n_{max}W}{\rho S C_{L_{max}}}\right]^{\frac{1}{2}} \tag{13}$$

Moreover, a turn must be coordinated in order to keep the radius of turn constant. For the requirements of a coordinated turn, you may refer to references, such as [3]. The trajectory smoother must take into account all of these performance constraints to convert an initial path into a smooth trajectory.

V. Sense and Avoid

Collision avoidance is a primary concern and a critical challenge in full integration of unmanned aircraft systems. One of the major limitations to the widespread use of unmanned vehicles in teaming with manned aircraft has been the detect-and-avoid problem. When a group of UAVs (e.g., three Reapers) are following a manned aircraft (e.g., F/A-18), a sense-and-avoid system will be needed to prevent collision between UAVs.

In general, there are five functions required in a sense-and-avoid system: 1. Detect the intruder/obstacle, 2. Track, 3. Evaluate, 4. Calculation, 5. Command, 6. Execute. There is currently a large amount of research projects [16] being conducted in the area of sense-and-avoid. In selecting a surveillance system, a number of factors should be evaluated. They are range, timeliness (update rate), field of view, simplicity, cost, design challenge, reliability, accuracy, size, weight, technology level, flexibility, and integration.

When a conflict resolution algorithm is feasible, various guidance laws may be employed for a collision avoidance. For instance, the proportional navigation guidance with a proportional navigation constant less than one (i.e., $N < 1$). In such case, the UAV will be turning slower than the LOS, thus continuously falling behind the target (i.e., another aircraft). Another appropriate guidance law for a collision avoidance (as in a formation flight) is the line of sight guidance law. This law may be implemented by assuming the goal (i.e., target) of the follower UAV to be constantly at a desirable distance behind or at the side of the leader UAV. This paper is mainly focusing on the sense-and-avoid system of one UAV to follow a manned aircraft.

VI. Teaming Law

In order to begin the synthesis of the teaming law, the design requirements relative to both parties must be technically established. Based on handling qualities [14], and also airworthiness standards [15], the following items are typical design requirements to be used in the design process: cost, stability of the overall teaming system; output (or state tracking) performance; accuracy from command to response; overshoot; steady state error; rise time; and settling time. In addition, the law must be robust with respect to aircraft type, communication elements, and mission.

A fully autonomous UAV should be capable of trajectory tracking, defined as tracking a time-parameterized reference. However, for trajectory tracking there exist fundamental performance limitations that cannot be overcome by any control system. Moreover, to meet temporal specifications, the airspeed profile often needs to be controlled independently. To overcome this challenge, temporal constraints are not frequently imposed in path-following problems, and the vehicle is allowed to converge to and follow a path without imposing any temporal specifications. This will result in a smoother convergence to the path, and the control signals are less likely to be saturated. This approach must also avoid collision in multi-vehicle cooperative missions.

In a path following problem, the designer is required to design an algorithm for a given path satisfying the given bounds such that the generalized error converges to a neighborhood of the zero. There are fundamental principles which govern an efficient teaming law; some of which are presented in this section. As the most important principle, the safety of the manned aircraft (in fact, the human pilot) is of much higher priority compared with the UAV airworthiness. Thus, the collision avoidance and sense or detect are two primary concerns to teaming success. Moreover, when the leader aircraft is out of sight of the follower, the follower aircraft must circle around to detect the leader.

The teaming law is established based on three fundamental principles: 1. Keep the UAV at a line of sight, 2. Keep UAVs at a safe distance from the leader aircraft and each other, 3. Each team member should fly within its safe flight envelope. Sections IV, V, and VI provide the concept and governing equations for each principle. The guidance system will generate a command for the control system to maintain the LOS. Ref. [20] has presented a modeling and decentralized control for the multiple UAVs formation based on Lyapunov design.

The sense-and-avoid system subsystem should make the necessary correction to keep the follower UAV at a safe distance (D_{TU}) from leader aircraft (i.e., target) by sending the proper signal to the control system.

$$C_1 \le D_{TU} \le C_2 \tag{14}$$

In addition, the sense-and-avoid subsystem should make the necessary correction to keep the follower UAVs at a safe distance (D_{UU}) from each other.

$$C_3 \le D_{UU} \le C_4 \tag{15}$$

The C_1, C_2, C_3, and C_4, are constant values and are given by the designer. These constants are functions of many factors including UAV vision sensor features, the UAV maneuverability, weather conditions, and flight altitude. When the UAV is at a safe distance (D_{TU}) from the leader aircraft, it must follow every flight maneuver of the leader aircraft. The only difference is that every maneuver is performed by the follower UAV after a time delay (T_d), which is the ratio of the safe distance (D_{TU}) to the target speed (U_T):

$$T_d = \frac{D_{TU}}{U_T} \tag{16}$$

For two reasons of 1. UAV airworthiness, and 2. Successful payload application (e.g., aerial photography); the trajectory must be smooth. A well-designed smooth trajectory has ideally no abrupt and significant changes on the movement of the UAV. The trajectory smoother should apply changes to make the assigned trajectory kinematically feasible in terms of constraints.

A limitation of this algorithm is that the trajectory is composed of a number of time-stamped curves, which specify the desired location of the UAV at a specified time.

Tracking the movement state estimation of an UAV basically concerns inferring the latent state of interest based on discrete time series noisy observations. The time of interest may be the past (namely, smoothing), the present (tracking) or the future (forecasting).

VII. Simulation

Two sets of simulations are presented to demonstrate the efficacy of the proposed algorithm and teaming law: 1. A UAV is following a manned aircraft in longitudinal plane (i.e., xz), 2. A UAV is following a maneuvering manned aircraft in the xy plane (i.e., turning flight). In the first simulation, the UAV (as the follower) with a conventional configuration, has a wing span of 20 m, length of 15 m, a stall speed of 70 knot, and a maximum speed of 250 knot. Moreover, the manned aircraft (as the leader), with a conventional configuration has a wing span of 15 m, length of 12 m, a stall speed of 100 knot, and a maximum speed of 400 knot. For this formation flight, the UAV is required to stay behind and follow the manned aircraft and keep a safe distance. The distance between the UAV and the manned aircraft should be between 100 to 120 meters. Hence,

$$100\,m < D_{TU} < 120\,m$$

Next, the UAV is required to follow a random trajectory (as if a manned aircraft is flying/leading) to simulate a manned-unmanned aircraft teaming flight. For this mission, the UAV is required to stay behind the manned aircraft at a safe distance. For the initial conditions, the leader aircraft is flying at a constant altitude with a velocity of 130 knot. The follower UAV is right behind the manned aircraft with a distance of 200 m, and an initial velocity of 120 knot. The UAV performance limits and constraints are tabulated in Table 1.

TABLE 1. UAV PERFORMANCE LIMITS AND CONSTRAINTS

No	Parameter	Value	Remarks
1	Maximum load factor	2	Structural limit
2	Maximum bank angle	60 deg	Structural limit
3	Maximum airspeed	250 knot	Engine limits
4	Minimum airspeed	1.2 V_s	Airworthiness, stall
5	Maximum bank angle	60 deg	Structural limit, camera view
6	Maximum possible turn rate	20 deg/sec	Fastest turn limit
7	Minimum turn radius	50 m	Tightest turn limit

A linear state-space dynamic model for both the manned aircraft and the UAV have been employed. For both vehicles, typical stability and control derivatives for a dynamically stable vehicle are utilized.

$$\dot{x} = Ax + Bu \qquad (17)$$
$$y = Cx + Du$$

The A, B, C, and D matrices are generated by a matlab code. The four state-variables are airspeed (V), climb angle (γ), heading angle (ψ), and sideslip angle (β). Furthermore, four control-variables are throttle (δ_T), elevator (δ_E), aileron (δ_A), and rudder (δ_R). Thus, the state variables are: $x = [V, \gamma, \psi, \beta]^T$ and input variables are $u = [\delta_T, \delta_E, \delta_A, \delta_R]^T$.

Four PID control laws (one for each controller) are employed for controlling the UAV in the three dimensional space. A Simulink model (Fig. 9) is developed to model all subsystems of both the follower UAV and the leader manned aircraft including LOS, navigation, guidance and control systems.

A. LONGITUDINAL FLIGHT TEAMING

The first simulation is to examine a team of one follower UAV and a manned leader aircraft in a 50 second longitudinal flight maneuver (cruise/climb/cruise). The leader aircraft will cruise for 20 seconds, and then, climb to 100 meters in another 20 seconds.

Fig. 4 shows velocities, distance, and heights of UAV and manned aircraft for this teaming flight operation. The top Figure shows the velocities of UAV and manned aircraft, and the middle Figure demonstrates the heights of UAV and manned aircraft. The bottom Figure illustrates the distance between UAV and manned aircraft. As the Fig. 5 demonstrates, the follower UAV is perfectly following the leader aircraft, and performs every flight operation by a delay of 1.5 seconds.

As the simulation results indicate, the UAV accelerates in the beginning to reduce the distance of 200 m to the desired value of 100 m. Then, it will keep the velocity equal to the velocity of the leader aircraft. Due to the desired distance of 100 m, and the velocity of the leader aircraft (130 knot), the time delay is about 1.5 seconds (i.e., 100/(130×0.5144)).

Fig. 5 illustrates the elevator deflections and throttle settings of the UAV for this teaming flight operation. The initial elevator angle is -2 deg, but during the flight, it varies to maintain the longitudinal trim. The initial throttle setting is 20 deg, but during the flight, it varies to maintain the forward velocity.

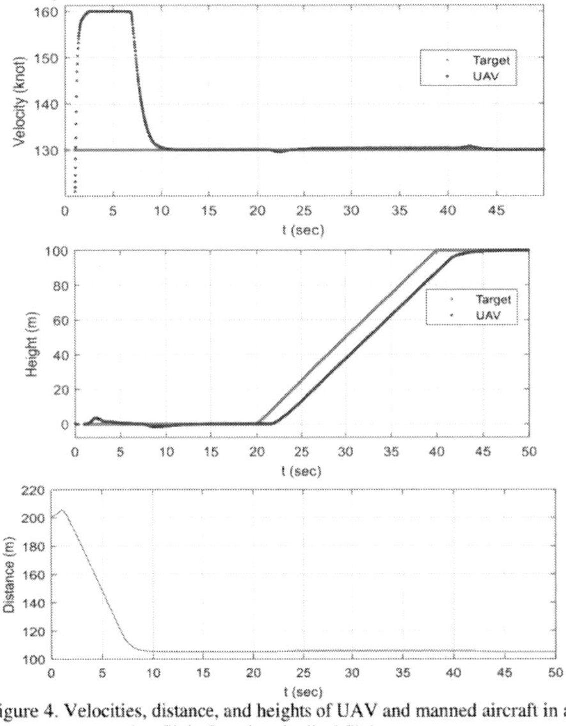

Figure 4. Velocities, distance, and heights of UAV and manned aircraft in a teaming flight for a longitudinal flight maneuver

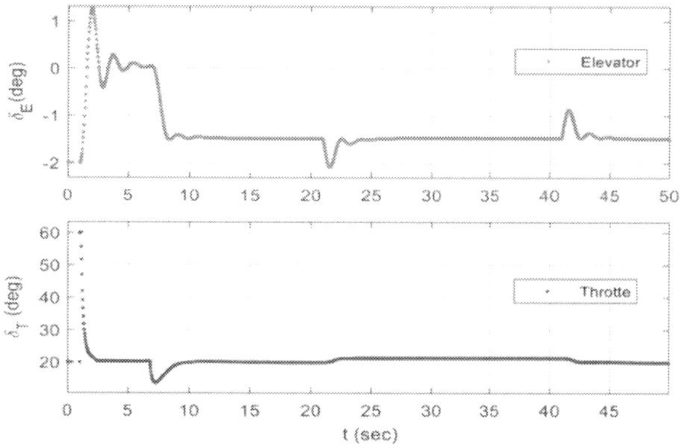

Figure 5. Elevator deflections and throttle settings of the UAV in a teaming flight for a longitudinal flight maneuver

Both UAV elevator and engine throttle are varying to change the velocity and altitude to follow the manned leader aircraft.

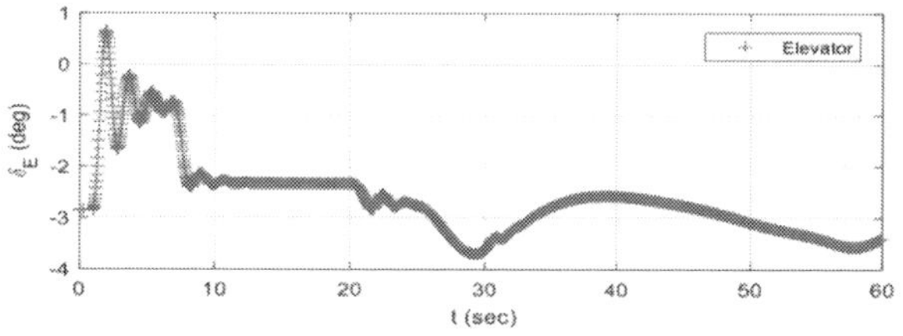

a. Elevator deflections

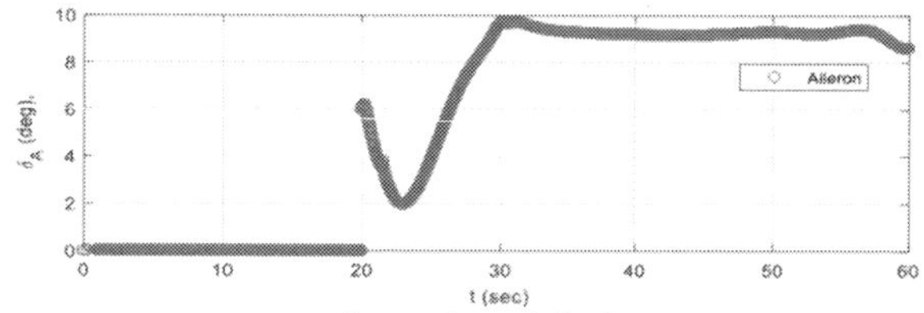

b. Aileron deflections

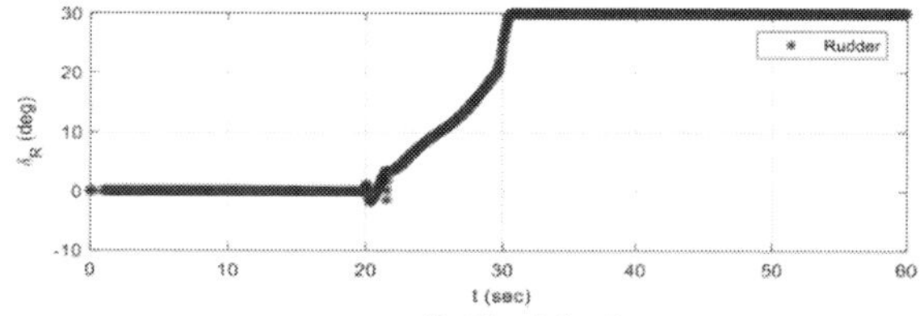

c. Rudder deflections

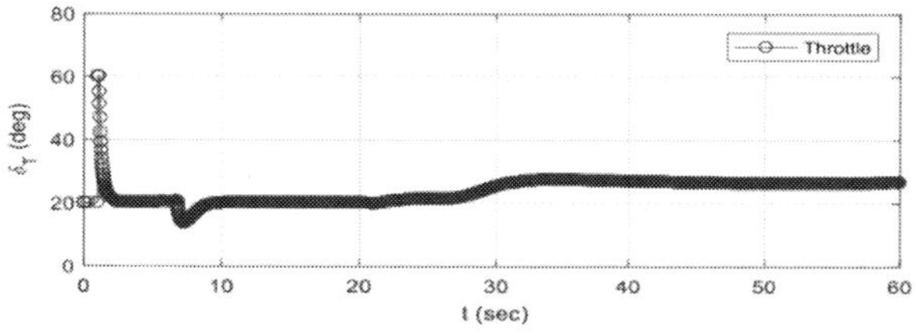

d. Throttle setting

Figure 6. Control surfaces of UAV in a teaming flight for a turning flight maneuver

B. Turning Flight Teaming

The second simulation is to examine a team of one follower UAV and a manned leader aircraft in a 60 second turning (lateral-directional) flight. The leader aircraft will cruise for 20 seconds, and then, have a 360 level turn to the left (one full turn in 40 seconds). Fig. 6 shows control surfaces (i.e., elevator, aileron, and rudder) deflections and throttle settings of the UAV in a teaming flight for a turning flight maneuver.

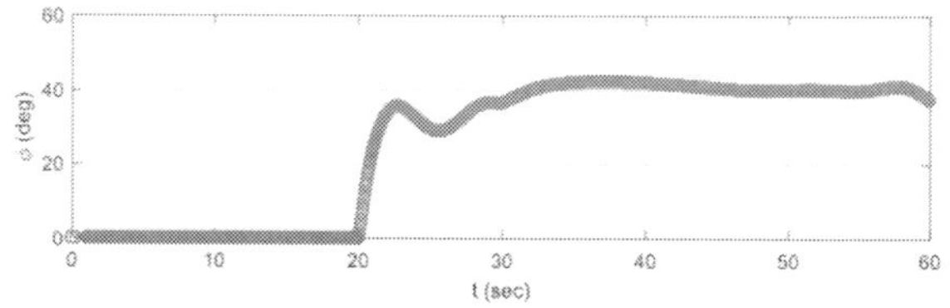

a. Bank angle

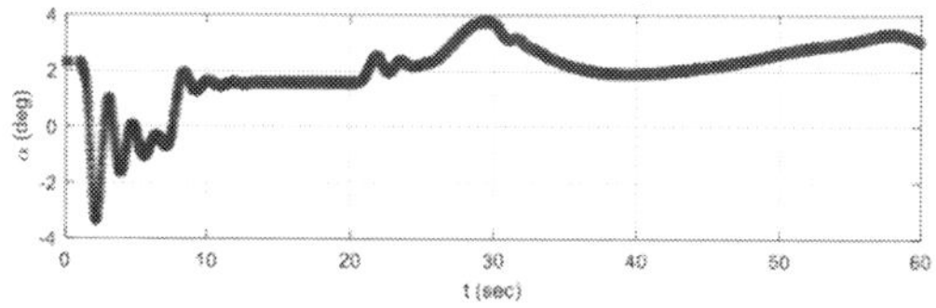

b. Angle of attack

Figure 7. Control surfaces and flight parameters of UAV in a teaming flight for a turning flight maneuver

The UAV accelerates in the beginning to reduce the distance of 200 m to the desired value of 100 m. Then, it will decelerate to keep the velocity equal to the velocity of the leader aircraft.

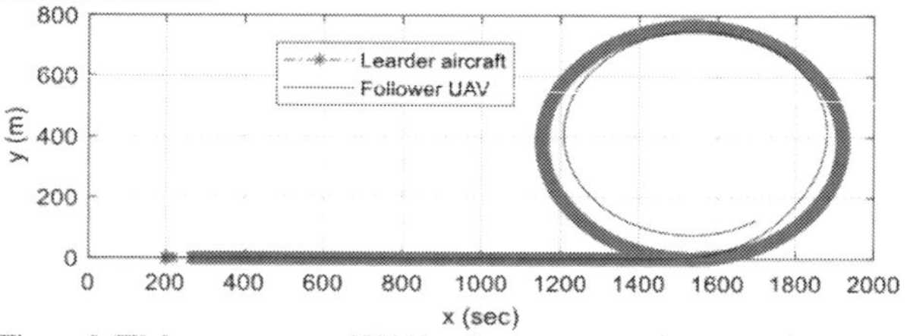

Figure 8. Flight parameters of UAV and manned aircraft in a teaming flight for a turning flight

During the turn, the UAV bank angle is about 40 degrees (Fig. 7), while the angle of attack is about 3 degrees. Fig. 8 illustrates the flight path of both UAV and leader aircraft. As the Figure demonstrates, the follower UAV is perfectly following the leader aircraft, and performs every flight operation by a delay of 1.5 seconds.

As the flight simulations indicate, both teaming operations are successful, and the UAV is tracking and following the manned aircraft for both longitudinal and direction flight maneuvers. In both flight missions, the UAV continuously keeps a distance of 100 m from leader aircraft to avoid a collision. In all flight motions, the UAV maneuverability constraints were observed, and the UAV did not fly beyond the flight envelope.

The simulation employs a UAV linear state-space dynamic model with four PID controllers. However, in reality, the dynamics of a UAV is nonlinear. Moreover, other control laws (e.g., robust nonlinear) may offer better outcomes. The objective of the paper is to present the fundamentals of the teaming technique with an application. This technique may employ UAV nonlinear model with more complex control laws. Each dynamic model and each control law has unique advantages and disadvantages. The current application is simple and efficient, but may not handle nonlinearities.

VIII. CONCLUSION AND FUTURE WORK

This paper explores the manned-aircraft-leader, unmanned-aircraft-follower teaming architecture. There are various challenges and techniques for manned-unmanned aircraft collaboration. This paper develops the concept of manned-unmanned aircraft teaming, as well as teaming architecture. The technical requirements for a manned-aircraft-leader, unmanned-aircraft-follower teaming are discussed. In addition, the teaming formulation, teaming laws, and sense-and-avoid system are presented. A particular teaming law and a guidance algorithm for manned-aircraft-leader, unmanned-aircraft-follower teaming architecture are developed.

At the end, the efficacy of the teaming architecture and performance of the sense-and-avoid/guidance systems are examined through formation flight simulations. The simulation results confirm that the suggested teaming law is applicable and efficient in following the flight team mission and in avoiding any obstacle. In future, the teaming law will be redesigned to improve the efficiency of the team. Moreover, the future work will include a team of three UAVs to follow a manned aircraft in 3d flight maneuvers.

REFERENCES

[1] A. Freedy, E. DeVisser, G. Weltman, and N. Coeyman, "Measurement of trust in human-robot collaboration", International Symposium on Collaborative Technologies and Systems, 0-9785699-1-1, IEEE, 2007.

[2] S. Jameson, J. Franke, R. Szczerba, and S. Stockdale, "Collaborative Autonomy for Manned/Unmanned Teams", American Helicopter Society, 61th Annual Forum, Grapevine, TX, June 1-3, 2005.

[3] S. J. Gaydos and I. P. Curry, "Manned-Unmanned Teaming: Expanding the Envelope of UAS Operational Employment", Journal of Aviation, Space, and Environmental Medicine, Vol. 85, No. 12, December 2014.

[4] M. M. R. Mostafa, "Accuracy Assessment of Professional Grade Unmanned Systems for High Precision Airborne Mapping", ISPRS Archives of the Photogrammetry, Remote Sensing and Spatial Information Sciences, Presented at the UAVg 2017, Bonn, Germany, September 4 – 7, 2017.

[5] M. Clough and T. Bruce, "Unmanned Aerial Vehicles: Autonomous Control Challenges, A Researcher's Perspective", Journal of Aerospace Computing, Information, and Communication, 1542-9423, Vol. 2, No. 8, 2005.

[6] R. W. Beard et al., "Autonomous Vehicle Technologies for Small Fixed-Wing UAVs," Journal of Aerospace Computing, Information, and Communication, 1542-9423, Vol. 2, No. 1, 2005.

[7] H. Friehmelt, "Some Consequences of UAV Design Requirements Especially on UAV Modeling and Simulation", AIAA-2003-5688, AIAA Modeling and Simulation Technologies Conference and Exhibit, Austin, Texas, Aug. 11-14, 2003.

[8] B. F. Gore, "Man–machine integration design and analysis system, V5: Augmentations, motivations, and directions for aeronautics applications", In P. C. Cacciabu, M. Hjalmdahl, A. Luedtke, & C. Riccioli, Human modelling in assisted transportation, Heidelberg, Germany, Springer, pp. 43–54, 2010.

[9] E. DeVisser, R. Parasuraman, A. Freedy, E. Freedy, and G. Weltman, "A Comprehensive Methodology for Assessing Human-Robot Team Performance for Use in Training and Simulation", Proceedings of the Human Factors and Ergonomics Society Annual Meeting, October 2006, Vol. 50.

[10] B. S. Blanchard, and W. J. Fabrycky, "Systems Engineering and Analysis", Fourth Edition, Prentice Hall, 2006.

[11] P. Zarchan, "Tactical and Strategic Missile Guidance", 6th Ed., American Institute of Aeronautics and Astronautics, Reston, VA, 2013.

[12] B. L. Stevens, F. L. Lewis, and E. L. Johnson, "Aircraft Control and Simulation: Dynamics, Controls Design, and Autonomous Systems", 3rd ed., John Wiley, 2015.

[13] C. Kaufman, R. Perlman, and M. Speciner; "Network Security: Private Communication in a Public World", 2nd Edition, Prentice Hall, 2002.

[14] MIL-STD-1797A, "Flying Qualities of Piloted Aircraft", Department of Defense Interface Standard, 2004

[15] US Department of Transportation, Federal Aviation Administration (www.faa.gov), "FAR 23, FAR 25", retrieved: Feb. 2019.

[16] P. Angelov and P. Angelov, "Sense and Avoid in UAS: Research and Applications", Wiley, 2012.

[17] M. Sadraey, "Manned-Unmanned Aircraft Teaming", International IEEE Aerospace Conference, Big Sky, Montana, March 3-10 2018.

[18] M. A. Goodrich and R. W. Bear, "Semi-Autonomous Human-UAV Interfaces for Fixed-Wing Mini-UAVs", Brigham Young University, 2004.

[19] V. Cichella, et al., "A 3D Path-Following Approach for a Multirotor UAV on SO(3)", 2nd IFAC Workshop on Research, Education and Development of Unmanned Aerial Systems, Compiegne, France, November 20-22, 2013.

[20] H. Zhicheng, F. Isabelle, and Z. Arturo, "Modeling and Decentralized Control for the Multiple UAVs Formation based on Lyapunov design and redesign", 2nd IFAC Workshop on Research, Education and Development of Unmanned Aerial Systems, Compiegne, France, November 20-22, 2013.

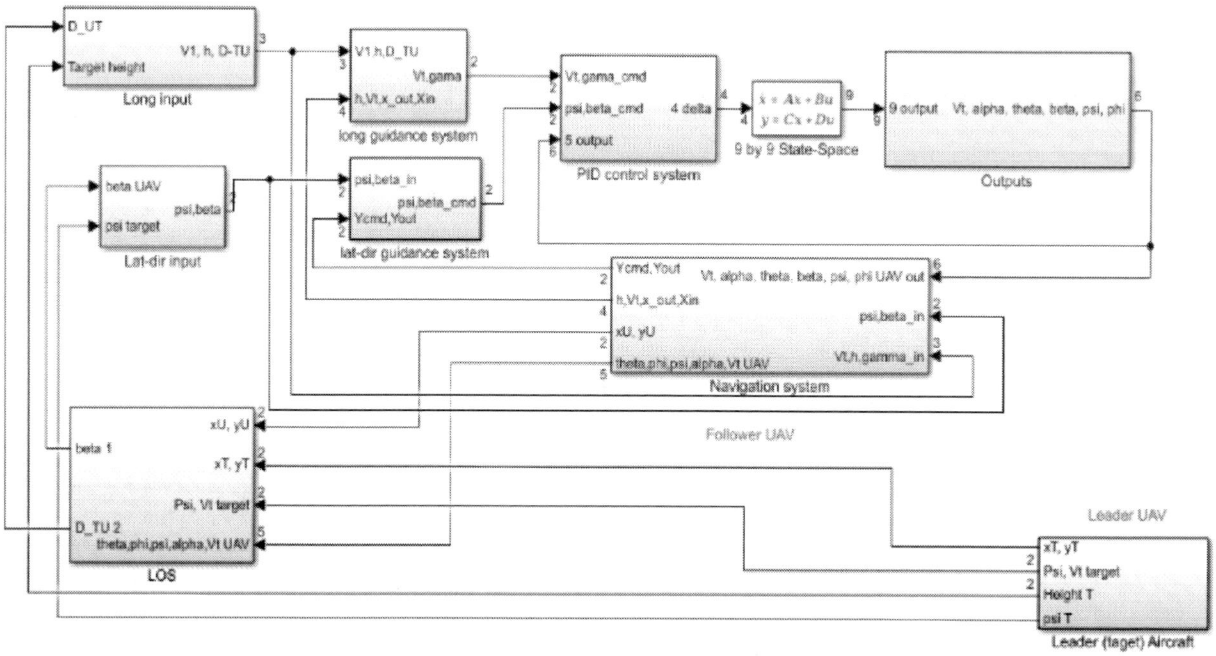

Figure 9. Simulink model for subsystems of the follower UAV and the leader manned aircraft

Evaluating LTL Formulas for On-Board Unmanned Vehicle Health Monitoring

Michael Poteat

Modeling, Simulation, and Visualization Engineering
Old Dominion University
Norfolk, VA, United States
Email: me@mpote.at

Yiannis Papelis

Virginia Modeling, Analysis and Simulation Center
Old Dominion University
Suffolk, VA, United States
Email: ypapelis@odu.edu

Abstract—**The proliferation of unmanned vehicle technologies has drastically increased their use in multiple domains. In the maritime domain, unmanned surface vehicles often pose special requirements for on-board health monitoring and fault mitigation due to long endurance, which increases the likelihood of failures when operating without human oversight. Whereas such vehicles can be equipped with numerous on-board sensors, detecting actual or impending failures is often more complicated than simply thresholding values of a sensor reading. In this paper, we will consider the use of Linear Temporal Logic (LTL) as a means to specify and then evaluate in real-time, the health status of an unmanned surface vehicle. This is accomplished by capturing nominal conditions in LTL formulas and then evaluating these formulas in real-time. The advantage of LTL is that it allows capturing value-based as well as time-based expectations for sensor readings when evaluating system status. We define a formal language which is an extension of LTL, and a corresponding software evaluation method with bounded performance. An example demonstration of the feasibility of the process is presented.**

Keywords–Linear Temporal Logic; safety; logic; model checking

I. Introduction

Monitoring the on-board status of unmanned maritime vehicles can prove challenging, for many reasons. Maritime vehicles operate in a relatively difficult environment in which debris, water spray, corrosion and other factors can degrade the performance of the system in ways that are not always immediately apparent. Furthermore, the use of automatic controllers often hides the onset of problems by compensating for such errors. Addressing such issues is often done by installing sensors that monitor for error conditions; however, there are difficulties in properly interpreting their readings. For example, consider an engine temperature gauge with a pre-set maximum safe limit. Shutting down the system based on that reading alone runs the risk of making an incorrect choice should the gauge itself fail and provide erroneous readings. A different but equally problematic scenario is gauge failure that displays a nominal temperature even though the actual temperature exceeds the safe limit. Because of the propensity of individual sensor failures, it is necessary the cross reference multiple sensor readings over time before making a determination of a fault. When under human supervision, sensor information is typically aggregated by the vehicle and transmitted to a monitoring/control station that displays all sensor readings, pushing the responsibility for making fault assessments and evaluating mission readiness to the human operator. Not only is this a difficult task for a human, but it is not transferable to unsupervised operations during which a vehicle must be able to make a determination of its ability to accomplish its mission autonomously.

Our approach is based on using Linear Temporal Logic (LTL) formulas Section III as a means of capturing nominal performance of the overall system. One advantage of LTL over other approaches is that LTL can capture the element of time in addition to fixed-in-time reading. Use of LTL formulas hence allows evaluating the behavior of the system over time and assessing if it operates within nominal parameters based on richer information when compared to point-in-time sensor readings. A key contribution of the paper is an efficient approach to evaluating the LTL formulas allowing their evaluation to be performed on-board the unmanned vessel.

The remaining of the paper is organized as follows: Section II overviews related work, Section III describes the LTL formalism in general and the specific portion used in our proposed system. Section IV outlines the method by which LTL formulas are evaluated in real-time based on sensor readings. Section V presents a test case of using LTL formulas to identify a nuanced failure in a maritime unmanned system and Section VI concludes.

II. Related Work

LTL has been used to model correctness properties of low-level software programs [1] and robotic motion planning [2] [3]. Safety properties can be falsified but not proved in general, as in sufficiently complex systems these statements are undecidable [4]. In practice, this is avoided by using a *bounded* variant of LTL known as metric temporal logic. This has been used to find the trajectory of safety properties over time [5]. Effectively, the decidability problem is avoided by evaluating safety expressions on a single system trajectory (i.e., a *trace*) in real-time.

On-board fault detection is also accomplished by using Bayesian networks [6], which consider the probability of the actual fault event as well as the reliability of the sensor, and thus makes a probabilistic estimate of a fault based on multiple sensor readings. One drawback is that a priori probability estimates of faults are needed, as well as relative sensor reliability weightings.

Another common approach for safety monitoring is the "residual method", whereby a real-time simulated version of the system is compared against the real system [7]. The residual (e.g., squared error) between the simulated and real system is computed; if the residual is too large, this indicates that some non-optimal state has been reached. A drawback of the residual approach is that you must model the system, and any errors in doing so, whether arising from system complexity or computational difficulty, may lead to false-positives. As well, it is not obvious how one would in general detect the exact problem that has occured solely from the residual, and indeed that problem has been an area of active research.

Our implementation is an alternative to both the residual and Bayesian methods, whereby one explicitly specifies invariants of how system variables must temporally relate to one another. In this "LTL approach", an explicit system model or simulation is not necessary, allowing it to be applied to systems intractable or uneconomic to explicitly model.

III. LTL Overview

LTL is essentially a generalization of Boolean logic, which adds a capability to model "propositions whose truth or falsity may depend on time" [8]. Practically, this adds a number of operators which specify temporal relationships between propositions. One way of thinking about temporal logic is that unlike first-order logic, it operates on countably infinite ordered sets [9] (i.e., sequences). In convention with the literature, we use the term *trace* to refer to these sequences, and the term *finite trace* when the sequence in question has finite size.

Since LTL is a generalization of Boolean logic, it inherits by default all of the common logical connectives intrinsic to that logic, which are enumerated by Table I. The so-called "application syntax" refers to the form used in application, chosen due to programming convention, as opposed to the symbolic form used in presentation of this document.

TABLE I. Common Logical Connectives

Operator	*Symbol*	*Application Syntax*
Not	$\neg p$	`!p`
And	$p \wedge q$	`p && q`
Or	$p \vee q$	`p || q`

In that predicate logic models quantification (e.g., $\forall$, $\exists$), temporal logic models temporal relationships (e.g., A:, E:).The best way to understand the LTL formalism is by example. The arguably simplest temporal operation is A:(p), such that p is an arbitrary boolean proposition with values across time (i.e., a trace). This expression is read as "always", and simply specifies that p is always true across the trace. Figure 1 shows a case where A:(p) evaluates to true or false, respectively. In the first example, A:(p) evaluates to false because there exists a time in the past where p was false. In the second example, A:(q) evaluates to true for the opposite reason.

The second most basic operator is E:(p), which is the dual of A:(p). It is read as "eventually", and has much the same mathematical meaning: E:(p) is true if p was true at any point in time. These two operators are dual due to the relation $\neg$A:$(p) \Leftrightarrow$ E:$(\neg p)$. This should make intuitive sense: p was not always true if, and only if, there was a point at which p was false. That operator relationship is a salient similarity between temporal and first-order logic. In much the same way, Figure 2 exemplifies a set of traces where E:(p) evaluates to true or false, respectively.

The full set of temporal operators considered in our application is described in Table II. In addition to the ones already

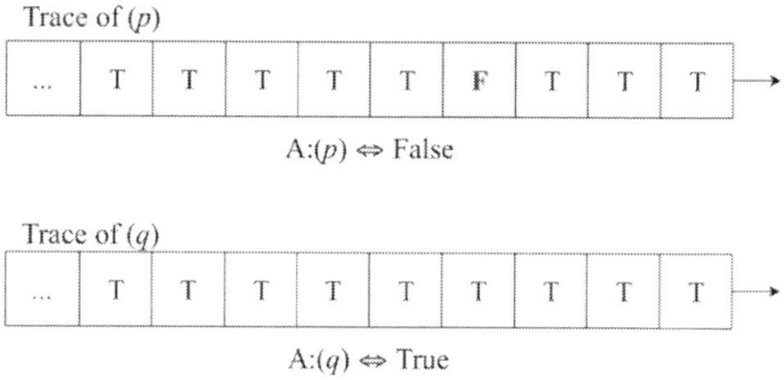

Figure 1. Always Operator on Two Example Traces.

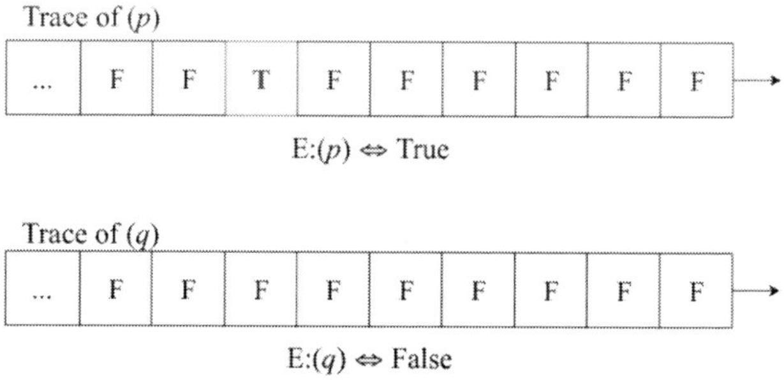

Figure 2. Eventually Operator on Two Example Traces.

described, there exist three other operators whose illustrated explanation we will omit.

TABLE II. Listing of Temporal Operators

Operator	*Syntax*	*Description*
Next	N: p	p was true one time-step ago.
Always	A: p	p was always true.
Eventually	E: p	p was eventually true at some point.
Until	p U: q	p was true up until just before q was true.
Release	p R: q	q was true up until p was true, after which q was false.

A. Introduction of Boolean Combinations

The true expressiveness of LTL arises from the ability to nest logical connectives and temporal operators in arbitrary ways. Referring back to Figure 1, the result of A:$(p \vee q)$ is true, because for every false entry in the trace of p, there exists a corresponding q entry that is true at the same time. The expression acted upon by a temporal operator may be any LTL expression, including other temporal operators. For example, in Figure 3, we see the intermediate values involved in the expression E:(A:(p)) operating upon a finite trace. A finite trace for this example was chosen only to keep the example simple; it works for general traces equivalently.

The key to understanding this nested temporal expression is that each temporal operator possesses its own trace (Boolean values through time), corresponding to whether or not the subsequence formed by taking the past at each point would result in a true value. However, the proper result of a temporal expression is the last value of the trace; This is indicated by the bottom arrow in Figure 3. A conceptual justification for this is that the last value of the trace is what the value is "now".

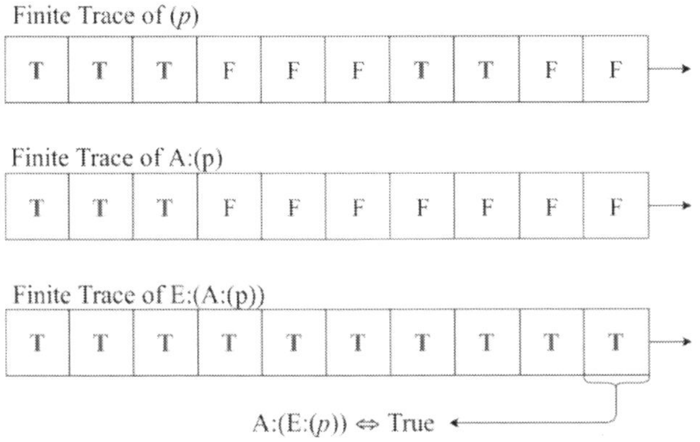

Figure 3. Nested Operator on Finite Trace.

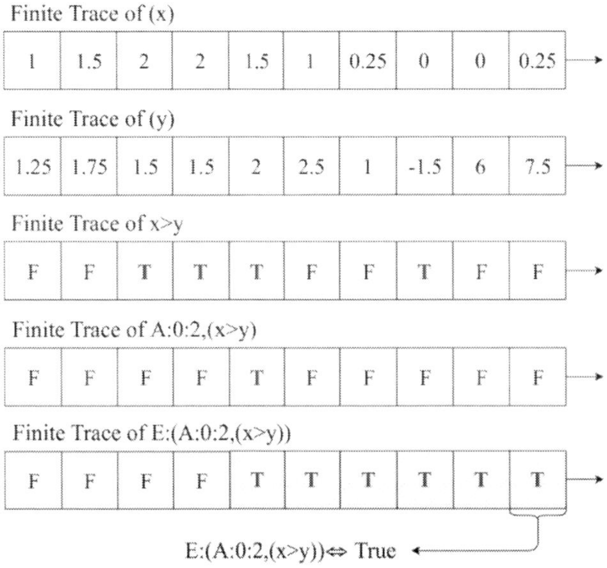

Figure 4. Bounded Temporal Expression on State Variables.

It is important to note that this interpretation is not unique; it is equally as valid to take the first value of the trace as "now" and consider all other trace values to be future values.

B. Introduction of Metric Temporal Logic

A common way to introduce real-time in the (LTL) syntax is by "replacing the unrestricted time operators by time-bounded versions" [10]. This allows for temporal operators to factor a metric of time, and to have essentially a time-bounded range of concern. In addition to making the logic much more expressive, it also has important considerations for real-time evaluation of the logic for practical applications.

We utilize MTL operators by defining some slightly modified syntax. For example, the time-bounded version of "always" is $\text{A}:_s^t(p)$ where $s, t \in \mathbb{Z}^{\geq}$. In our formulation, the 0th entry corresponds to "now", and all other entries incrementally refer to past values. Table III defines the application syntax and mathematical symbology used to denote the metric temporal operators.

TABLE III. SYNTAX OF METRIC TEMPORAL OPERATORS

Operator	*Symbol*	*Application Syntax*
Always	$\text{A}:_s^t(p)$	`A:s:t, (p)`
Eventually	$\text{E}:_s^t(p)$	`E:s:t, (p)`
Until	$p\text{U}:_s^t q$	`p U:s:t, q`
Release	$p\text{R}:_s^t q$	`p R:s:t, q`

C. Introduction of State Variables

The final extensions we include in our formalism are basic arithmetic and relational operations, as well as numerical state variables. State variables are real numbers which possess a real-valued trace (i.e., values through time). Effectively, this allows us to construct expressions which model the temporal relationship of real-valued variables through time. These values can represent sensor readings or other on-board state varibles. A comprehensive example of this capability is illustrated by Figure 4, which shows the intermediate values associated with evaluating $\text{E}:(\text{A}:_0^2(x > y))$, given that $x, y \in \mathbb{R}$. This expression is equivalent to the existence of a three-unit contiguous time region during which x is larger than y.

IV. METHOD

Real-time evaluation of the LTL formalism described by Section III was implemented via a Robot Operating System (ROS) package developed for the purpose. ROS is a commonly used middleware for developing robotics applications, providing algorithms and visualization tools. Some of the basic functionality provided is message-passing, which is implemented through so-called "ROS topics", and serves as the basis of the application.

Given user-specified LTL formulas and associated topic names, the program parses and evaluates the formulas, publishing the truth result to the rest of the ROS system. The flow of inputs and outputs involved in this process is illustrated in Figure 5. Dotted arrows represent external interfaces to the system.

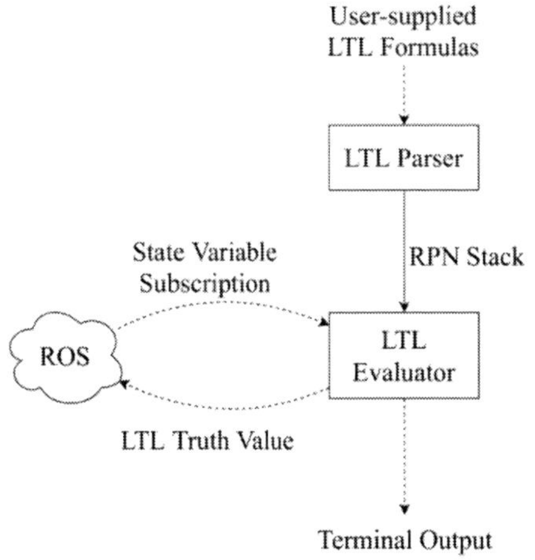

Figure 5. System Diagram of LTL Parser and Evaluator.

The evaluation of an LTL expression occurs in two steps, as illustrated in Figure 6. Of note is that explicit construction of the abstract-syntax tree is not performed during parsing, but is provided here only for explanation.

1) The expression is parsed while converting from infix to RPN.
2) Variable tokens are replaced with the corresponding data, and the stack machine is executed.

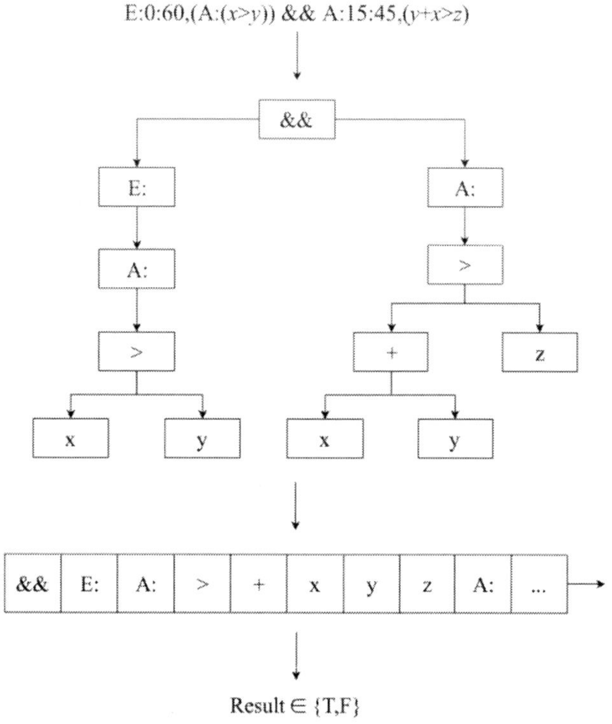

Figure 6. Generation of RPN Stack Machine.

Parsing is performed via Dijkstra's shunting-yard algorithm, converting the expression string to an array of Reverse Polish Notation (RPN) tokens. The evaluator then, on each arrival of new data, evaluates the RPN expression using a stack-based postfix evaluation algorithm. Each element of the stack is a trace, and each operator is a function of one or more traces.

When a real number is encountered in the execution, it is interpreted as a trace consisting solely of that real number. Hence, when a variable is introduced and compared to that number, the result is a boolean trace representing the result of that comparison over time. For all arithmetic, relational, and logical operators the result is simply that operator applied pair-wise to each element of the two corresponding traces. In the case of 1-arity operators e.g., $!p$, the operator is simply applied to each element of the trace. For temporal operators, each trace element's result is a function of the previous elements in the same way as described in Section III. Each element of every trace is of real type, and is automatically type cast depending on the operator.

The internal procedure used to calculate the 'Always' operator is described by Algorithm 1. If a boundedness operator

Algorithm 1: 'Always' operator. Resultant array is true up until x_i is false.

function A (x);
Input : Array of reals x of size n
Output: Array of reals, size n
`boolean` : α = `true`;
α = `false`;
for $x_i \in x$ **do**
    $\alpha = x_i \wedge \alpha$;
    $x_i = \mathbb{R}(\alpha)$;
end
return x;

is applied the procedure described by Algorithm 1 will operate only on a contiguous subsequence of the input trace. All non-zero real numbers (approximated by floating point) are type cast to `true` if acted upon by a boolean operator.

We achieve bounded performance by allowing the user to specify the maximum trace size for each LTL formula. Once the trace reaches that size, all LTL formulas, whether they are ultimately bounded or not will only act upon data within the specified time window of the current time. This is to ensure that the computation required to evaluate a given LTL formula is sublinear with respect to the current time of operation. One future work considered is automatic generation of an appropriate maximum trace size given an LTL formula.

V. RESULTS

This method was applied to an autonomous sea vessel in order to detect motor misalignment conditions, which occur when there exists an offset between the steering control value and the angle between the vessel and one, or both, of the motors. The control interface is a four-vector, with each element controlling the rotation (with respect to the craft) and effort of each of the two motors respectively. We use the term "effort" a percentage of the total power available to the system for acceleration that abstracts away physical details. For context, a simplified diagram of the physical placement of the motors can be seen in Figure 7. The controls values are subject to the constraints defined by (1) and (2).

$$-100 \geq E_N \leq 100 \tag{1}$$

$$-90^\circ \geq \theta_N \leq 90^\circ \tag{2}$$

The method was implemented as a configurable ROS component, which subscribes to the topics necessary to detect the suboptimal condition. The implementation allows for multiple LTL formulas each corresponding to a set of ROS topics. (3) specifies the LTL formula written to detect the motor misalignment condition, where $|x|$ specifies the absolute value operation.

$$\text{A:0:60,}(E_L = E_R \wedge |S_L| < 3 \wedge |S_R| < 3 \wedge V_{yaw} > 0.3) \tag{3}$$

We may break (3) into three logical clauses. If the following three conditions are true for the last sixty time units, the motor is misaligned.

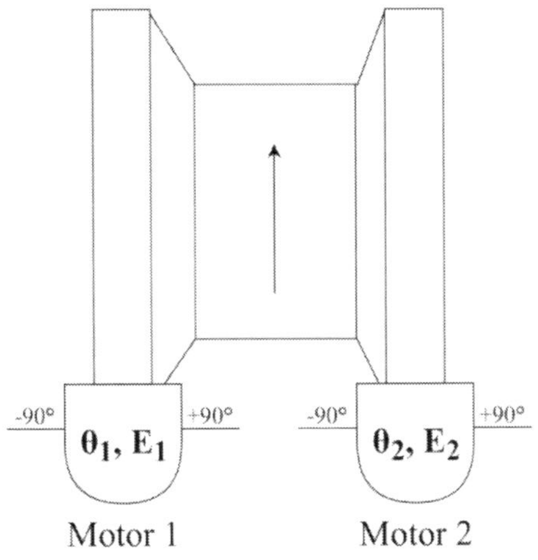

Figure 7. Diagram of Autonomous Vessel in Overhead View.

1) The efforts from both motors are equal.
2) The steering angles from both motors are less than 3 degrees, and...
3) The yaw-velocity of the craft is above a certain threshold.

The LTL formula was applied to two simulations of the autonomous vessel, each under an equivalent control trajectory. In the first (control) simulation, both motors are correctly aligned. In the second, the left motor is misaligned by 10°. The resultant angular velocity of both 10-second simulations is illustrated by Figure 8. The difference in yaw velocity, and particularly the spike at 2 seconds in the misaligned case can be attributed to the alignment discrepancy.

The control trajectory applied was generated by a simple driver code. For 2 seconds, an effort value of 50 and 100 was applied to the left and right motors respectively. Then, for the next 2 seconds, an effort value of 100 was applied to both motors for 2 seconds. Finally, the vehicle was allowed to coast under no effort. The control trajectory was chosen to be deterministic and not unlikely to occur during user operation.

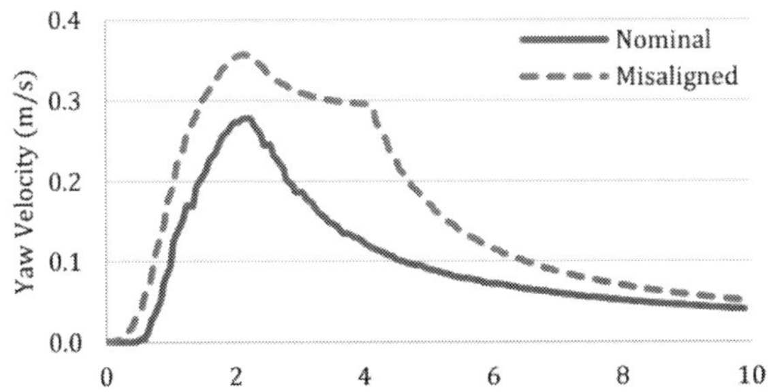

Figure 8. Angular Velocity of Nominal vs. Misaligned Case.

The resultant boolean signal for both the nominal case and misaligned case is seen in Figure 9. Due to the to the structure of the LTL formula used, there is a delay present in the result. It is possible to decrease the delay, but at risk of causing false-positives. As in most forms of signal processing, a tradeoff in delay and accuracy is present.

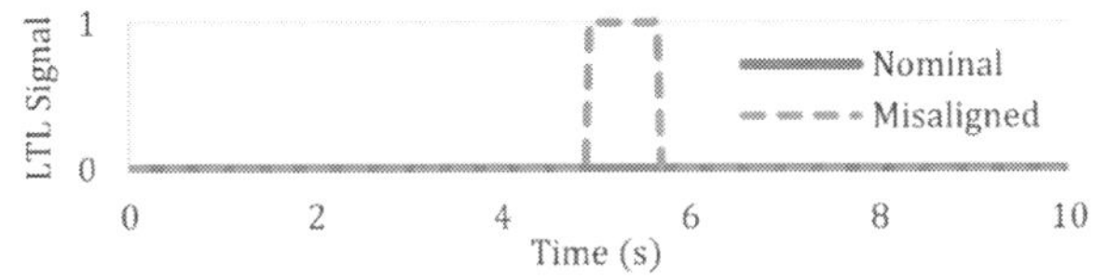

Figure 9. LTL Signal of Nominal vs. Misaligned Case.

Instead of integrating the squared error between what is expected to happen (via a physics model) with what was observed, i.e., the "residual method", we write specific temporal scenarios, which would only occur if the condition is present. The LTL approach allows us to both be more specific about error detection, and can be deployed in scenarios where an accurate physics model is intractable to compute.

VI. Conclusion and Future Work

Autonomous systems require ways to detect, interpret, and even anticipate problems. On-board sensors provide information, but unless there is a trivial interpretation (i.e., battery voltage dropping below a threshold), it is difficult to make a singular assessment about on-board status based on several sensor readings. Furthermore, proper interpretation of sensors cannot be done only for a single time, but must be done over a history. Proper sensor values may be temporally correlated in non-trivial ways. LTL is a convenient formalism for capturing the expected behavior of the system via mathematical modeling. Failures in the system can be directly inferred from evaluating these LTL expressions.

In this paper, we have demonstrated a practical LTL evaluation method that has bounded performance with respect to temporal formula evaluation at given time-points. For tele-operated systems, we view this as a compression scheme to encode high-dimensional temporal data into a form parsable by a human operator controlling the system. For on-board systems, this method effectively addresses the problem of autonomously capturing the nominal performance of the overall system.

There are three major directions planned for future work of this method. Currently, maximum trace size is manually set in order to provide bounded performance. However, it seems possible to automatically derive the maximum trace size from a provided LTL formula. As well, memoization of certain intermediary values may improve on the computational complexity of the method. Finally, a large part of the effort expended in using this method is coming up with a LTL formula that captures the desired behavior. Supervised machine learning techniques could be used to automatically generate an appropriate LTL formula given examples of nominal and "problem" mission trajectories, enabling rapid development of status assessment systems.

References

[1] J. Morse, L. Cordeiro, D. Nicole, and B. Fischer, "B.: Context-bounded model checking of LTL properties for ansi-c software," in *SEFM 2011. LNCS.* Springer, 2011, pp. 302–317.

[2] G. E. Fainekos and H. Kress-gazit, "Temporal logic motion planning for mobile robots," in *In Proceedings of the 2005 IEEE International Conference on Robotics and Automation*, 2005, pp. 2020–2025.

[3] A. Albore and P. Bertoli, "Safe ltl assumption-based planning," in *In Proc. 16th Int. Conf. on Planning and Scheduling (ICAPS-06*.

[4] T. A. Henzinger, P. W. Kopke, A. Puri, and P. Varaiya, "What's decidable about hybrid automata?" in *Journal of Computer and System Sciences*. ACM Press, 1995, pp. 373–382.

[5] J. Schumann, K. Y. Rozier, T. Reinbacher, O. J. Mengshoel, T. Mbaya, E. Al, J. Schumann, K. Y. Rozier, T. Reinbacher, O. J. Mengshoel, and T. Mbaya, "Towards real-time, on-board, hardware-supported sensor and software health management for unmanned aerial systems," in *in Proceedings of the 2013 Annual Conference of the Prognostics and Health Management Society (PHM2013*, 2013.

[6] R. Zhang, X. Hu, H. Wang, and H. Yao, "Fault diagnosis method in complex system using bayesian networks sensitivity analysis," *Information Technology Journal*, vol. 14, pp. 24–30, 01 2015.

[7] R. Reiter, "A theory of diagnosis from first principles," 1987.

[8] F. KrÃűger, *Temporal Logic of Programs*, ser. EATCS Monographs on Theoretical Computer Science. Springer, 1987, vol. 8.

[9] E. A. Emerson, "Temporal and modal logic," in *Handbook of Theoretical Computer Science*. Elsevier, 1995, pp. 995–1072.

[10] R. Alur and T. A. Henzinger, "Logics and models of real time: A survey," 1992.

Dynamic, Model-based Reconfiguration for Flexible Robotic Assembly Lines

Niki Kousi, Christos Gkournelos, Sotiris Aivaliotis, George Michalos, Sotiris Makris
Laboratory for Manufacturing Systems & Automation
Department of Mechanical Engineering and Aeronautics, University of Patras
Patras, Greece
e-mail: makris@lms.mech.upatras.gr, kousi@lms.mech.upatras.gr, gkournelos@lms.mech.upatras.gr, saival@lms.mech.upatras.gr

Abstract—**The European industry is becoming more customer centric in an approach to meet the varying customers' demand and minimize the costs of large inventories. The optimized production capacity that is achieved by the fixed production model can no longer guarantee the sustainability inside a fluctuating market that constantly requests new models. This creates the need to deploy flexible production systems exploiting the capabilities of multiple resources including both robots and human operators. Motivated by this need, this paper introduces the usage of mobile dual arm robots that are able to autonomously navigate in different workstations to undertake multiple operations, acting as assistants to human workers. A digital world model infrastructure for enabling this dynamic performance achieving process level reconfiguration, through robot's behavior adaptation is discussed. This system is based on a multiple sensor data synthesis mechanism that facilitates the real time shopfloor status digital representation. Static objects and moving obstacles, as well as human presence are identified inside this model enabling the robots' behavior adaptation through reasoning upon them. The suggested infrastructure has been deployed and tested in a case study from the automotive industry.**

Keywords-Mobile robots; flexibility; perception; digital world; sensor data synthesis.

I. INTRODUCTION

Robots have been considered as a major enabler for autonomous assembly systems. However, in current robot-based production systems, flexibility [1] and reconfiguration are still constrained due to [2]: a) the rigidity of the used stationary robotic units, b) the use of fixed and product model dedicated equipment, c) the use of fixed robot control logic and d) the absence of perception abilities that would allow the robots to dynamically adapt their behavior to the production needs.

Overcoming these limitations may be realized through the introduction of flexible robot workers enabling autonomy and collaboration between all production resources (including human operators and robot resources). Mobility both in resources and product level can play a vital role towards the realization of such production concepts as discussed in [3]. To this end, a hybrid and dynamically reconfigurable shopfloor is suggested employing mobile dual arm workers, namely *Mobile Robot Platforms (MRP)*, and *human operators*.

The last decades, extensive research has been made in the field of mobile robotic systems, either in the field of mobile robot manipulators or simple mobile platforms [4]. However, existing applications have limited perception capabilities not allowing real time adaptation of the system and robot behavior to dynamic environments [5][6]. Most of the manipulators are restricted to performing off-line programmed tasks only when they are in fixed positions, thus not fully exploiting their mobility.

On the other hand, digital representation and simulation of the production environment and process have emerged over the last decades as a means of partially handling the optimization of the production system performance [6]. In this era of digitalization in manufacturing, the Digital Twin concept has gained a lot of attention given the advantages that it may offer in terms of system autonomy [7]. The main principle of this concept relies on the digital representation of the physical world using multiple data input formats, such as Computer aided design – CAD files or other unified formats [8] as well as real time update of the virtual world based on real-time data (e.g., shopfloor/resource sensors, process related data, etc.). This is a very promising approach for providing perception and cognition abilities towards more autonomous and intelligent robotic systems [9].

Existing applications of dynamic robot control based on digital modelling and sensor data for ensuring collision free paths are based on the functionalities provided by Robot Operating System (ROS) [10]. The latter provides a rich content of data types and formats to virtually represent various hardware devices and multi-sensor data as well as a network of services and topics for broadcasting the captured knowledge. However, existing infrastructures are not mature enough to support the representation of the discussed hybrid production paradigm given the complexity of the various automated devices used, such as multiple mobile dual arm workers and products as well as human operators.

To overcome the existing limitations, this paper introduces a Digital World model infrastructure for supporting the effective introduction of MRPs in assembly environments. A unified semantic representation of the geometrical and the workload state on top of the ROS provided data structures is proposed so for the model to be able to support real time planning and MRP behavior optimization based on the shopfloor status.

The paper is organized as follows: Section II discusses the MRPs structure and capabilities while section III is focusing on the Digital World model description. In Section IV, the implementation of the robot's behavior adaption in different levels is presented. The performance of the system is analyzed on an automotive case study in Section IV. The last section is dedicated to drawing the conclusions and providing an outlook towards future work.

II. MOBILE ROBOT PLATFORMS (MRPS)

The present work considers as flexible robotic assembly lines the production paradigm presented by Kousi et al. [3]. Under this paradigm, mobile dual arm workers are introduced as the main enables for the flexibility of the system. These so-called MRPs can autonomously navigate inside the shopfloor localizing themselves into different workstations for a) performing multiple assembly operations, such as handling, insertion, screwing, drilling, etc. and b) acting as assistants to human operators. Figure 1 presents MRPs' hardware structure.

The main hardware components integrated under the MRPs can be summarized as follows:

- Two collaborative robot arms undertaking the assembly tasks execution;
- An omnidirectional mobile platform enabling the autonomous navigation;
- A torso adding two degrees of freedom to the robot arms in terms of rotation and elevation;

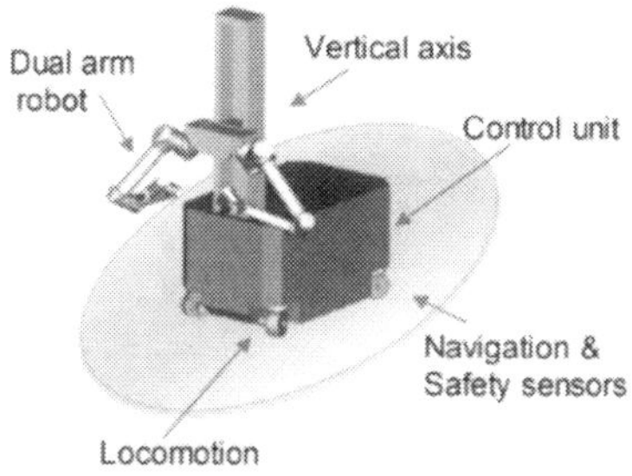

Figure 1. Mobile Robot Platforms (MRPs).

- Safety certified 2D laser scanners allowing the single plan obstacle detection, and
- Depth sensors allowing the 3D environment understanding.

These components aim to provide the hardware infrastructure allowing the safe navigation and localization of the robot into the different workstations as well as flexibility in terms of the process by dynamically identifying the product variants that need to be processed.

III. DYNAMIC DIGITAL WORLD MODEL

To enable the dynamic behavior and communication among these MRPs, the discussed Digital World model aims to provide the infrastructure for enabling the shopfloor data acquisition as well as combine them in a common representation to be consumed by the different decision-making mechanisms involved in the execution. A continuous feedback from the actual shopfloor (using resource and sensor data) will enable the dynamic update of digital twin involving two main functionalities:

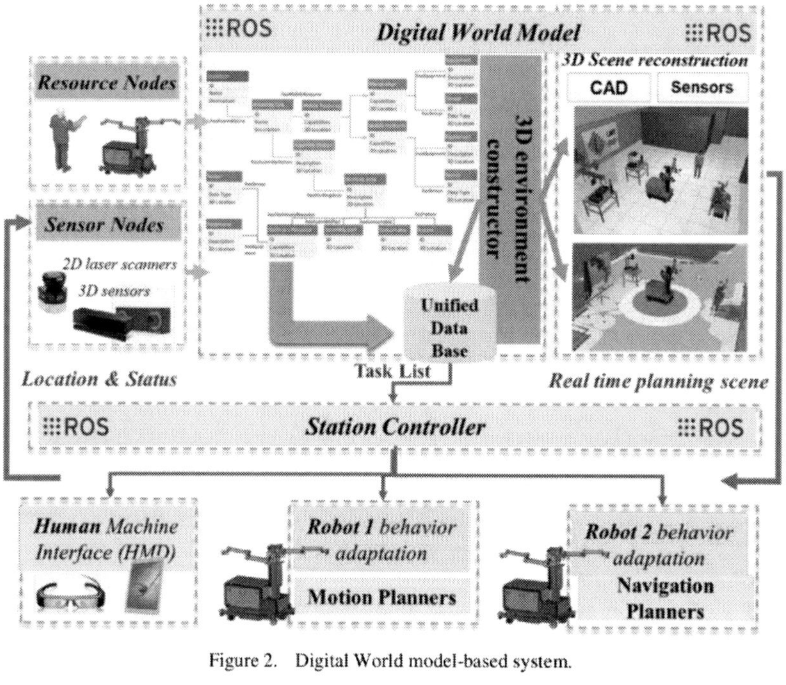

Figure 2. Digital World model-based system.

- Virtual representation of the shopfloor using multiple sensor data combination and CAD models. The digital shopfloor is rendered in the 3D environment using the capabilities provided by ROS.
- A unified data model will be implemented in order to semantically represent the geometrical as well as the workload state. This data model should be generic enough in order to be able to address multiple cases as well as to be consumed by multiple components inside execution system.

The overall system structure is presented in Figure 2.

A. 3D environment constructor – sensor data synthesis

The 3D environment constructor, composed by a set of sub-components, is responsible for registering the various entities included in the assembly, such as resources, parts, equipment, sensors, etc. A dedicated monitoring mechanism records the online location of these entities. These locations are used for constructing the complete working environment under a global world frame. This construction is performed based on the ROS Tf library [11] as visualized in Figure 3. The involved software components were developed on top of ROS provided functionalities enabling the scalable network communication and easy integration with existing robotic applications. In more detail, existing ROS interfaces for various robot models and sensor types make the developed infrastructure re-usable in multiple robotic systems.

During the set-up phase, the configuration of the resources, sensors and static objects takes place. In particular, the Resource configuration sub-component is managing the registration of the existing resources in the system. A set of attributes describing the resources have been defined as a universal resource model, such as transform configuration (.urdf format), path (.yaml format) and motion (.srdf format) configuration, payload, velocity, location, etc. These are populated for each resource instance introduced in the system. In a similar way, the involved Sensors are registered in the system through interfacing with the ROS drivers and recording their configuration data. The multiple

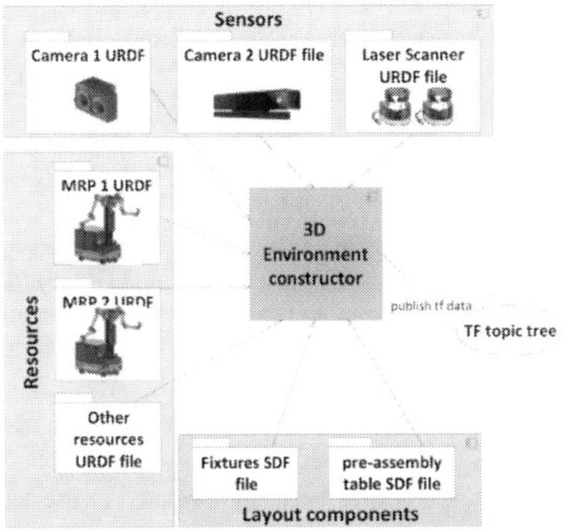

Figure 3. 3D environment constructor.

sensor data are shared with the robots' motion and path planners though dedicated topics following a predefined naming convention for each new sensor. Collecting the data from the available sensors, a data synthesis mechanism is responsible for publishing the 2D–3D combined sensor data. In that way, the 3D scene is reconstructed based on the sensors and this scene is consumed as a cost map for the standards motion and path planning algorithms (e.g., gmapping, amcl, ompl). The static objects, are loaded in .sdf that is uses by robot simulators, such as GAZEBO [12].

During the real-time execution phase, a Resource location and status monitoring sub–component is deployed for regularly publishing this online information on the digital twin. These data are retrieved through dedicated interfaces in each resource controllers. Nevertheless, apart from the static parts whose position is defined at the configuration phase, there are also moving objects and obstacles whose position is not well fixed and need to be identified during the execution.

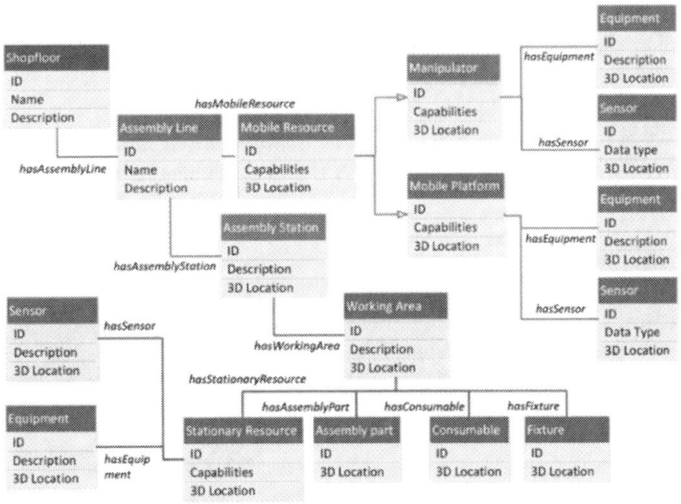

Figure 4. Unified semantic world model.

B. *Unified semantic model*

To handle the complexity of hybrid production systems, this study suggests a structured way to model the process and the environment following the principles of hierarchical modelling as shown in Figure 4.

IV. ROBOT BEHAVIOR ADAPTATION

Under this study robot behavior is specified as the set of low-level actions, such as *navigation*, *move arm* actions that the robot needs to perform for performing a task such as *pick and place* of an object. Thus, the concept of adapting robot behavior relies on the realization of ad-hoc changes in the MRP's planned navigation and motion paths so that it may perform the high-level task successfully.

A lot of research has been done related to the avoidance of collisions among resources and unmapped obstacles inside the shopfloor environment. Exploiting existing algorithms, the Digital twin provides interfaces with robot's path and trajectory planners, to achieve online re-planning based on fused real-time information from shopfloor. The MRP structure has been modelled through a ROS based description file describing the link the inter-robot connections among the robot arms, the platform and the torso. Thus, inter-robot conflicts such as collision of the robot with itself are not allowed.

A. *MRP platform online path planning*

MRP online path planning is implemented based on ROS navigation stack for mobile robots, thence, is essential the use of ROS Topics for sending transforms using tf, publishing odometry information, publishing sensor data. Digital World model resource manager handles the appropriate information for the correct configuration of each MRP unit as follows:

- Transform configuration: The transform tree for every coordinate frame of each resource is described inside the .urdf file. Worlds model's repository contains all the URDF files for each resource.
- Sensor and Odometry Information: Resource manager is responsible for defining which sensors are used by each robot.
- Map: Inside world model's repository 2D and 3D maps of the shopfloor are stored. In case of simple 2D navigation as visualized in Figure 5, the map_server node publishes periodically the map data in */map2d* topic.
- Planner Configuration: For the MRP's navigation two planners are responsible based on the ROS 2D SLAM navigation module. The first is the global planner and is responsible for finding a minimum cost plan from a start point to an end point. The second is the base local planner, which is responsible for computing velocity commands to send to the mobile base of the robot given a high-level plan from global planner.

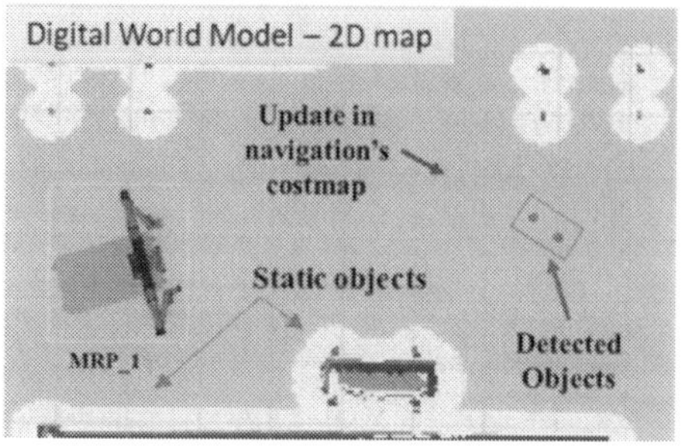

Figure 5. Digital World Model – 2D map.

B. *MRP robot arm online motion planning*

For the motion planning and controlling of the MRP arms ROS MoveIt! [13] is used. MoveIt! communicates with the MRP through ROS and it requires the existence of a dedicated ROS package for its configuration. The resource manager for the registration of a robot, such as MRP needs three type of information in order to setup the motion planning and export the MoveIt! package.

- Robots Universal Robot Description File (URDF);
- Robots Semantic Robot Description Format (SRDF) file created from MoveIt! setup assistant tool, and
- MoveIt! configuration files including among others joint limits, kinematics, motion planning, perception.

The digital world model through the Sensor Manager provides to MoveIt! the configuration for the occupancy 3D map created in occupancy grid using the OctoMap library as represented in Figure 6. This map is used as cost map with real time obstacles. Enhancing the environment knowledge with the occupancy map, the online motion planning component is aware of the existing objects / obstacles and uses this knowledge to ensure a collision-free trajectory planning.

V. CASE STUDY

The proposed Digital World model infrastructure has been implemented and tested through a case study coming from the automotive sector. In particular, the pilot case scenario involves the assembly of a passenger's vehicle suspension. This assembly scenario involves a set of assembly operations in three different workstations: a) the damper pre-assembly area, b) the damper compression area and c) the damper assembly on the disk area.

Following the analysis made in [3], an MRP is introduced in this assembly line, navigating among these

Figure 6. Digital World model – 3D map.

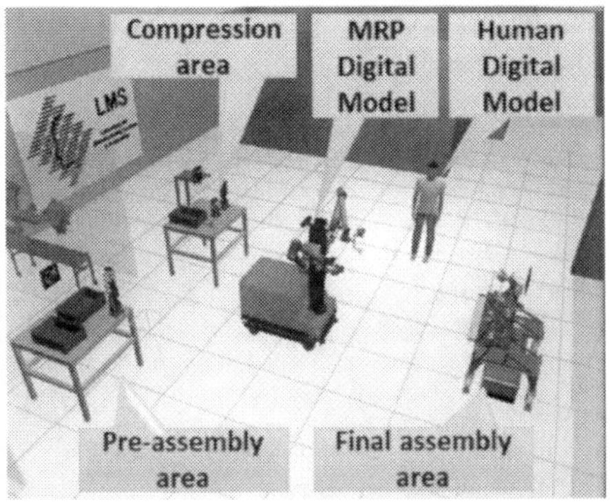

Figure 7. Assembly enviroment simulation.

workstations for performing a) the transferring of the damper from the pre-assembly to the compression area, b) small parts assembly on the compression area and b) the assembly of the compressed damper on the disk. In parallel, one human operator is working on the same workspace performing the pre-assembly of the damper as well as a set of cabling operations on the disk assembly area.

To be able to test the application in a realistic robotics set up in terms of 3D layout, a GAZEBO ROS-based simulation was set up replicating the assembly environment as shown in Figure 7. The digital models of the MRP (URDF) and human (CAD) where added in the simulation integrating the human side interface and robot controller in the backend. Figure 8 visualizes the Digital World model of the assembly environment based on the sensor data: a) two laser scanners located in the mobile platform of the MRP and b) one Kinect located on its torso. A Station Controller mechanism is responsible for dispatching the assigned tasks to the MRP, as well as the human operator and monitoring their progress so to coordinate the execution.

For the efficient execution of the scenario, the MRP needs to perceive the: a) damper and working tables to compensate the localization errors that cannot be foreseen offline, using a Kinect depth sensor, b) static obstacles and moving humans / obstacles for ensuring collision free navigation, using 2D laser scanner data.

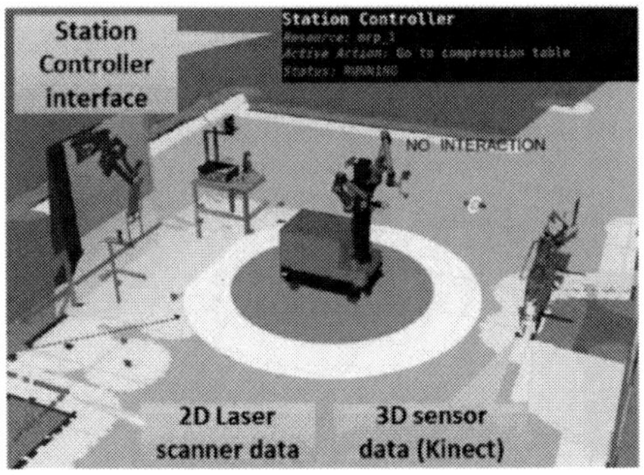

Figure 8. Digital World model visualization.

Figure 9. MRP 2D SLAM navigation.

Each time the robot is re-located by the Station Controller to a different workstation it needs to autonomously navigate from its current location to the new one. 2D SLAM based navigation is an existing solution for resolving the path generation aspects as visualized in Figure 9.

In this specific use case, the Digital World model provides the 2D map based on the combined sensor data from the two laser scanners located on the MRP platform. This map includes the static obstacles existing during the map creation procedure. Nevertheless, as mentioned in Section II, apart from the static obstacles recorded during the map creation procedure, during actual execution several other moving obstacles may be in conflict with MRP's navigation path. The dynamic nature of the Digital World model allows the real time update of the planning scene, so for the navigation planners to consider in the local plan generation the new, unmapped obstacles. Figure 10 presents an instance where the human operator interferes to MRP's planned path. The respective visualization of the Digital World model instance during this case is also presented.

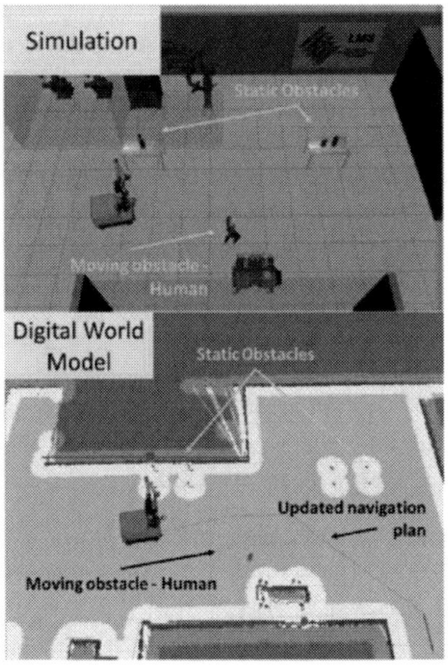

Figure 10. Collision avoidance with moving obstacles – humans.

In that way, the MRP may avoid collision with humans in a dynamic way while both are in motion.

VI. Conclusions and Future Work

Shopfloor uncertainty is a key aspect that limits the flexibility potential of nowadays manufacturing systems. Modular robotic systems are considered as a main enabler for production system reconfigurability. However, their fixed control logic, based on pre-programmed operations, does not allow the effective exploitation of their capabilities. Robots' perception abilities and reasoning upon the perceived environment so to adapt their behavior are key prerequisites for overcoming the existing limitations. To this end, this work, introduces the deployment of a dynamic Digital World model enabling the a) multiple sensor data synthesis into a common scene and the online update of the scene based on the real time data, b) the integration of the involved resources and hardware components allowing the robots to understand the real time environment and apply cognition techniques to transform the sensor based scene into useful information for optimizing their behavior.

The discussed infrastructure has been tested in an assembly case study form the automotive sector, employing one MRP and one human operator. The deployment of the Digital World model allowed the reconfiguration of robot behavior by compensating the real – world uncertainty. Combining 2D and 3D sensor data information increases shopfloor's real time knowledge and eventually leads to higher accuracy in robot actions.

Considering a production system with more workstations and more humans and MRPs the complexity and unpredictability of the system increases a lot. In these cases, the suggested Digital World model may have a greater impact when applied in the completed manufacturing system. To achieve that, technical issues such as the computational requirements for processing big amounts of data need to be overcome as a future step. In addition, under the era of Industry4.0 data security is an important aspect to be addressed. Future version of this platform needs to be enhanced a secure communications framework that can ensure that connections between resources and systems are private (or secure) by using approaches such as symmetric cryptography.

Nevertheless, the validation of the developed infrastructure under a physical set up involving the actual MRP is already an ongoing work by the authors. Future work should also focus on the integration of a higher-level decision-making mechanism that will be able to dynamically re-distribute the work among the available robot and human resources based on their capabilities and the production needs.

Acknowledgment

This work has been partially funded by the EC research project "THOMAS – Mobile dual arm robotic workers with embedded cognition for hybrid and dynamically reconfigurable manufacturing systems" (Grant Agreement: 723616) (www.thomas-project.eu/).

References

[1] G. Chryssolouris, Manufacturing Systems: Theory and Practice, second ed. Springer-Verlag, New York , 2006

[2] G. Michalos, N. Kousi, S. Makris, and G. Chryssolouris, "Performance Assessment of Production Systems with Mobile Robots" 48th CIRP Conference on Manufacturing Systems (CMS 2015) Procedia CIRP, 2016, pp. 195-200, ISSN 2212-8271

[3] N. Kousi, G. Michalos, S. Aivaliots, and S. Makris, "An outlook on future assembly systems introducing robotic mobile dual arm workers" 51st CIRP Conference on Manufacturing Systems, (CMS 2018), Procedia CIRP, 2018, pp. 33-38 ISSN 2212-8271

[4] N. Kousi, S. Koukas, G. Michalos, and S. Makris, "Scheduling of smart intra – factory material supply operations using mobile robots", International Journal of Production Research. Vol. 57, pp. 801-814, Jul 2018, doi.org/10.1080/00207543.2018.1483587

[5] J. Váncza and L. Monostori, "Cyber-physical Manufacturing in the Light of Professor Kanji Ueda's Legacy", 50th CIRP Conference on Manufacturing systems (CMS 2017) Procedia CIRP, 2017, pp. 631-638, ISSN 2212-8271

[6] G. Michalos, S. Makris, N. Papakostas, D. Mourtzis, and G. Chryssolouris, "Automotive assembly technologies review: challenges and outlook for a flexible and adaptive approach", CIRP Journal of Manufacturing Science and Technology, vol. 2, pp. 81-91, 2010, doi.org/10.1016/j.cirpj.2009.12.001

[7] R. Rosen, G. V. Wichert, G. Lo, and K. D. Bettenhausen, "About The Importance of Autonomy and Digital Twins for the Future of Manufacturing", IFAC-PapersOnLine, vol. 48, pp. 567-572, 2015, ISSN 2405-8963

[8] S. Makris, G. Michalos, and G. Chryssolouris, "Virtual Commissioning of an Assembly Cell with Cooperating Robots", Advances in Decision Sciences, vol. 2012, Aug 2018, 11 pages, doi:10.1155/2012/428060

[9] S. Giordani, M. Lujak, and F. Martinelli, "A distributed multi-agent production planning and scheduling framework for mobile robots", Computers and Industrial Engineering, vol. 64, pp. 19-30, Jan 2013, doi.org/10.1016/j.cie.2012.09.004

[10] URL Robot Operating System http://www.ros.org/, last accessed April 2019

[11] URL ROS Tf library http://wiki.ros.org/tf. last accessed March 2019

[12] URL GAZEBO SIM http://gazebosim.org/, last accessed March 2019

[13] URL ROS MoveIt! https://moveit.ros.org/, last accessed March 201

A Robust Polyurethane Depositing System for Deployment on Disaster Scenario Robotics

Alec John Burns
School of Engineering
University of Liverpool
Liverpool, UK
Email: sgaburns@liv.ac.uk

Sebastiano Fichera
School of Engineering
University of Liverpool
Liverpool, UK
Email: Sebastiano.Fichera@liv.ac.uk

Paolo Paoletti
School of Engineering
University of Liverpool
Liverpool, UK
Email: paoletti@liv.ac.uk

Abstract—**Robotic platforms have been widely recognised as potential tools for mitigating the aftermath of natural catastrophes. However, their ineffectiveness in traversing highly unstable and irregular terrains is a key bottleneck in their deployment and usage in real world scenarios. In this work, a Polyurethane Foam depositing system is proposed to allow ground vehicles to overcome obstacles and navigate on challenging substrates. The proposed system is designed as in independent modular mechanism that can be attached to various robotic platforms to enable material deposition and thus to increase their ability in overcoming obstacles. The materials used are inexpensive and their properties can be tuned on board by a simple control system, allowing the device to vary its output type according to situational requirements. Four different deposit types have been characterized, with expansion ratios varying from $20\times$ to $33\times$, compressive strengths from $0.16MPa$ to $2MPa$, and full expansion and set times below 6 minutes, allowing application in real-time. The system has been fitted to a tracked rover equipped with some basic sensors to allow autonomous responses when faced with obstacles. The system allows successful traversing of previously insurmountable obstacles such as large frontal objects and chasms. The results show that the amount of foam deposited can be well controlled and multiple layers can be stacked on top of each other to significantly increase altitude.**

Keywords–Robotics; Overcoming Obstacles; Disaster Scenario.

I. Introduction

A natural catastrophe is an unexpected event caused by nature, which results in a great deal of suffering, damage and death. These include but are not limited to events such as, tornadoes, hurricanes, earthquakes, etc. According to a U.N. report [1], since 1995 over $600,000$ people have been killed, $4.1billion$ injured or left homeless and $\$2trillion$ in economic damages have been caused by such natural catastrophes. When natural disasters strike, the primary concern is human life and therefore it is critical to reach the victims and the survivors as soon as possible. People left stranded in the wake of these events are often stuck for days without food, water or medicines. They find themselves cut off from all support, typically due to collapsed infrastructure, making it impossible for teams to easily and safely reach them. This results in first responders being some of the most at risk during any relief efforts [2], often entering highly unstable areas with little knowledge of the interiors.

It is widely acknowledged that robotic platforms will play a key role in mitigating the after effects of such disasters. Major progress has been made in the developments of aerial, terrestrial and maritime robotic platforms specifically designed for use for disaster relief, search and rescue and salvage operations [3]. This is because robots can be deployed quickly in areas deemed too hazardous for human operation. Terrestrial platform specifically can be used to collect interior data, deliver supplies and support first responders. Many projects have been developed in recent years to achieve some of these functions, see for example [4]–[6]. However, when taking ground based platforms from the even surface of a lab to the unpredictable and often unstable terrain expected in disaster zone environments, they typically encounter major difficulties.

TABLE I. SYNTHETIC COMPARISON OF LOCOMOTION SYSTEM FEATURES, TAKEN FROM [8]. LeW = LEGGED WHEELED, LeT = LEGGED TRACKED, WT = WHEELED TRACKED, L=LOW, M=MEDIUM and H=HIGH

	W	T	Leg	LeW	LeT	WT
maximum speed	H	M/H	L	M/H	M	M/H
obstacle crossing	L	M/H	H	M/H	H	M
step climbing	L	M	H	H	H	M
slope climbing	L/M	H	M/H	M/H	H	M/H
soft terrain	L	H	L/M	L/M	M/H	H
uneven terrain	L	M/H	H	H	H	M/H
energy efficiency	H	M	L	M/H	M	M/H
system complexity	L	L	H	M/H	M/H	L/M

Numerous robotic architectures have been developed for the very purpose of overcoming rough terrain. Current approaches can be classified into roughly five categories according to [7]: single-tracked, multi-tracked, wheeled, quadruped-platforms (or biologically inspired systems) and humanoid. Each of these unique solutions can perform well in particular conditions, but there is no one of these categories that performs exceptionally in every circumstance. As a result of this, more focus has been recently put on the development of hybrid platforms to maximise the advantages of multiple architectures. However, such systems are expensive and their added benefits often limited. A comparison of tracked, wheeled, humanoid and their respective hybrids was performed in [8] and is reported in Table I. This overlooks quadruped and biologically inspired platforms as these represent a very diverse array of systems which are difficult to generalise. Table I shows that no architecture nor hybrid system can tackle all of the considered environments, therefore development of one particular locomotion style will not result in a system that is the most apt in all scenarios. Due to this, material deposition systems have been suggested as methods for augmenting robotic platforms to increase their ability of navigating uneven terrain.

In this paper, a novel Polyurethane (PU) Foam deposition system is proposed to increase a robotic platforms ability to traverse uneven terrains and overcome obstacles. The paper is structured as follows. In Section II, an overview of Polyurethane foam and the related works are given. In Section III, a brief description of the design for the depositing module, a characterisation of the deposited material and the integration with a tracked rover is reported. Section IV contains an illustration of the experimental setup used to test the effectiveness of the depositing systems, whereas the results obtained in these experiments are discussed in Section V. Finally, some final remarks and suggestions for further work are reported in Section VI.

II. Background

A. Polyurethane Foam

Polyurethane Foam (PU) is a synthetic resin in which the polymer units are linked by urethane groups; when combining the two part constituents (PU-5800, Polycraft), the mix quickly expands and then sets rigid. The ratio between these two parts alters the final properties of the PU foam and therefore maximum values for such properties are the best way to characterise the material. Two key material characteristics for the purpose of this paper are:

- Compressive strengths - over $2MPa$ are possible, which can easily support the weight of a human standing thereon.
- Expansion ratios - over $30\times$ the original volume, meaning $25dm^3$ of final structure foam can be generated from $840cm^3$ of the two part liquid constituents [9].

The final properties depend largely on two factors: the mix ratio and the mix style. Therefore, different mixing mechanisms, such as manual stirring, syringe pumping and aerosol deposition, will result in very different final material properties. The importance of this will be further discussed in Section II-B. The final material form is a closed-cell and thus, water-proof foam when set and all mix types are lighter than water, yet strong enough to support the weight of a human. Additionally, these foams attach to a variety of materials including wood, iron, and concrete, among others. Based on these characteristics, this material is deemed suitable for use in disaster scenarios in real-time.

B. Related Work

Two projects have utilised a robotic PU foam depositing system for traversing obstacles. The first platform was proposed in [10] and utilised a motorised syringe prefilled with the two parts of PU. As the syringe is actuated, the two parts are driven through a series of static mixing chambers to increase turbulence and initiate reaction. This allows the system to deposit small amounts of PU foam to create a ramp which allowed it to traverse an object larger than its original capability. There are several major drawbacks of this system. Firstly, the style of deposition provides little mixing and thus very low expansion ratio of the foam, meaning a significant amount of material extrusion was needed to create the desired ramps. This low expansion ratio, coupled with the single rigid nozzle deposit system, resulted in a very complex build requirement, which would be difficult to implement autonomously and was thus manually controlled by a human operator. Further, continuous deposition was required if the syringe was to remain unblocked before using all of the material. For the ramp demo shown in this project, multiple syringe cartridges and mixing devices were manually replaced on the system to allow continuous usage.

An alternative approach was proposed in [9], where a robotic platform utilised an aerosol depositing system mounted on a gimbal, with both single part and two part PU tested. The two part PU resulted in much more effective outputs and a more flexible deposition than [10], and therefore an autonomous ramping system was possible upon detecting an object. However, the use of aerosol depositing system gives little control over the material being deposited, as the mix ratio and outlet speed are determined with the systematic design and cannot be controlled by the platform or even altered simply offline. Also, the use of prepackaged aerosols bring into questions how well this system could be scaled.

To overcome the drawbacks of existing platforms, this paper proposes an on board pumping and mixing system to drive the two part liquids of PU foam to reaction. The proposed approach provides complete control over the deposition process and over the final material properties of the PU foam, thus eliminating the issues described above.

III. Design

A. PU Foam Deposit System

The PU foam deposit process is illustrated in Figure 1. Three separate reservoirs are used to contain the required components: PU part one, PU part two and a solvent. Peristaltic pumps are used to drive PU parts one and two to an external mixing chamber. This chamber ensures the two parts are fully diffused without increasing turbulence to induce reaction. This is a necessary step when multiple outlets are required as in the platform described in this paper, otherwise the flows would not mix and develop into separate channels due to the viscous nature of the individual parts, see Figure 2. The now combined PU is separated toward two different nozzles and passed through a static mixing nozzle (MA6.3-21S, Adhesive Dispensing Ltd.) before the outlet. As mentioned, previous systems utilising PU frequently become blocked after, and even during, use due to residue building up in the system and expanding. The proposed system therefore makes use of a a solvent flushing mechanism. By using a third perilstaltic pump, a solvent is pumped through the system to inhibit the reaction and eject any potential blockages. This procedure allows the system to be used numerous times without issue.

The proposed design results in a number of benefits when compared to systems available in the literature:

1) Basing the system around peristaltic pumping mechanisms results in a fixed amount of liquid being driven at any one time. The amount of liquid being actuated is equal to that being pumped within the tubing and mixing devices and is thus independent of the reservoir size from which it is being drawn. This, unlike syringe and aerosol driven designs [9], [10], allows significant scaling of reservoirs with no system alteration.

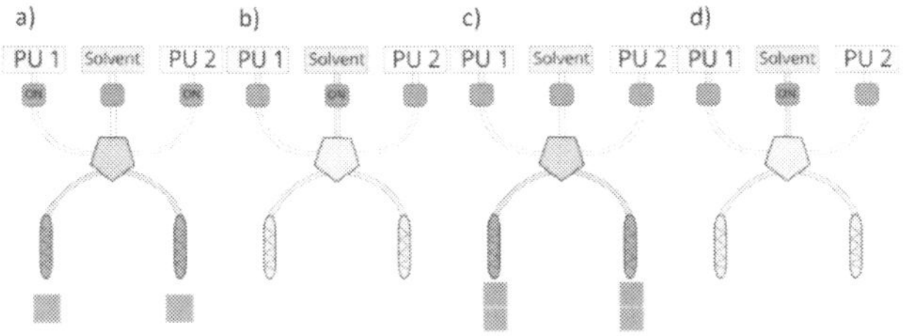

Figure 1. Stages of PU foam synthesis and solvent flush: a) Pumping of PU part one and two to create first batch, b) flush of solvent, c) Pumping of PU parts to create second batch, d) flush of solvent. Peristalstic pumps are represented by red symbols, central pentagon represents the mixing chamber and crossed cylinder represent the static mixing nozzles.

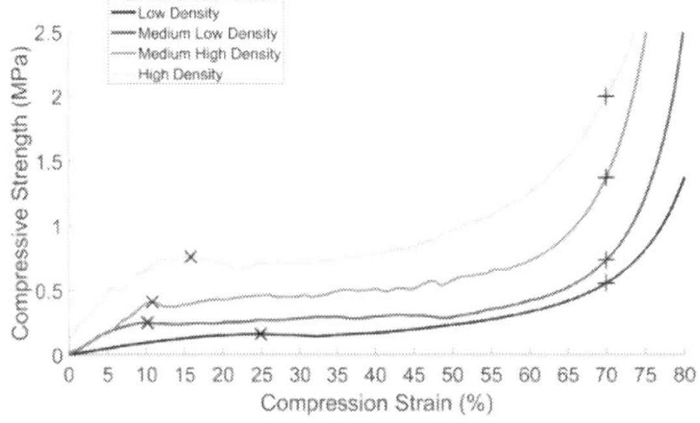

Figure 3. Stress-strain curves of the foam for different mix ratios, see also Table II.

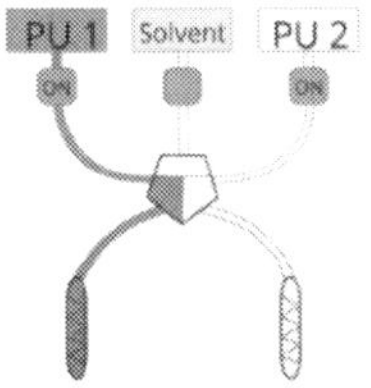

Figure 2. Illustration of PU parts one and two not mixing, which occurs without a suitable mixing chamber.

2) The system can independently control the flow rate of each PU part via the individual peristaltic pumps. This allows complete control over the mix ratio and therefore the final mechanical properties of the deposited PU foam. For example, increasing the ratio of PU part two would increase expansion ratio; this could be used to maximise volumetric output if material was low. Conversely, if the system required a harder deposit, it could autonomously increase the ratio of PU part one to the mix.
3) Flow rate control allows control of fluid turbulence within the mixing devices. Increasing overall flow velocity increases the turbulence with which the chemicals are mixed, thus reducing the time taken to begin expansion. This has the potential to allow outputted material to be less fluid-like and more immediately sticky, where obvious applications would be to allow foam deposition on vertical walls. However, making the deposit more liquid-like on exit allows the substance to be deposited into crevices and cracks which would not be possible for syringe or aerosol deposited systems.
4) Finally, the system allows two pumps to drive the liquids to two outlets, although it is possible to increase this number. The importance of this will be mentioned in Section III-C.

B. *Foam Characterisation*

To demonstrate the control ability on the final material properties of the PU foam, four different PU foam types have been characterised according to: mix ratio, expansion ratio, initial compressive strength, final compressive strength, rise time and set time. Higher compressive strengths and expansion ratios are possible from this deposition system. However, mixes that result in higher expansion ratios, for example, result in compressive strengths that are too low to be considered useful for the envisaged applications, and vice versa.

PU foam is a high ductility material, hence it tends to experience large shape deformation instead of exhibiting brittle cracking behaviour under load. Therefore, two non standard definitions of compressive strength are used: initial compressive strength and final compressive strength. The former is defined as the pressure applied before permanent plastic deformation occurs, and is highlighted with the symbol $'\times'$ in Figure 3. The latter is defined as the pressure at which the height of the deposit is reduced by 70%, as shown in Figure 3 with the symbol $'+'$. Beyond this value the deposit is considered to have failed. Controlled compression tests were conducted on an extracted cubic test sample from a free rise foam deposit. Force and compression/tension were measured with a material testing machine (Instron 3345) loading the specimens at a rate of $2mm/min$.

Set time is measured from initial deposition until the foam has fully solidified, and is calculated by removing multiple samples at set times and recording their compressive strength. Full set time is considered the point at which compressive strength no longer increases with increased reaction time.

Whilst absolute values of the properties have been measured and are of importance per se, the relative differences are the primary quantities of interest, as they demonstrate the capability of the proposed system to deliver enhanced control characteristics. A summary of properties of the deposited foams are reported in Table II, where each foam is defined by the mix ratio of part one to part two. Such table shows, for example, that the proposed device can create PU foams with compressive strengths ranging from $0.56MPa$ to $2MPa$.

C. *Robotic Platform*

The modular design proposed for the depositing system allows easy deployment on already existing robotic platforms, enabling their increased range of operation. For the purposes of testing, the simple low cost ground rover shown in Figure 4 was used. This platform is a two-tracked vehicle with a track height of $100mm$ and a track length of $300mm$. The maximum pressure exerted by the rover on the terrain is about $0.02MPa$ ($15kg$ rover on the total surface area of its tracks), therefore the PU foam can easily sustain the weight of the whole platform. The rover is driven by two large stepper motors (RB-Phi-266, Robotshop) controlled by a central Arduino Mega 2560 board which actuates the motor speeds via two Arduino

TABLE II. CHARACTERISATION OF FOUR TYPES OF PU FOAM DEPOSITION.

	Low Density	**Medium-Low Density**	**Medium-High Density**	**High Density**
Mix Ratio (one:two)	$1 : 0.74$	$1 : 1$	$1 : 1.4$	$1 : 1.6$
Expansion Ratio	$33\times$	$29\times$	$25\times$	$20\times$
Initial Compressive Strength	$0.16MPa$	$0.25MPa$	$0.41MPa$	$0.76MPa$
Final Compressive Strength	$0.56MPa$	$0.74MPa$	$1.37MPa$	$2MPa$
Rise Time	37 seconds	46 seconds	52 seconds	55 seconds
Set Time	$210 - 270$ seconds	$240 - 300$ seconds	$270 - 340$ seconds	$310 - 380$ seconds

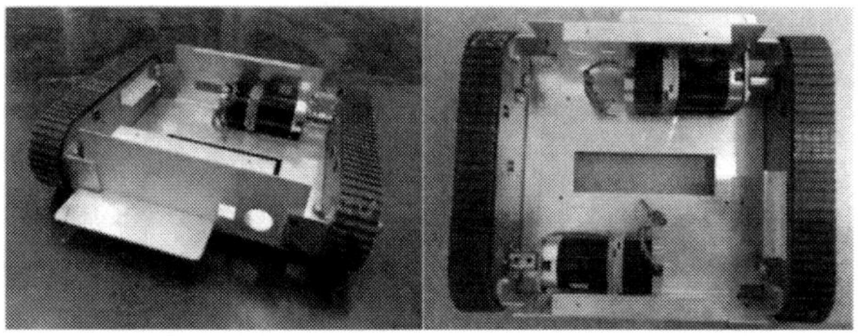

Figure 4. Images of the rover platform used for testing.

Nano boards and the pumping systems via another Arduino Mega 2560. A digital compass is connected to the central control board to feed orientation information back to the controller and positional information is estimated based on encoder information from the motors. The PU Foam depositing system was mounted on top of the rover with the two outlets positioned directly behind the tracks. As the rover moves, the foam will be deposited, forming two distinct extrusions which are aligned with the rovers tracks. Once the foam has expanded and solidified, the rover can simply climb on said extrusions to increase or maintain altitude. When depositing foam in a straight line, controlling either deposit speed or rover speed allows the platform to create ramp structures as will be demonstrated in Section IV. This is an efficent approach compared to the complex depositing mechanism proposed in [9] and to the complicated ramp structure required in [10].

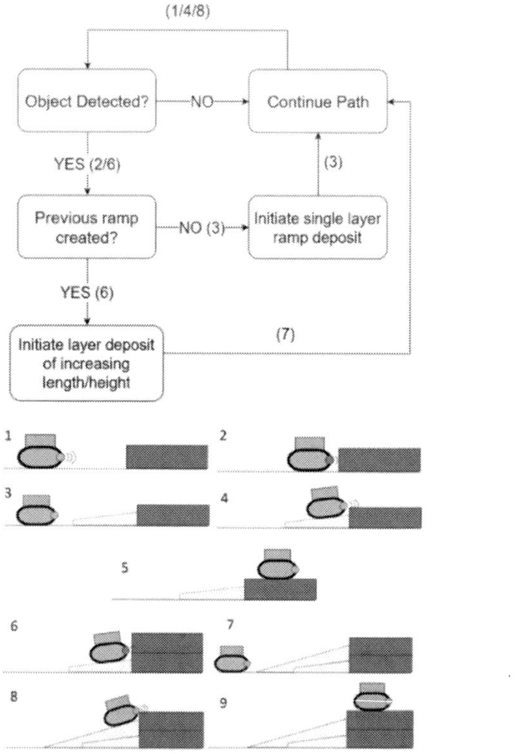

Figure 5. Flowchart and illustration of the frontal obstacle detection system and ramp building process.

IV. EXPERIMENTAL SETUP

Two main simulated scenarios are designed to demonstrate the effectiveness of the proposed PU foam depositing system in allowing ground vehicles to navigate in a disaster scenario: obstacle climbing and chasm traversing. To this end, the robotic platform described in Section III-C was fitted with ultrasonic distance sensors (HC-SR04) pointing in the direction of travel and toward the ground to detect obstacles and/or chasms. If the sensors detect a scenario that would prevent the ground vehicle from proceeding on the planned path, a PU foam deposition protocol is initiated.

A. *Frontal Obstacle Detection and Climbing*

Frontal obstacles are defined as objects that are placed on the rover planned path and are too high to be overcome by the vehicle itself. Through testing, it was determined that the rover cannot overcome obstacles that are above half the rover track height. The frontal ultrasound sensor was then placed at this height and, once an obstacle is detected, the rover initiates a ramp depositing procedure in order to climb onto the obstacle. In particular, following detection of an obstacle, the rover will begin to move forward at a low motor torque to align the rover front face with the straight edge of an object upon contact. The ramp building protocol, described in the flowchart of Figure 5 is then initiated, giving rise to the responses illustrated in the same figure.

B. *Chasm Detection and Filling*

A chasm is defined as a gap in the floor that is long enough to prevent the rover from moving over it without falling in. Through testing it was determined that the rover can overcome chasms of up to $100mm$ (one third of the total length) without falling into said gap. Longer gaps would prevent the vehicle to move along the planned path. Two ultrasound sensors were then placed on the underside of the chassis, pointing to the ground. One sensor was positioned at the front of the undercarriage and another one was placed at one third of the length from the front, in other word $100mm$ behind. These two sensors are necessary as some gaps in the floor, of less than $100mm$ in length, can be overcome by the rover without need for material deposition. However, if both undercarriage sensors detect a continuous gap, the rover will stop moving

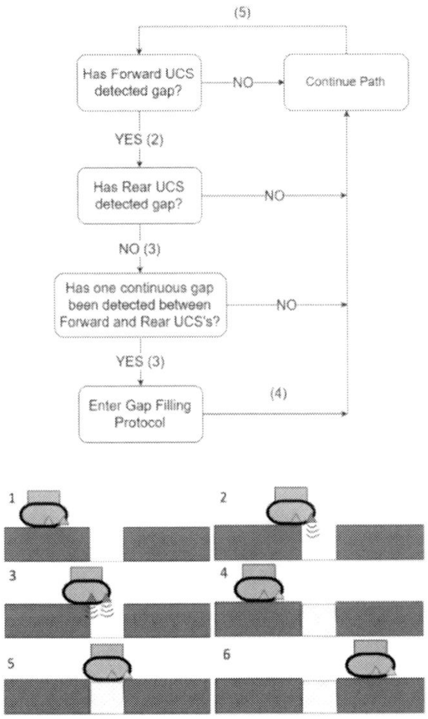

Figure 6. Flowchart and illustration of the chasm detection and filling system.

and initiate a void filling procedure. At first, the rover uses depth measurements of the chasm to estimate the amount of deposit required. However, if it is under deposited (for example if the foam expanded less than expected) then it would once again detect the chasm and repeat the filling procedure. Over-depositing typically leads to foam overflowing the chasm, but the extra amount is usually trivial for the rover to overcome. A flowchart of autonomous response to chasms and respective illustration for the responses are shown in Figure 6. Chasm detection is overridden when climbing a ramp produced by the system described in Section IV-A.

V. Results

Three experiments were carried out with both detection systems being operational. In all experiments, the rover is instructed to move in a straight line and the detection systems will determine whether or not they should activate the PU foam deposit procedures in order for the rover to continue to navigate along it planned s path. All experiments require the on-board autonomous decision system to:

1) Identify an obstacle or a chasm preventing forward movement.
2) Deposit the PU foam to overcome said obstacle according to the procedures described in Section IV.
3) Flush the system with solvent to ensure blockages do not occur.
4) Wait an appropriate amount of time for the PU foam to set.
5) Climb onto the obstacle or move over the filled chasm using the deposited PU foam.

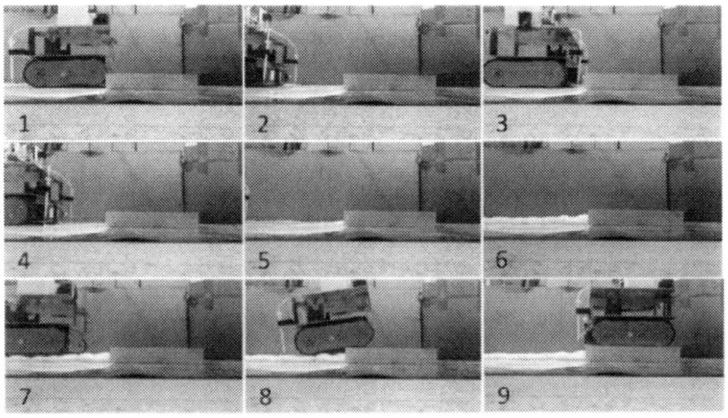

Figure 7. Small obstacle test: the stages of the rover detecting a $60mm$ high block and depositing a foam ramp to climb onto the obstacle.

The mix ratio of PU Part one:Part two was fixed at $1:1$ (Medium-Low Density foam) for all three tests. The first two experiments consider frontal obstacles and the third considers chasm detection. In all the scenario the vehicle could not navigatr along the planned path without the aid of the PU foam depositing system. For the frontal obstacles, the rover would either topple or slip when trying to climb on the objects. In the case of the chasm, the rover would simply fall into it.

A. *Small Frontal Obstacle Test*

The first experiment considered a $60mm$ high block - 60% of the $100mm$ rover height - blocking the rovers path. As can be seen from Figure 7, the rover detected the object and initiated its ramping procedure. The system created a sloped ramp by varying the peristaltic pump speed, effectively decreasing flow rate with increased distance from the obstacle. The system then waited for the foam to expand and solidify before using the deposit to climb onto the obstacle. The total time to run this experiment was 6 minutes and 42 seconds.

B. *Large Frontal Obstacle Test*

In the second experiment, a $130mm$ high block - 130% times the rover height - was placed along the planned path. Upon successfully detecting the object, the rover initiated the ramp building procedure as in the previous scenario. However, upon climbing the ramp it detects the object again. The system, knowing it has previously created a ramp, then enters its ramp filling procedure but deposits for an increase distance, creating a two tiered construct, as shown in Figure 8. After curing, the platform used the two-layer ramp to climb onto the obstacle. Total time for this experiment was 13 minutes and 42 seconds.

C. *Chasm Test*

In the final experiment, a $160mm$ long chasm was placed along the rover's path - over half the $300mm$ rover tracks length. The chasm was $80mm$ deep and $400mm$ wide. Once the forward undercarriage sensor detected a gap, the rover reduced its speed to ensure it had sufficient time to detect a potential chasm. Once the second sensor detected the same continuous gap, the decision logic inferred that no flooring is present between the two sensors, hence the chasm filling procedure was initiated. The material depositing system estimated the amount of material to be deposited from the knowledge of the depth of the chasm (measured by the undercarriage

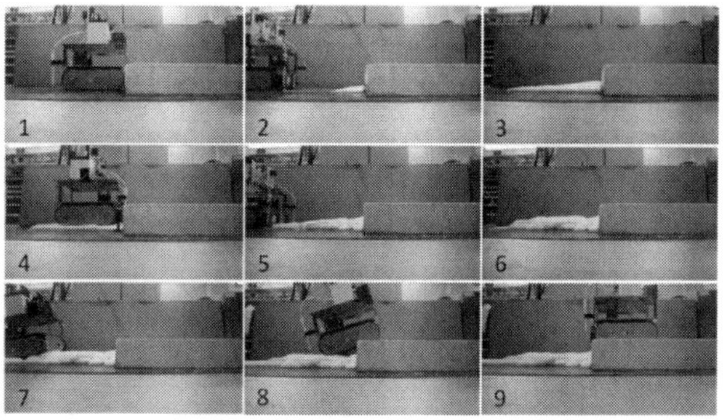

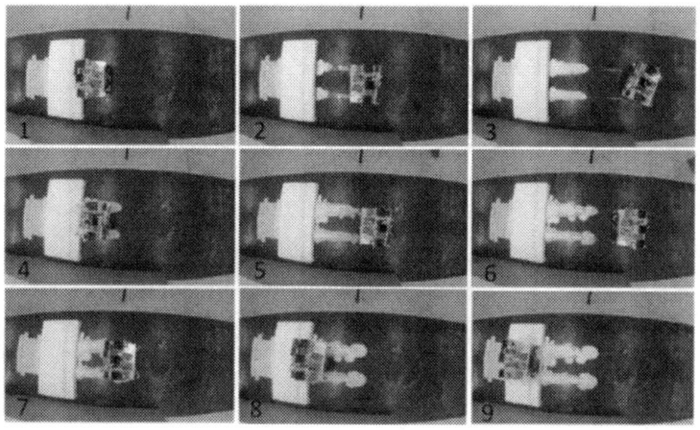

Figure 8. Large obstacle test: the stages of the rover detecting a $130mm$ high block and depositing a two-layer foam ramp to climb onto the obstacle. Left: side view, Right: top view.

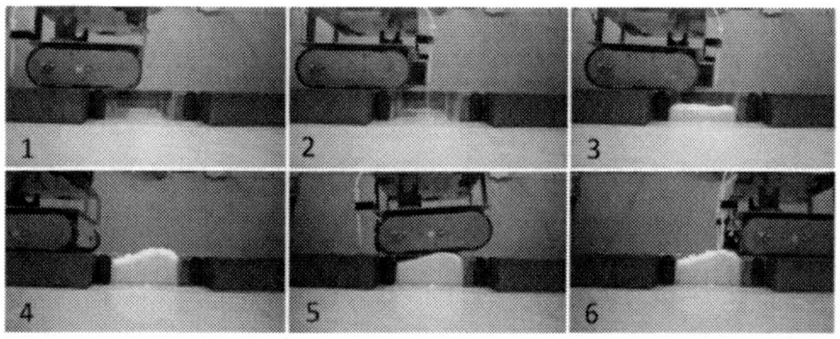

Figure 9. Chasm test: the stages of the rover detecting a $160mm$ long chasm and depositing PU foam to fill the gap and traverse the chasm.

sensors), performed the deposit and then waited for this to expand and solidify. The rover successfully filled the chasm and traversed the gap as shown in Figure 9. Total time for this experiment time was 5 minutes and 60 seconds.

VI. Conclusions and Future Work

In this paper, an inexpensive and easy-to-use PU foam depositing system is proposed. The system is designed as an independent module that can easily be integrated into existing robotic platforms to broaden their navigation capabilities on uneven terrains. This system does not require any complicated control systems, but it allows significant obstacles and chasms to be overcome. The primary benefit of this system when compared with others available in the literature is the complete control over the mix ratio and the deposit process. This allows control over the mechanical properties of the deposited material, allowing the PU foams expansion ratio and final compressive strength to be altered autonomously according to the situational requirement. Furthermore, the embedded flush system allows the long term use of the module without blockage, a typical drawback of existing platforms. The proposed device mitigates the main obstacle for using ground robots in disaster scenarios: traversing uneven terrain. Future developments may include the development of intelligent algorithms for optimising mix ratios according to the situation detected by sensors, scaling of system for increased range of applications, and collaborative robotics to tackle more complex and large scale efforts.

Acknowledgment

This research was supported by Apadana Management 3 Ltd.

References

[1] Centre for Research on Epidemiology of Distasters and United Nations Office for Disaster Risk Reduction, "The human cost of weather related disasters 1995-2015," 2016, retrieved: May, 2019. [Online]. Available: https://www.unisdr.org/2015/docs/climatechange/COP21_WeatherDisastersReport_2015_FINAL.pdf

[2] D. A. Alexander and S. Klein, "First responders after disasters: A review of stress reactions, at-risk, vulnerability, and resilience factors," Prehospital and Disaster Medicine, vol. 24, no. 2, 2009, p. 87–94.

[3] R. R. Murphy, S. Tadokoro, D. Nardi, A. Jacoff, P. Fiorini, H. Choset, and A. M. Erkmen, Search and Rescue Robotics. Berlin, Heidelberg: Springer Berlin Heidelberg, 2008, pp. 1151–1173.

[4] K. Nagatani et al., "Redesign of rescue mobile robot Quince," in 2011 IEEE International Symposium on Safety, Security, and Rescue Robotics, Nov 2011, pp. 13–18.

[5] R. R. Murphy, J. Kravitz, S. L. Stover, and R. Shoureshi, "Mobile robots in mine rescue and recovery," IEEE Robotics Automation Magazine, vol. 16, no. 2, June 2009, pp. 91–103.

[6] F. Matsuno and S. Tadokoro, "Rescue robots and systems in japan," in 2004 IEEE International Conference on Robotics and Biomimetics, Aug 2004, pp. 12–20.

[7] M. Brunner, B. Brüggemann, and D. Schulz, "Towards autonomously traversing complex obstacles with mobile robots with adjustable chassis," in Proceedings of the 13th International Carpathian Control Conference (ICCC), May 2012, pp. 63–68.

[8] L. Bruzzone and G. Quaglia, "Review article: locomotion systems for ground mobile robots in unstructured environments," Mechanical Sciences, vol. 3, 07 2012, pp. 49–62.

[9] R. Fujisawa et al., "Active modification of the environment by a robot with construction abilities," ROBOMECH Journal, vol. 2, no. 1, 2015, p. 9.

[10] N. Napp, O. R. Rappoli, J. M. Wu, and R. Nagpal, "Materials and mechanisms for amorphous robotic construction," in 2012 IEEE/RSJ International Conference on Intelligent Robots and Systems, Oct 2012, pp. 4879–4885.

DART Project: A High Precision UAV Prototype Exploiting On-board Visual Sensing

Michele Basso, Luca Bigazzi, Giacomo Innocenti

Dipartimento di Ingegneria dell'Informazione
Università degli Studi di Firenze
via S. Marta 3, 50139, Firenze, Italy.
Email: {michele.basso,giacomo.innocenti}@unifi.it

***Abstract*—This work explores a way to achieve high precision in the positioning of a 250-class aerial drone by means of only on-board sensors. The proposed technology is still in development, and its basic idea is to compensate the errors of the sensors by fusing together strongly correlated data streams. The main players are a 6 Degrees of Freedom (DoF) Inertial Measurement Unit (IMU) and a computer vision system, arranged to work together as a "virtual sensor" providing the pose of the drone relative to one or more markers acting as reference points of known position and orientation. The proposed advance sensing exploits complementary filters to merge inertial and visual data. Such a refined positioning is then used to feed a custom control strategy acting as auto-pilot for implementing autonomous navigation. Preliminary results on the developed technologies are reported.**

Keywords*–*Advance sensing; Drone; Computer Vision; Sensor Fusion.

I. INTRODUCTION

Thanks to their versatility, small drones like multirotor Unmanned Aerial Vehicles (UAVs) have received more and more interest over the last few years, both in the academic and industrial communities. In the scientific literature the use of drones is getting very popular and applications are increasing in pace with the technological development of these systems. Moreover, recent advances in microelectronics have made single-board microcontrollers and embedded systems economically affordable, making their use widespread to add advanced features in many small and medium-sized systems such as drones. In the context of UAV systems, for example, the availability of these advanced single-board computers is important in applications where extreme positioning precision is required. In this regard, interesting applications that have been proposed recently concern precision agriculture, where drones equipped with Real-Time Kinematic Global Navigation Satellite Systems (GNSSs-RTK) [1] are used to minimize human intervention [2] [3]. Other recent usage scenarios see drones equipped with specific scientific equipment, for example for the reconstruction of 3D environments through LIDAR (Laser Remote Sensing) techniques [4], or for monitoring road traffic [5]. These systems often use Vision-Based Navigation (VBN) algorithms to improve positioning accuracy [6]–[8]. However, currently in the scientific literature there are no direct references to the precision achieved by these multirotor systems, since in almost all of today's applications high precision specifications are not required, while for applications that require it, alternative solutions are sought. In particular, at the current technological level there are no drones capable of following trajectories with sub-centimetric precision and this precludes the use of these drones in many potential novel applications.

The main purpose of this work consists in the development of a high-precision positioning system for UAV multirotors, which makes these devices usable in a wide class of applications where high accuracy is the main requirement. To increase the level of accuracy of the currently available solutions, the proposed approach integrates and extends the performance of computer vision and inertial sensor navigation techniques, where position, velocity and attitude data extracted simultaneously from video streams and inertial sensors are merged together by filter fusion algorithms for error compensation. The above task involves the development of software and hardware dedicated to video processing. In particular, by exploiting a single camera mounted on-board, the main task is based on the identification of specific markers in the environment, from which it is possible to extract with high precision the information of attitude and position relative to the drone. Through appropriate algorithms, it is then possible to determine in real-time the 3D coordinates of the drone with respect to the marker, which can be used as a position virtual sensor for controlling the drone trajectory. This visual sensor has been designed to be employed as an on-board autonomous navigation system add-on for commercial drones. Indeed, the developed prototype has been implemented on a low-cost hardware board (Raspberry PI), which is able to process video and inertial sensor data to autonomously pilot a 250-class multirotor for tracking specific trajectories.

The rest of the paper is structured as follows. In Section II, the hardware and software architectures are illustrated. In Section III, the computer vision technique developed for the advanced sensing of the drone's position is presented. We conclude the paper in Section IV reporting some preliminary results.

II. PROTOTYPE ARCHITECTURE

A. *Hardware*

The DART prototype is a 250-class aerial drone developed at the Systems & Control Lab of the Department of Information Engineering of the University of Florence (see Figure 1). The drone features a flight controller CC3D Revo running the open-source LibrePilot software as low-level interface to the hardware. This very basic architecture has been extended by

(a)

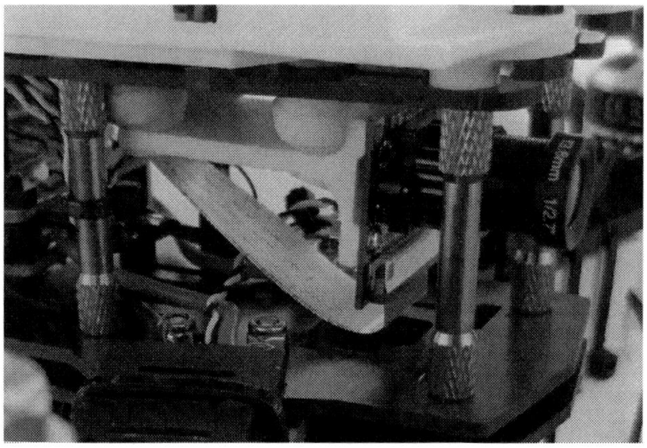

(b)

Figure 1. (a) DART prototype. (b) Zoom of the camera suspension support.

two additional board: A Raspberry PI 3 B+ and a Arduino nano. The first board is equipped with an Pololu 2739 IMU and a Raspicam camera module, and it implements the autonomous driving commands based on image processing and data from the onboard IMU. The second board, instead, implements a Pulse Position Modulation mixer (PPM-mixer) between the commands coming from the 2.4 GHz receiver, and those generated by the autonomous driving module. The mixer allows also for hybrid driving modes, and it is responsible of the safety during transitions from manual to autonomous flight modes and vice-versa. Figure 2 illustrates the related functional scheme. The Raspberry module communicates with the PPM-mixer via a bidirectional Universal Asynchronous Receiver Transmitter (UART) protocol, while the commands from the receiver arrive to the Arduino nano via its native PPM protocol. PPM is also the kind of signal expected by the LibrePilot interface, and so this has to be the nature of the mixer output, thus explaining its name. Regarding the commands from the receiver, then, the mixer operates just as a pass-through, while the commands from the autonomous driving module have to be transformed into proper PPM signals. In the Raspberry board, API V4L2 are exploited to handle the signals from the connector of the camera, whereas data from the IMU arrive via I2C bus.

B. Software

All the necessary software runs on the three boards described in the previous subsection according to the following scheme. The CC3D Revo board executes the LibrePilot software [9], which provides access to the drone IMU sensors and motors, thus acting as low-level interface to each single device on the drone. The Raspberry module, instead, executes the software for image processing, and it is also responsible for generating the commands of the autonomous driving. In particular, the developed computer vision software is based on OpenCV [10] and Visp [11] libraries. In the proposed version, the computer vision software is designed to recognize special markers. Figure 3 depicts the result of the image processing that allows the module to detect the marker, and to compute its orientation. The autonomous driver implements an in-house control algorithm, described in more details later. The Arduino nano board, finally, runs UART and PPM protocols specifically designed for it objective function, i.e. the hardware switch.

C. Control algorithm

The autonomous driving module computes the commands in the same form of those coming from the receiver, i.e., as proper reference values for roll, pitch, yaw and thrust. At this stage of the project, they are simply conceived to have the drone maintaining a desired position $\overline{Q}$ with a zero yaw angle $\psi = 0$, such that the drone is facing the marker. The image processing module provides both relative orientation and relative position with respect to the marker. This information is further integrated by means of a fusion algorithm with data coming from the onboard IMU to improve the estimate of the image processing. It is worth stressing that with the implemented algorithm and hardware platform the image processing module works at about 30-40 Hz, while the IMU can provide data at higher frequency. Therefore, the sensor fusion algorithm also synchronizes the two different information streams in order to use the right samples from each sensor. The final result is a refined estimate of the drone position Q with respect to the marker, whose details will be described in the next section. The extension to multiple markers is still under development, but early results are promising.

The information on the drone pose errors $(\overline{Q} - Q)$ and $(0 - \psi)$ are used to feed four distinct controllers, which generate the driving commands as references for roll and pitch angles, yaw angular velocity, and thrust. Such a preliminary solution is not expected to provide the best performance, since it does not consider the mutual connections between the drone pose components, but it allows one to design the autonomous driver by composition of simpler modules. The resulting control architecture is illustrated in Figure 4.

III. ADVANCED SENSING

A. Virtual sensor

The vision algorithm takes care of detecting one or more known markers present in the environment in order to obtain their poses (positions and orientations) with respect to the camera reference frame (body frame). To achieve this task, the algorithm computes the gradient for each pixel of the image such that pixels with similar gradient directions are grouped into sets. The latter sets identify edges in the image from which

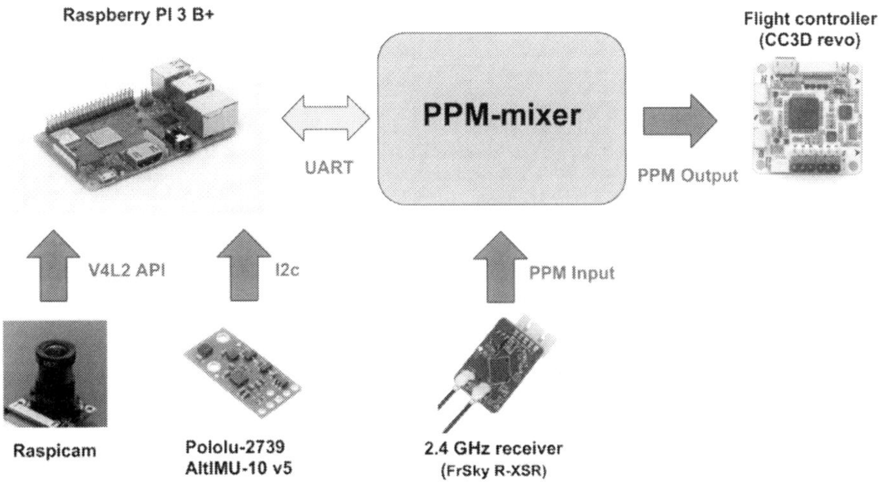

Figure 2. Hardware configuration and dependencies.

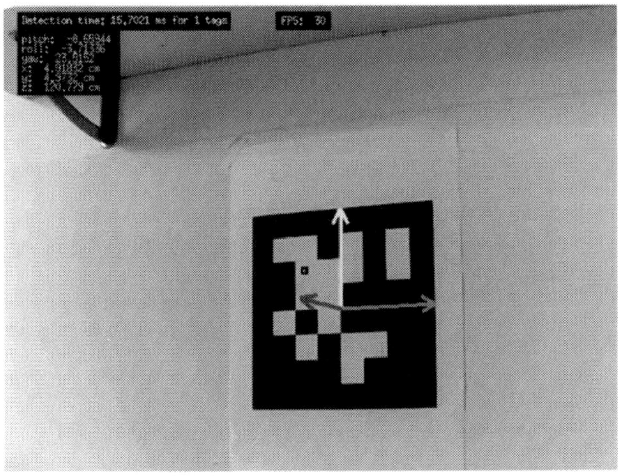

Figure 3. Marker as seen from the image processing module.

the algorithm searches for the correct sequence that recognizes the two-dimensional position (u, v) of each marker in pixel coordinates.

The marker coordinates (x_m, y_m, z_m) in body frame can be computed through the relations for barrel distortion

$$y_m/z_m = \frac{(v - v_0)(1 + k_{ud}R^2)}{p_y} \tag{1}$$

where

$$R^2 = \frac{(u - u_0)^2}{p_x^2} + \frac{(v - v_0)^2}{p_y^2}, \tag{2}$$

(u_0, v_0) represents pixel coordinates of the image center, whereas parameters p_x e p_y are the focal length to pixel dimension ratios. Finally, k_{ud} and k_{du} are parameters needed to correct lens distortions. Therefore, k_{ud}, k_{du}, p_x and p_y are intrinsic camera parameters which can be obtained through an iterative evaluation process that involves the acquisition of frames of a known image in different poses.

If the geometrical properties of the marker are known, it is possible to retrieve additional information such as the distance z_m and orientation of the marker itself which, in turn, provide the full pose of the marker frame with respect to the body or camera frame. Indeed, the following change of coordinates provide the drone 3D-position Q with respect to the marker frame

$$Q = \begin{bmatrix} x \\ y \\ z \end{bmatrix} = R_{XYZ}(\Phi) \begin{bmatrix} x_m \\ y_m \\ z_m \end{bmatrix} \tag{3}$$

where

$$\Phi = \begin{bmatrix} \varphi \\ \theta \\ \psi \end{bmatrix} \tag{4}$$

is the vector of the roll, pitch and yaw angles between the frames (computed in the experiments by using the Homography method), and

$$R_{XYZ}(\Phi) = \begin{bmatrix} c_\varphi c_\psi & c_\varphi s_\psi s_\theta + s_\varphi c_\theta & -c_\varphi s_\psi c_\theta + s_\varphi s_\theta \\ -s_\varphi c_\psi & -s_\varphi s_\psi s_\theta + c_\varphi c_\theta & s_\varphi s_\psi c_\theta + c_\varphi s_\theta \\ s_\psi & -c_\psi s_\theta & c_\psi c_\theta \end{bmatrix}$$

is the corresponding rotation matrix.

B. Sensor fusion

The use of an addition 6-DoF IMU makes it possible to merge the information of the drone attitude with the estimate provided by the vision, considerably increasing performance, especially at high frequencies.

At first, the algorithm running on the software platform prefilters both the attitude and position data coming from the vision and the angular velocities measured by the IMU gyroscope. Then, to improve the estimation accuracy, at each iteration k the attitude vector Φ_k computed by the vision system is fused with the angular velocities Ω_k measured by the gyroscope, through the use of the following first order complementary filter

$$\hat{\Phi}_{k+1} = \rho(\hat{\Phi}_k + T_k\Omega_k) + (1 - \rho)\Phi_k \tag{5}$$

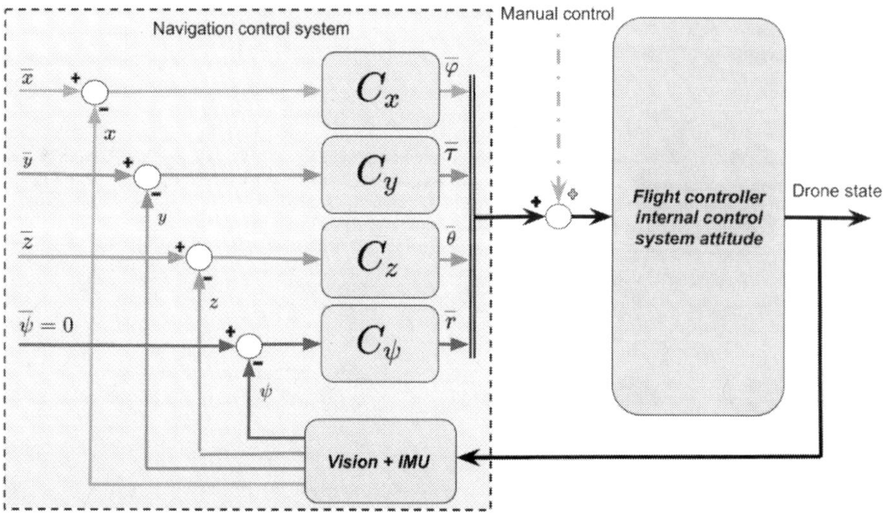

Figure 4. Architecture of the autonomous driving module. Blue blocks stands for custom made functions, while the green block represents the CC3D Revo board programmed with the LibrePilot software.

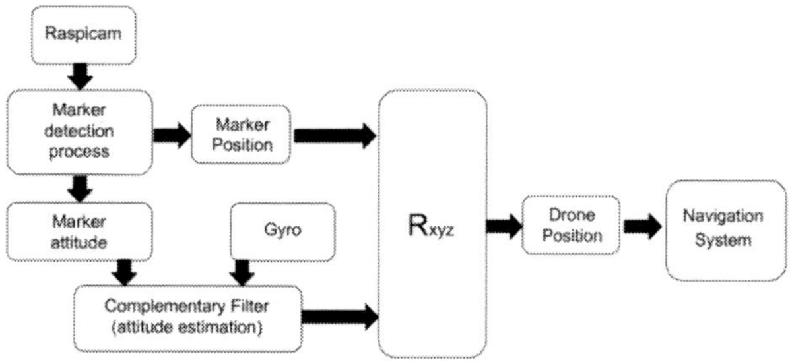

Figure 5. Schematic of the estimation process for the drone position and orientation.

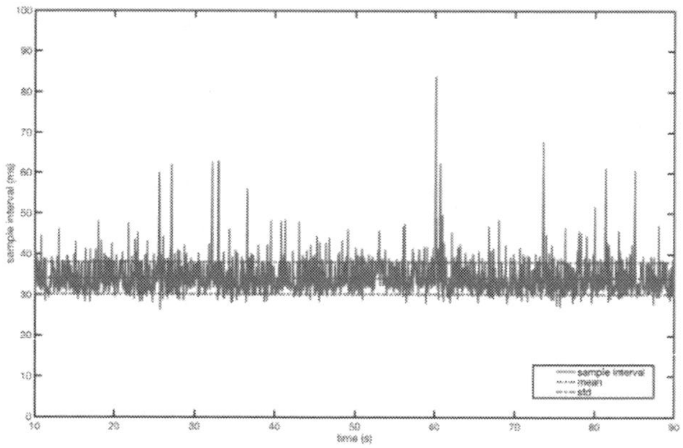

Figure 6. Measured sample interval of the navigation system.

where T_k is the actual sample interval and

$$\Omega_k = \begin{bmatrix} p \\ q \\ r \end{bmatrix} \tag{6}$$

is the vector of the angular velocities around the three main drone axes. The new orientation estimate $\hat{\Phi}$ of equation (5) can now be employed in the coordinates transformation (3) providing a refined position estimate Q. The schematic of the complete filtering and estimation process is depicted in Figure 5.

IV. Conclusion and Future Developments

In this section, some preliminary results will be reported and commented. A depiction of the next development of the project will be illustrated, as well.

Figure 6 depicts how the sampling time varies during a test flight. It is worth observing that its average is around the already mentioned 34ms (i.e., about 30Hz) with a sufficiently narrow standard deviation less than 2.5ms. Nevertheless, since the control board in not meant for real-time computing, the varying computational burden and the variable power supply to the processor generate relatively small oscillation of the sampling time. In Figure 7, the trend of positions x, y, and z are shown as they evolve during a test flight in auto-piloting mode. The experiment is meant to provide a glimpse of the output coming from the virtual sensor based on computer vision techniques. The comparison with the real position of the drone would require a special environment (such as a set of ground cameras), which will be developed later in the project to assess the final result quality. Still, a simple visual inspection of the diagrams suggests that the virtual sensor may be able to catch sufficiently rapid variations of the position without introducing relevant noise. In this respect, Figure 8 reports the position estimate while the drone stands still on a test bench. Since the position is constant, the plot shows the trend of the estimation errors and it provides a good graphical representation of the system intrinsic noise (appraisable in only few centimeters for a 2.72m distant marker) and its related power. Looking at Figure 8, the result turns out particularly encouraging once the absence of a gimball for the camera is stressed, since such a solution would strongly reduce the

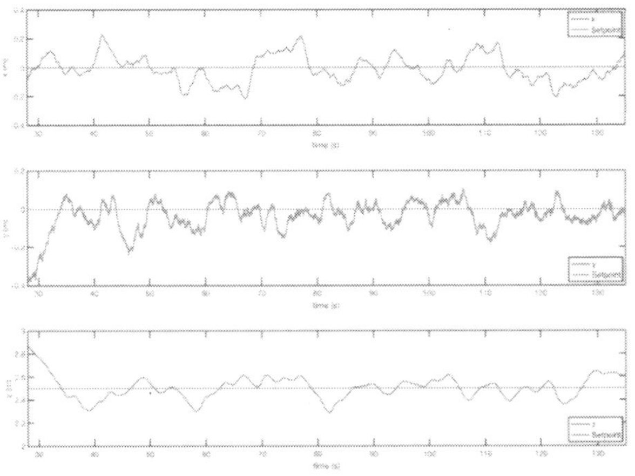

Figure 7. Drone detected position during an autonomous flight.

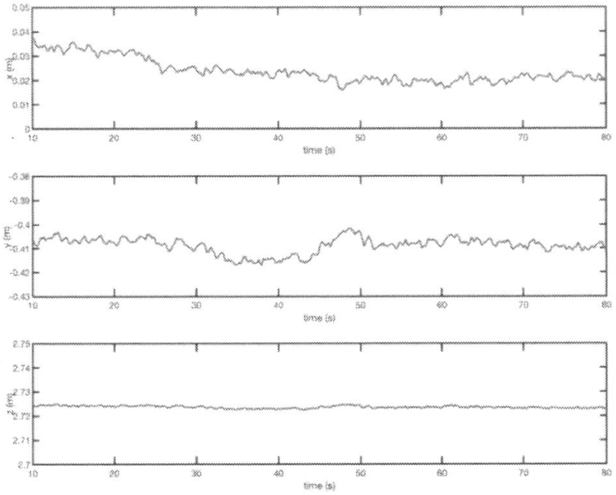

Figure 8. Drone detected position in static conditions.

compensation needed to refine the pose estimate. The addition of a gimball is planned as one of the next improvements.

Other tests have already been planned to check the reliability of the proposed technology up to this stage of the project. Experiments aimed at testing the auto piloting functionality, instead, are scheduled later on, because they are more complicated to perform due to the many precautions needed to ensure the drone safety during an autonomous flight. Most likely, better performance could be achieved by using model based controllers. Therefore, an accurate physical model of the drone will be top priority for the continuation of the project.

REFERENCES

[1] P. Henkel, U. Mittmann, and M. Iafrancesco, "Real-time kinematic positioning with GPS and GLONASS," in 2016 24th European Signal Processing Conference (EUSIPCO), Aug 2016, pp. 1063–1067.

[2] P. Tokekar, J. V. Hook, D. Mulla, and V. Isler, "Sensor planning for a symbiotic UAV and UGV system for precision agriculture," IEEE Transactions on Robotics, vol. 32, no. 6, Dec 2016, pp. 1498–1511.

[3] B. Reshma and S. S. Kumar, "Precision aquaculture drone algorithm for delivery in sea cages," in 2016 IEEE International Conference on Engineering and Technology (ICETECH), March 2016, pp. 1264–1270.

[4] M. Sanfourche, B. Le Saux, A. Plyer, and G. Le Besnerais, "Environment mapping & interpretation by drone," in 2015 Joint Urban Remote Sensing Event (JURSE), March 2015, pp. 1–4.

[5] H. Zhou, H. Kong, L. Wei, D. Creighton, and S. Nahavandi, "Efficient road detection and tracking for unmanned aerial vehicle," IEEE Transactions on Intelligent Transportation Systems, vol. 16, no. 1, Feb 2015, pp. 297–309.

[6] F. Samadzadegan and G. Abdi, "Autonomous navigation of unmanned aerial vehicles based on multi-sensor data fusion," in 20th Iranian Conference on Electrical Engineering (ICEE2012), May 2012, pp. 868–873.

[7] A. G. Kendall, N. N. Salvapantula, and K. A. Stol, "On-board object tracking control of a quadcopter with monocular vision," in 2014 International Conference on Unmanned Aircraft Systems (ICUAS), May 2014, pp. 404–411.

[8] P. Rudol, M. Wzorek, and P. Doherty, "Vision-based pose estimation for autonomous indoor navigation of micro-scale unmanned aircraft systems," in 2010 IEEE International Conference on Robotics and Automation, May 2010, pp. 1913–1920.

[9] "LibrePilot open source project," 2019, URL: https://www.librepilot.org [accessed: 2019-04-02].

[10] "Open Source Computer Vision Library," 2019, URL: https://opencv.org/ [accessed: 2019-04-02].

[11] "Open source visual servoing platform library," 2019, URL: https://visp.inria.fr/ [accessed: 2019-04-02].

A Navigational System for Quadcopter Remote Inspection of Offshore Substations

Elisabeth Welburn*, Hassan Hakim Khalili†, Ananya Gupta‡, Joaquin Carrasco§ and Simon Watson¶
School of Electrical and Electronic Engineering
The University of Manchester, Manchester, UK M14 9PL
*Email: Elisabeth.Welburn@manchester.ac.uk
† Email: Hassan.Hakimkhalili@manchester.ac.uk
‡ Email: Ananya.Gupta@manchester.ac.uk
§ Email: Joaquin.Carrasco@manchester.ac.uk
¶ Email: Simon.Watson@manchester.ac.uk

Abstract—**Effective and safe maintenance of offshore infrastructure is hampered by its remote location. Robotic inspection can provide a retrofit solution, improving safety for human personnel by removing them from a potentially hazardous environment, and also reduce operational costs. There are three primary challenges for navigation around an offshore substation: low visibility, high electromagnetic fields and the absence of Global Positioning System (GPS) signals. This paper details a navigational system that enables Unmanned Aerial Vehicles (UAVs) to operate within a dark and GPS-denied environment.**

Keywords–Robotics In Hazardous Fields; Aerial Robotics; SLAM; Sensor-based Control.

I. Introduction

The remote inspection and asset management of offshore wind farms and the connection to shore will be worth up to 2 billion pounds annually by 2025. However, current methods of inspection are dangerous for human personnel and introduce high costs for the industry as a whole [1].

Currently, Supervisory Control and Data Acquisition (SCADA) systems and thermal imaging inspections are being used in data management to inform substation operations and maintenance. However, the limited number of qualified inspectors coupled with the high demand leads to common unexpected failures. Automation could potentially alleviate this by increasing inspection frequency and standardizing procedures [2].

Robotic inspection platforms have the potential to ensure the maintenance of vital infrastructure, reducing associated expenditure and hazards [1]. However, this endeavour presents unique challenges that must be overcome for it to become a viable commercial method. Considering the offshore substation environment in the context of a navigational system, the inherently symmetrical nature coupled with the occlusion of GPS signal may attribute to difficulty ascertaining an accurate estimation of the robot's global 6 Degree of Freedom (DoF) pose. The high electromagnetic fields necessitate the use of shielding, limiting external sensor hardware [3]. The presence of high electromagnetic fields could potentially interfere with the nominal operation of the propulsion motors [4]. To circumvent this, the use of a magnetometer within the proposed navigational system will be neglected. Moreover, the sensor payload must also be minimal to extend battery life, facilitating the implementation of autonomous capabilities in this remote location. Also, the absence of visible light limits the use of vision-based odometry.

Three levels of autonomy can be defined: pure tele-operation, safe-guarded tele-operation and autonomous navigation [5]. The navigational system presented within this paper provides a method of remote tele-operation. However, the aim is to extend this system to full autonomy in the future with more sophisticated obstacle avoidance capabilities that account for the electromagnetic fields.

This paper presents a navigational system for UAVs to operate inside a High Voltage Direct Current (HVDC) valve hall. The quadcopter is equipped with two 2D Light Detection and Ranging (LiDAR) devices that are mounted perpendicularly to each other, the combination of which provides a 3D estimation of the robot pose. However, this estimation is, in part, based upon relative movement of the surrounding landmarks between frames and so is subject to a certain amount of drift. This is further exacerbated by the repetitive and symmetrical nature of these landmarks. To remedy this, the implementation of Quick Response (QR) codes were investigated as global reference points to correct for this accumulated error. Sensor fusion was accomplished with the use of an Extended Kalman Filter (EKF).

The remainder of this paper is structured as follows: Section II of this paper will consider related works and Section III will detail the system architecture, while Section IV will analyse the collated results and several conclusions will be drawn concerning further extensions of this work and the viability of this system within industry.

II. Related Work

To inform system design, the state-of-the-art navigational techniques were considered for UAVs as well as ground vehicles, with the view of adapting these methods for UAV navigation of a GPS-denied and dark environment.

A. *Current Navigational Techniques*

In [6], an autonomous navigational system was developed for a ground vehicle deployed within a GPS-denied greenhouse. This system used the Hector Simultaneous Localisation and Mapping (SLAM) Robot Operating System (ROS) package, that is also used within this system, and combined this with a potential fields path planning algorithm. Structural changes due to the growth of crops were accounted in the path planning algorithm while being safe to operate in the presence of humans. This is reminiscent of faults occurring and causing a fluctuation of electromagnetic fields inside the HVDC valve hall environment, changing the required clearances to maintain nominal operation of the UAV.

In [7], a UAV was deployed into a GPS-denied, dark tunnel where a perception system comprising of a near-infra-red stereo camera, flashing LEDs, inertial sensors, and a 3D depth sensor to derive the geometry of the environment. A horizon-based planner accounted for the system's uncertainty during mission execution and generated collision-free exploration paths. However, the environment here was unknown and static, whereas the valve hall geometry is known and faults within the racks can cause a fluctuation of the electromagnetic fields.

In [2], a robot transverses substations with the use of a rail system and collects IR and visible images, positioning, time and component description and transmits this, as well as energy, to a control centre with the use of the rails. This mitigates faults caused by intermediate electromagnetic interference between the robot and the control centre. Also, magnetic references on the rails negate the need for markings implemented onto the substation infrastructure. Also, the use of the commercial voltage for Brazil facilitates installation in other locations. However, the rail-based robot requires the installation of an extensive rail system in existing substations to operate [2]. The system proposed within this paper provides a retro-fit solution that could potentially accomplish the same task.

B. Vision-Based Odometry Techniques

The dark nature of the valve hall restricts the perception within the visible spectrum. However, a Near-Infrared (NIR) camera will be fitted to the drone for fault detection purposes and also a LED spotlight can provide limited ambient lighting in the immediate vicinity.

In general, though visual odometry is useful for local position control and stability, these methods often suffer from long-term drifts and are not suitable for building large-scale maps [8]. RGB-D cameras provide both a colour image and per-pixel depth estimates and are prominent within mobile robotic platforms due to their richness of the data collected coupled with their reducing cost. In [8], a system for the navigation of a micro-air vehicle within a cluttered, GPS-denied indoor environments with the use of an on-board RGB-D camera and an Inertial Measurement Unit (IMU) was developed. This system periodically corrected for the drift present within the local state estimation based upon visual odometry with results from the RGB-D mapping algorithm [9]. However, this system was unsuitable for real-time situations as the loop closing and SLAM algorithms were not sufficiently fast to be run on an on-board processor.

The use of Quick Response codes within absolute localisation methods for indoor mobile robots is widespread due to their large data storage capabilities, small size, low cost and simple implementation. A possible issue with their use is that the recognition rate is reduced if the QR code is small within the camera's field of view or the robot moves too fast. Considering this application in real-time, the processing resources are sufficiently low to enable use of the QR codes, as it was found within [10], that the time taken to calculate the relative position of the robot was between 20 to 30 ms.

Within [10], an industrial camera was mounted onto a mobile ground robot pointing upwards in order to identify QR codes mounted to the ceiling. Meanwhile, a laser range-finder was used for object detection as well as the construction of a 2D map with the use of a Rao-Blackwellized particle filter. The Dijkstra algorithm, as well as the Dyanmic Window Approach were used to implement both local and global path planning capabilities [10]. However, this system is not usable in situations where the QR codes were occluded from the camera's field of view due to sheltering obstacles or ambient light. Odometry data was used to compensate for the drift occurring within the short time interval travelling between the QR codes, whereby the error accumulation was mitigated with the use of additional sensor inputs [10].

In [11], a tailored extended H_∞ filter (EHF) was implemented. This filter fused both odometry and gyroscope data with pose estimates based upon QR code landmarks. However, this method is more computationally expensive compared to an EKF, taking longer to converge on an accurate estimate [11], which is paramount when instructing real-time control as in this scenario.

III. System Architecture

Within this section, the architecture of the navigational system as depicted in Figure 1 is discussed.

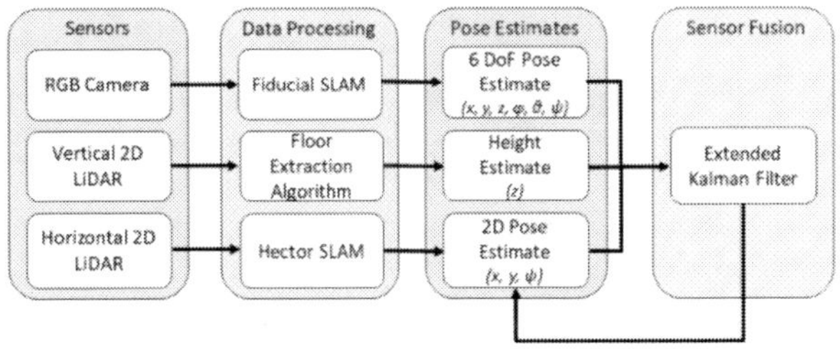

Figure 1. Software Architecture for the Proposed Navigational System.

A. Mobile Robotic Platform

The quadcopter utilised for the proof-of-concept system is the Hector quadrotor Robot Operating System (ROS) package [12] due to its pre-existing and well-documented integration with the Gazebo simulator. The visual geometry was written within COLLADA format and the collision geometry was modelled as a STL mesh. A low polygon count reduced the demand from rendering the model, allowing simulations to be ran at a higher percentage of real-time. The propellers were represented by actuator discs to facilitate the maintenance of boundary conditions [12]. The hector quadrotor is depicted below in Figure 2.

Figure 2. The Hector quadrotor rendered within the Gazebo simulator. Image taken from [12].

The CAD model of an offshore substation, as shown in Figure 3, with the correct clearances as the real-time environment was constructed and used to collate results.

Figure 3. CAD model of the HVDC valve hall

B. 2D SLAM Algorithm

Low-cost laser range-finders are prevalent in autonomous robot applications due to their low price and ability to trace terrains and structures in the contiguous area, while consuming relatively little power [13].

In the proposed system, two Hokuyo utm-30lx LiDARs were mounted perpendicularly to each other. It was assumed that the z-axis was out-of-plane relative to the ground plane and the x-axis was pointing in the forward direction of the quadcopter. The horizontal, planar LiDAR was used within the 2D SLAM algorithm to construct a map of the surroundings.

A ROS node, Hector Mapping [14], was selected as the 2D SLAM algorithm, of which the only requirement was a high frequency laser scanner, such as the Hokuyo utm-30lx LiDAR in this scenario.

C. Floor Extraction

For height estimation and greater spatial understanding, a secondary LiDAR was mounted, perpendicular to the primary LiDAR, onto the underside of Hector quadrotor. The vertical LiDAR produced a 2D vertical laser scan of the environment. A split-and-merge algorithm [15] was then implemented to differentiate the walls and floor using the relative angle of the incident laser endpoints. The roll and pitch recorded by the EKF was processed and the calculated relative angles of the identified line segments were rotated to avoid falsely recognising the walls as the floor during operation.

A laser pointing vertically downwards was also considered as the method of height estimation, however this is a less robust method than the aforementioned secondary LiDAR. This is because if the quadrotor turned near the boundaries of the space, the singular laser point could potentially rotate to be incidental on walls or substation racks. This could be mitigated with the use of fusion with the orientation from the IMU device to account for the laser rotation. However, IMU data suffers from drift and so a secondary LiDAR was used in the implementation to provide more information of the transformation of the laser scan points relative to the quadrotor.

D. QR Codes as Global Landmarks

Vision-based odometry is generally computationally intensive and also suffers from robustness under varying lighting conditions [11]. However, in this scenario there is an absence of visible light and so ambient light levels are constant. Also, vision-based odometry was implemented with the view to periodically correct for drift in the 2D SLAM algorithm pose estimations.

A FLIR One Near-Infrared (NIR) camera of a spectral range between 8 - 14 μm will be utilised to enable simultaneous QR code detection and faults within the infrared spectrum. An infrared LED emitting light between 750 - 950 nm will be mounted on top of the camera, illuminating the proximal field of view. However, for the purposes of this simulation, a generic camera is created within a virtual world lit by ambient lighting to ensure an accurate estimation of the nominal accuracy of the vision-based odometry.

The QR codes were generated with the use of the open-source library, arUco markers. These were then placed on the racks within the virtual substation environment at regular intervals. The ROS package, fiducial SLAM [16], was used to both identify the unique identifier of the QR code as well as produce a 6 DoF pose estimation of the drone using the known global poses of the QR codes.

The QR codes could potentially be used in two capacities during drone operation. Correct identification of a unique QR code indicates the drone is within the correct general vicinity of the rack. These could form the basis of a command interface to set the goal destination that determines the generated path. The unique identifiers of visible QR codes in the camera field of view are shown in Figure 3.

Figure 4. The virtual UAV inspecting a substation rack. Inset is the camera field of view.

Alternatively, the pose of the visible QR marker in a known location can be processed to output a 6 DoF pose estimation of the drone that could have been later fused with the other sensor measurements within the EKF. However, this was found to produce erroneous estimations of 6 DoF pose, as discussed later.

IV. SENSOR FUSION

Sensor fusion was necessary within this system to identify the optimal estimate of the UAVs pose. Considering the sensor measurements modelled in this section, $(x_s, y_s, z_s, \phi_s, \theta_s, \Psi_s)$ was produced from the 2D SLAM performed using the planar LiDAR, z from the height measurement using the perpendicular LiDAR and, finally, $(x, y, z, \phi, \theta, \Psi)$ was produced from the vision-based odometry system based upon QR codes visible to the on-board camera.

First, the orientation measurements must be converted from a quarternion in the local frame to Euler angles that are relative to the global frame. A function available within the ROS python library tf was used for this conversion. For the purposes of this system, the starting pose of the spawned robot was assumed to be the global frame in terms of the way-point commands that were converted into command velocities. However, this coordinate frame was mapped onto the 2D occupancy grid constructed to utilise the A* path planning algorithm.

The measurements were taken at different unsynchronised rates. To accompany this, each sensor measurement was sampled with each new IMU measurement at a rate of 100 Hz. In this way, a sufficient sample rate was ensured.

Kalman filters are algorithms for the estimation of dynamic state variables by combining state predictions with measurements. For discrete systems, the future values of the state variables can be predicted using Kalman filters.

The EKF can overcome the linearity assumption of the Kalman Filter that both the motion model and sensor model are linear Gaussian [13]. Within this system, an extended Kalman filter was implemented, where the non-linearity is introduced with the continuously-variable rotation relative to the global frame.

For time-invariant systems, the function f computed the predicted state from the previous estimate, and the h function computed the output. The variables, w_k and v_k, represented the process and observation white noises, respectively, i. e.

$$x_{k+1} = f(x_k, u_k) + w_k \tag{1}$$
$$z_k = h(x_k) + v_k \tag{2}$$

The white noises w_k and v_k were assumed to be zero mean and covariances Q_k and R_k, respectively.

For the purposes of this Kalman filter, all variables were within the global frame. The values used for initialisation of the Kalman filter were the coordinates of spawning the robot model.

In the case of the Hector quadcopter, the state variables were updated with the use of inertial measurements from the IMU unit. The state vector, X, comprised of these state variables:

$$X = [x \quad y \quad z \quad \dot{x} \quad \dot{y} \quad \dot{z} \quad \phi \quad \theta \quad \Psi]^T \tag{3}$$

where x, y, z were the positions on the X, Y, and Z axes and ϕ was the roll, θ, the pitch and Ψ, the yaw of the quadrotor.

The global displacement, s, in each of the X, Y and Z axes was modelled using dead reckoning with the initial displacement, s_0, the rotation matrix that transforms between the body frame to the inertial frame, R, the initial velocity at the start of the time interval v_0, IMU acceleration within the IMU frame of reference, a, the gravitational constant, g, and the length of the time interval, t.

With some abuse of notation, this relationship was encapsulated in the dynamic matrix, f, that described how the state evolves to the next time step, as below:

$$f = \begin{bmatrix} s_0 + \dot{s}\Delta T + \frac{1}{2}R(a-g)\Delta T^2 \\ \dot{v}_0 + \Delta T\Big(R(a-g)\Big) \\ \alpha_0 + \Delta T\Theta \end{bmatrix}, \tag{4}$$

where Θ was the mapping of the angular velocities in the body frame (p, q, r) to the changes in the Euler angles within the inertial frame [17], e.g.

$$\Theta = \begin{bmatrix} 1 & \sin\phi\tan\theta & \cos\phi\tan\theta \\ 0 & \cos\phi & -\sin\phi \\ 0 & \frac{\sin\phi}{\cos\theta} & \frac{\cos\phi}{\cos\theta} \end{bmatrix}. \tag{5}$$

The measurement function, h, was given by

$$h = [x \quad y \quad z \quad \phi \quad \theta \quad \Psi]^T. \tag{6}$$

The linearisation of (1) provided the state transition matrix, F_k, by computing the Jacobian of the dynamic matrix f with respect to the state vector. Similarly, the observation matrix H_k was also be defined as the Jacobian of the measurement matrix, h with respect to the state vector.

The control inputs into the system were assumed to be the linear accelerations and the angular velocities as measured by the IMU, i.e.

$$u = [\ddot{x} \quad \ddot{y} \quad \ddot{z} \quad \dot{\phi} \quad \dot{\theta} \quad \dot{\Psi} \quad]^T \tag{7}$$

The time update of the EKF algorithm was given by

$$\hat{x}_{k|k-1} = f(x_{k-1}, u_{k-1}), \tag{8}$$
$$P_{k|k-1} = F_k P_{k-1|k-1} F_k^T + Q_k. \tag{9}$$

The measurement update steps were then computed to adjust the Kalman gain, K_k and to update the estimate with the actual measurement, z_k, and to update the error covariance, $P_{k|k}$. The measurement residual, $\widetilde{y}$ as well as the covariance residual, S_k were also calculated.

$$\widetilde{y}_k = z_k - h(\hat{x}_{k|k-1}) \tag{10}$$
$$S_k = H_k P_{k|k-1} H_k^T + R_k \tag{11}$$
$$K_k = P_{k|k-1} H_k^T S_k^{-1} \tag{12}$$
$$\hat{x}_{k|k} = \hat{x}_{k|k-1} + K_k \widetilde{y}_k \tag{13}$$
$$P_{k|k} = (I - K_k H_k) P_{k|k-1} \tag{14}$$

This method was less computationally expensive in comparison to other methods, such as the H_∞ filter (EHF) [11]. One of the drawbacks of an extended Kalman filter is that it is not an optimal estimator. Moreover, if the initial state vector is wrong, the filter will quickly diverge due to its linearisation. As a result, the EKF requires extensive tuning of these parameters.

V. Path Planning Algorithm

The final pose estimation from the EKF was fed into an A* path planning module [18]. The robot radius was considered greater than the nominal dimensions, ensuring clearances from the high electromagnetic fields present within the substation racks were maintained.

Prior to this, a 2D occupancy grid of the substation plan was constructed using the known dimensions of the CAD model. In terms of command way-points, height correction was performed first to adjust the drone to the specified goal height because of the largely constant geometry of the environment within the vertical plane. Then, an A* path planning algorithm was then used to generate the path shown in Figure 5 within the substation.

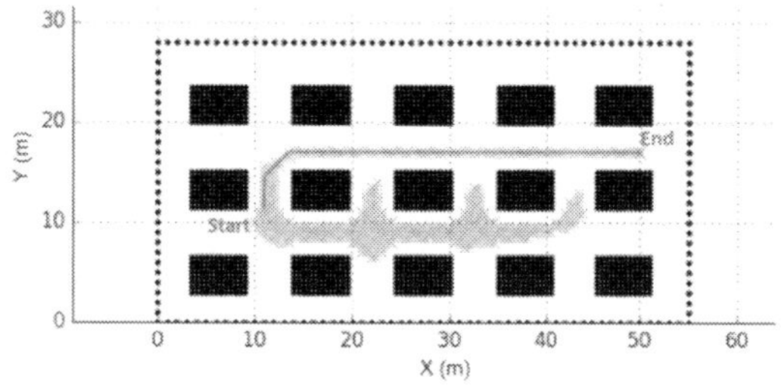

Figure 5. A 2D occupancy grid and path generated by the A* star algorithm

TABLE I. ERROR IN EKF OUTPUT

Global Axis	Distance Travelled (m)	Maximum Error (m)	Maximum Error (%)
x	39	0.65	1.67
y	5.5	0.3	5.45
z	5	0.015	0.3

This produced the optimal trajectory consisting of 0.5 m increments between the start position and goal position. After this, alterations to the orientation of the drone were made to enable 360 degree inspection.

VI. RESULTS

To ascertain a baseline and compute the errors of the constituent algorithms, the standard deviations of each of the measurements were calculated. These standard deviations were then used as a baseline for tuning of the Q and R matrices within the EKF.

The pose estimation generated from the EKF during the mapped trajectory in Figure 5 was used to gauge the viability of the proposed navigational system. The IMU measurements, as well as the *hector_mapping* 2D pose and extracted floor height were fused by the EKF. The 3D position of the UAV is compared to the ground truth within Figure 6. The error present within the EKF output is tabulated in Table I. An error of 1.67% in the x-axis throughout the course of a twenty-minute mission is tolerable. However, an error of 5.45% in the y-axis is unsatisfactory and further tuning of the EKF is required to alleviate this. The height estimation algorithm was found to produce the least error, with a 0.3% throughout the length of the mission. The average battery life of a UAV is between ten to fifteen minutes, depending on payload and so these figures represent a probable overestimation of the drift present within the EKF.

The camera stream was also recorded, whereby visible QR codes unique identifiers were overlaid, as seen in Figure 4. The 6 DoF pose estimation from the visible QR codes was also collated to evaluate whether this data should be incorporated into the EKF. However, as can be seen by Figure 7, these pose estimations are extremely erratic and will not contribute to the overall stability of the EKF upon fusion.

The inaccurate 6 DoF pose estimation produced from the *fiducial_slam* could potentially be due to the 2D nature of the QR codes hindering precise depth perception. It also may be due to the monocular nature of the camera.

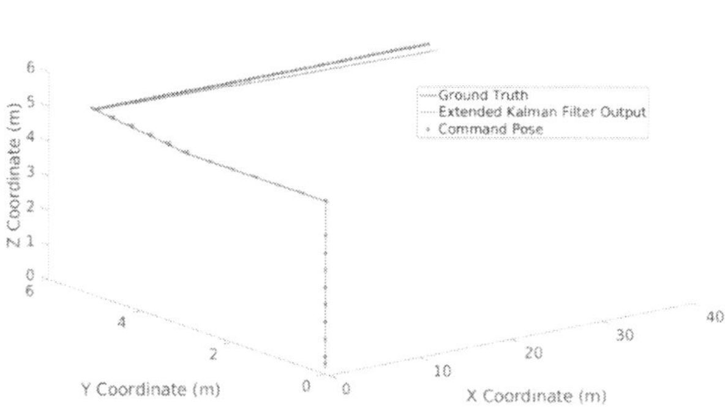

Figure 6. EKF pose estimation

Considering Figure 7, ultimately direct pose estimation from fiducial slam was not implemented within the EKF. However, the unique identifiers displayed within the camera stream could potentially facilitate inspection of substation racks by providing a visual verification of the current vicinity of the UAV.

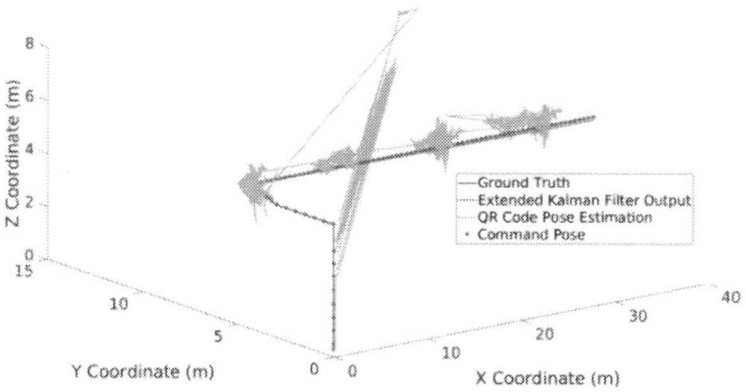

Figure 7. EKF pose estimation with the fiducial slam results

In summary, these set of results suggest that this framework could potentially be adapted for implementation into a real-world system.

VII. CONCLUSION

In conclusion, the proposed, proof-of-concept, navigational system paves the way for UAV navigation within dark, GPS-denied environments. This was acheived with the fusion of IMU data with processed LiDAR measurements. Possible mechanisms of correction via vision-based odometry upon the identification of QR codes within the environment were explored and it was concluded that though the QR codes provide visual cues of the drones current position they fail to act as reference points to generate an accurate 6 DoF pose. This system provides a retro-fit solution for the remote inspection of substations, merely requiring the careful placement of QR codes within the environment.

Future work includes the implementation of this navigational system onto a drone within an indoor, confined and dark environment. The computation and sensing required for local position control will be performed on-board the vehicle, reducing the dependence on unreliable wireless links [8]. The path planning capabilities will also be expanded to account for the presence of electromagnetic fields with the implementation of a modified potential fields algorithm. Moreover, this system could potentially pave the way for the use of thermal imaging to identify faults within the substation infrastructure. This is advantageous in comparision to existing methods because it involves non-contact precision temperature measurements and non-destructive testing [5].

ACKNOWLEDGMENTS

This work was supported by the Holistic Operation and Maintenance for Energy from Offshore Wind Farms (HOME Offshore) project (EPSRC Grant Number: EP/P009743/1) and the Robotics and Artifical Intelligence for Nuclear (RAIN) project (EPSRC Grant Number: EP/R026084/1). The authors would like to thank both Dr. Andrew West and Dr. Thomas Wright of the University of Manchester for their continued support.

REFERENCES

[1] E. M. Barnes et al., "Technology Drivers in Windfarm Asset Management Position Paper," 2018, pp. 1–46.

[2] B. P. Silva et al., "On-rail solution for autonomous inspections in electrical substations," Infrared Physics & Technology, vol. 90, May 2018, pp. 53–58. [Online]. Available: https://www.sciencedirect.com/science/article/pii/S1350449517307247

[3] M. Heggo et al., "Evaluation and mitigation of high electrostatic fields on operation of aerial inspections vehicles in hvdc environments," in EERA DeepWind19, Jan 2019.

[4] M Heggo et al., "Evaluation and mitigation of offshore hvdc valve hall magnetic field impact on inspection quadcopter propulsion motors," in EERA DeepWind19, Jan 2019.

[5] P. Rea and E. Ottaviano, "Design and development of an Inspection Robotic System for indoor applications," Robotics and Computer-Integrated Manufacturing, vol. 49, Feb 2018, pp. 143–151. [Online]. Available: https://linkinghub.elsevier.com/retrieve/pii/S0736584517300613

[6] E. H. Harik, A. Korsaeth, E. H. C. Harik, and A. Korsaeth, "Combining Hector SLAM and Artificial Potential Field for Autonomous Navigation Inside a Greenhouse," Robotics, vol. 7, no. 2, May 2018, p. 22. [Online]. Available: http://www.mdpi.com/2218-6581/7/2/22

[7] C. Papachristos, S. Khattak, and K. Alexis, "Autonomous exploration of visually-degraded environments using aerial robots," in 2017 International Conference on Unmanned Aircraft Systems (ICUAS). IEEE, Jun 2017, pp. 775–780. [Online]. Available: http://ieeexplore.ieee.org/document/7991510/

[8] Huang et al., "Visual Odometry and Mapping for Autonomous Flight Using an RGB-D Camera." Springer, Cham, 2017, pp. 235–252. [Online]. Available: http://link.springer.com/10.1007/978-3-319-29363-914

[9] P. Henry, M. Krainin, E. Herbst, X. Ren, and D. Fox, "RGB-D Mapping: Using Depth Cameras for Dense 3D Modeling of Indoor Environments." Springer, Berlin, Heidelberg, 2014, pp. 477–491. [Online]. Available: http://link.springer.com/10.1007/978-3-642-28572-133

[10] H. Zhang, C. Zhang, W. Yang, and C.-Y. Chen, "Localization and navigation using QR code for mobile robot in indoor environment," in 2015 IEEE International Conference on Robotics and Biomimetics (ROBIO). IEEE, Dec 2015, pp. 2501–2506. [Online]. Available: http://ieeexplore.ieee.org/document/7419715/

[11] P. Nazemzadeh, D. Fontanelli, D. Macii, and L. Palopoli, "Indoor Localization of Mobile Robots Through QR Code Detection and Dead Reckoning Data Fusion," IEEE/ASME Transactions on Mechatronics, vol. 22, no. 6, Dec 2017, pp. 2588–2599. [Online]. Available: http://ieeexplore.ieee.org/document/8066377/

[12] J. Meyer, A. Sendobry, S. Kohlbrecher, U. Klingauf, and O. von Stryk, "Comprehensive simulation of quadrotor UAVs using ROS and gazebo," in Simulation, Modeling, and Programming for Autonomous Robots. Springer Berlin Heidelberg, 2012, pp. 400–411. [Online]. Available: https://doi.org/10.1007%2F978-3-642-34327-8_36

[13] W.-C. Jiang, M.-Y. Ju, Y.-J. Chen, and W.-C. Jiang, "Implementation of Odometry with EKF in Hector SLAM Methods," International Journal of Automation and Smart Technology, vol. 8, no. 1, Mar 2018, pp. 9–18. [Online]. Available: http://www.ausmt.org/index.php/AUSMT/article/view/1558

[14] "Hector mapping," accessed: 2019-05-09. [Online]. Available: \url{http://wiki.ros.org/hector_mapping}

[15] "Laser line extraction," accessed: 2019-05-09. [Online]. Available: https://github.com/kam3k/laser_line_extraction

[16] "Fiducial slam," accessed: 2019-05-09. [Online]. Available: https://github.com/UbiquityRobotics/fiducials

[17] T. I. Fossen, Handbook of Marine Craft Hydrodynamics and Motion Control. Chichester, UK: John Wiley & Sons, Ltd, Apr 2011. [Online]. Available: http://doi.wiley.com/10.1002/9781119994138

[18] "Pythonrobotics," accessed: 2019-05-09. [Online]. Available: https://github.com/AtsushiSakai/PythonRobotics

Towards a Methodology to Test UAVs in Hazardous Environments

Vince Page
School of Engineering
University of Liverpool
Liverpool, United Kingdom
Email: v.page@liverpool.ac.uk

Matt Webster
Department of Computer Science
University of Liverpool
Liverpool, United Kingdom
Email: matt@liverpool.ac.uk

Michael Fisher
Department of Computer Science
University of Liverpool
Liverpool, United Kingdom
Email: MFisher@liverpool.ac.uk

Mike Jump
School of Engineering
University of Liverpool
Liverpool, United Kingdom
Email: mjump1@liverpool.ac.uk

ABSTRACT - This paper reports on the early stages of the development of a methodology to analyse and test autonomous systems in hazardous environments, with the aim of verifying both the safe decision-making and resulting actions of the system. The ultimate goal is to generate safety case evidence that a designer can provide to a regulator to show that the system to be used will likely operate safely.

Keywords – UAV; Hazardous Environments; Verification; Simulation.

I. INTRODUCTION

There is currently a drive in the UK toward using autonomous systems, and robotic systems in particular, in extreme or hazardous environments [1]. This paper is concerned with the Verification and Validation (V&V) of autonomous systems operating in hazardous (specifically offshore) environments.

Autonomous systems are systems which decide for themselves what to do [2]. Typically, these decisions are made using computer systems, which control the system in question and perform operations that might otherwise be performed by a person. For example, an autonomous Unmanned Aerial Vehicle (UAV) will need to contain a number of computer systems that can replace a human pilot operating the UAV using remote control [3].

In this paper, an autonomous system means the following:

A system that is given a goal and restrictions and fulfils this goal by planning, making decisions and carrying out actions without direct human interaction

Robotic systems are good for tasks in hazardous environments. Typically, robotic systems are used for Dull, Dirty and/or Dangerous missions, commonly known as the "three D's". Recently however, the need to use robots within Demanding, Distant and Distributed missions has also been established. Offshore environments, such as oil platforms and wind farms, are prime examples of these latter "three D's".

In all environments, but in particular for hazardous environments, autonomous systems must operate safely and be safe to operate. What is more, this must be demonstrable. Part of the process to demonstrate this safety case means that the decisions being made, by the system, the reasons why they have been made and the actions that result from these decisions need to be verified for all possible operating conditions. Furthermore, if a system fails, knowledge regarding why it fails is required. Thus, the question asked in this paper is as follows:

How can an autonomous UAV be analysed to determine the conditions under which it fails and to indicate why it failed?

This paper uses an example scenario of an UAV inspecting an offshore asset to demonstrate the development of tools and techniques that will be used to verify its safe operation.

The paper is organised as follows. Section II establishes the challenges of offshore environments for autonomous systems; how V&V can be used to ensure safety; how a system needs to be constructed to be verified; how the V&V outputs can be used to build certification evidence; and how the methodology presented contributes to this. Section III presents the methodology to analyse the UAV and provide explainable failures and Section IV shows the results of its application and interpretation. Finally, conclusions are drawn and future work is detailed in Section V.

II. BACKGROUND

A. *Offshore Operations*

For the purposes of this paper, 'the offshore environment' means the environment around energy generation assets, such as oil rigs and wind turbines.

UAV operations, e.g., remote inspections around oil rigs and wind turbines, pose many engineering challenges. A potentially significant source of operational difficulty for such tasks will be when flying in the disturbed/turbulent air flow near such structures, as shown in Figure 1. Such turbulent flow structures make flying in and around the offshore assets dangerous if the vehicle does not possess sufficient control authority to maintain its desired position, leading to a potential collision with the asset or its associated personnel.

A similar situation exists for ship-borne naval aviation operations. Helicopters are often operated from landing decks located at the ship's stern. The ship's motion and wind conditions create an area of disturbed air flow in the landing area. To determine whether a particular ship and helicopter combination is capable of landing/taking off from the ship under a given wind condition, flight trials are conducted to form a Ship Helicopter Operating Limit (SHOL) [4]. Previous work has investigated the replacement of part of the physical testing required to generate a SHOL with piloted simulations [4]. The method presented in this paper takes a similar simulation-based approach for autonomous UAV system missions.

The scenario considered in this paper is an inspection task for a UAV on an oil rig leg. This is a sufficiently complex task to allow the methodology to be rigorously tested. It will be applied to other, more diverse scenarios at a later date.

B. V&V of Autonomous Systems

Autonomous systems present a significant challenge for V&V. Many non-autonomous systems are designed to use a human operator who has overall responsibility for the safe and reliable operation of the system. Autonomous systems, on the other hand, cannot assume the presence of the responsible human, and therefore must manage safe and reliable operations themselves [5].

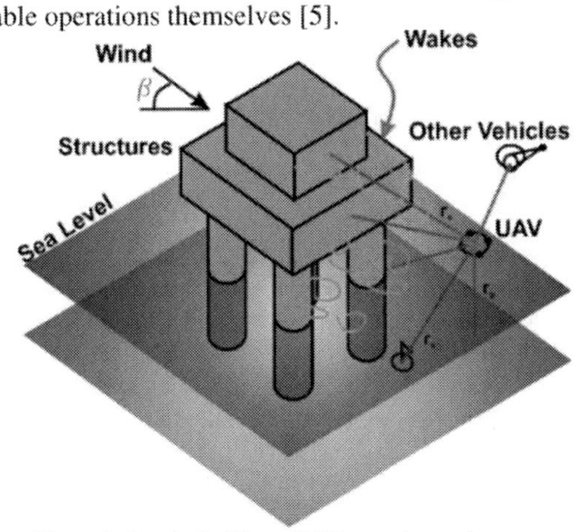

Figure 1. A typical offshore UAV operating environment.

V&V for autonomous systems uses many well-established techniques, as well as some that have been developed with autonomous systems in mind [5]. At the same time, experimentation within controlled environments is a mainstay of engineering best-practice, and is also used for autonomous systems. However, due to the significant challenges and added complexity of autonomous systems, experimentation can be expensive and dangerous. Therefore, high-fidelity simulation is often used as a separate V&V technique [6]. High-fidelity simulation involves incorporating accurate physical models of a system within a realistic synthetic environment. Trials within high-fidelity simulation provide a safer and potentially cheaper means to test than physical experiments. Of course, this comes at the cost of needing to understand the limitations of the models being used. The models of the system and the environment used within simulation must themselves be verified and validated [7].

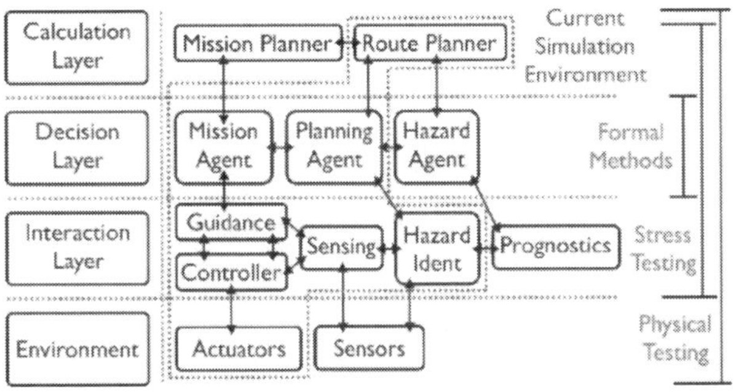

Figure 2. System Architecture of an Autonomous UAV with the separation of the component using layers which then indicates the verification method to be applied to each

A V&V technique commonly used for autonomous systems is formal verification, an application of Formal Methods [8]. Formal verification works by building abstract mathematical models of the system in question, and then exhaustively analysing the models using software to determine whether or not particular requirements hold. Formal verification is particularly useful for finite state systems, and has therefore found a natural application in the verification and validation of autonomous software.

There are, of course, many other V&V techniques not listed above, including hardware-in-loop testing [9], real-world operations and end-user validation [10], that are also used for V&V of autonomous systems.

C. Systems Architecture for V&V

To be able to apply V&V to a whole system, it needs to be constructed in a certain way. This is mostly due to the models used to describe a sub-system. In Figure 2, the systems architecture of an autonomous system that is to fly UAVs around oil rigs is shown. There are two important features in this architecture: the layers and the intra-layer separation of subsystems.

The layering is to group sub-systems, similar in construction rather than role or output. The calculation layer can be thought of as any task that reasons about the world in a non-abstract way, such as a route or mission planner. The decision layer is for those systems that make decisions based on information provided by the interaction and calculation layers. The interaction layer is the-low level autonomous tasks that translates plans and decisions into actions. The environment layer is the actual hardware that physically carries out the desired actions.

On the right of Figure 2, the verification methods are aligned with the components that they are best suited to testing. Formal methods are well suited to analysing and verifying decision making, but the abstraction required to apply them to planners or continuous controllers makes them less so for these elements. Simulation-based testing allows many permutations of the systems goals, initial conditions and even internal parameters, to be tested; thus allowing the actions of the systems to be rigorously tested. The physical testing of the system then checks the results of the formal methods and simulations against reality and will determine the validity of the abstractions and assumptions required to build them.

In short, with the system constructed in such a way, the following questions can be answered:

Formal Methods - *Has the safe decision been made?*
Simulation Based Testing - *Did it result in safe actions?*
Physical Testing - *How well do these answers match reality?*

D. Evidence for Safe Operations

For an autonomous system to be used in a real-world environment, its safe operation needs to be agreed with the regulator. In the UK, there is no standard method for assessing whether or not autonomous UAV operations are safe. Each request for operation is reviewed on a case-by-case basis using a submitted safety case/risk assessment for the planned operation.

V&V techniques can be used to generate evidence to prove that a system will operate safely and reliably. This paper proposes that formal methods and simulation based stress testing can be included to add strength to the safety case.

For the scenario considered in this paper, the operating envelope of the system, when being used in certain conditions is the addition to the safety case. An example of this is shown in Figure 3. This example is intentionally similar to that of a SHOL. The aim of simulation-based verification is to generate this operating envelope. The dotted lines represent the boundary between safe and unsafe operations.

As an example, for a UAV doing inspections of the legs of an oil rig, there will exist a set of wind speeds and directions under which the UAV is no longer able to operate. The operator of the UAV, oil rig and regulators will need to know the safe wind speed and direction operating envelope before any task can proceed.

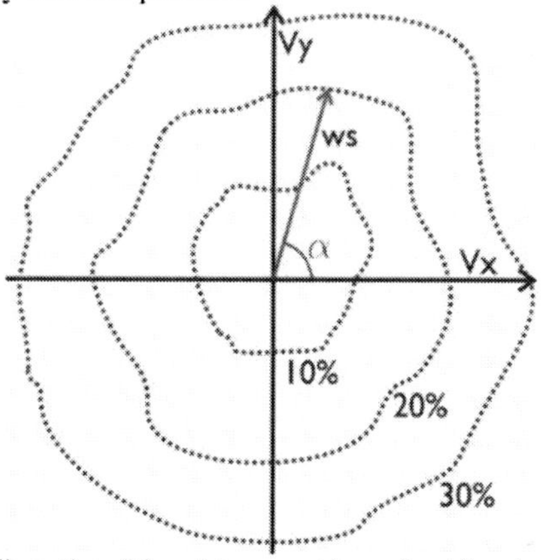

Figure 3. Illustration of the safety case evidence aimed for when using the methodology.

In addition, for this situation the variables that affect the safe operation of the UAV are not restricted to just the wind speed and direction. They could include, but are not limited to, the following:

- Initial position and goal
- Geometry of environment
- UAV performance capability
- Actuator/sensor performance/degradation
- Other environmental conditions e.g. ambient light, sea state etc.

This means that the real operating envelope will be a multi-dimensional surface.

It is important to note here that such a surface can not only be used as safety-case evidence, but also as a run-time safety monitor. The analogy is that the boundary is the equivalent of the prior experience of the human pilot, where they intuitively know what actions and decisions are a good idea or not. This can then be used, while the system is in operation, to inform the autonomous system of when it is feasible to carry out a plan or not; or as a monitor to tell the system that, as the environment changes, planned actions or current states (such as where it is) are no longer safe.

E. Understanding the System's Failure

If a system is tested under one set of conditions and is found to successfully complete the task assigned to it safely, this is good. If under slightly different conditions, the system fails to complete it safely, this is also good. This now informs both the user and the system itself, when it should and should not carry out particular actions. This is the essence of the operating envelope shown in Figure 3. However, this does not inform the user, or regulator, why the system failed.

It is far more useful to be able to say under what conditions a system can or cannot work and to also to be able to say why. This both directs any effort to redesign or improve the system, as the designer now knows which system to focus on; and it provides the regulator with a more concrete answer as to why it behaves in the way it does.

As an example, suppose there are measures of failure for an actuator, controller, guidance, and navigation of a UAV (more on this in Section III). After a simulation of a task, at a number of wind speeds and directions, these failure measures are then applied to the response, a possible result could be as shown in Figure 4 (a). Outside of this boundary, the system failed its task, while inside it succeeded. The aggregate of these failure results in Figure 4 (b).

This boundary is now the operating envelope of the system. However, by splitting the failure of the system into separate components, the colours shown can be added. This then indicates that the actuator, at least in this example, was the most likely cause of the system to fail its task.

III. METHODS

This section describes the cost functions and methodology used to apply V&V ideas to an autonomous systems.

A. *Cost functions for each component*

Four continuous autonomy components are considered. The responsibility of each component, what its job is, determines the definition of the cost function. The responsibilities of each component are as follows:

***Actuator**: To create the required output while leaving a margin of error as a contingency.*
***Controller**: To force the current states to follow the commanded states as closely as possible, while maintaining system stability.*
***Guidance**: To cause the system to follow the desired path to within a desired separation distance.*
***Navigation**: To generate a path between the start and goal, while avoiding collisions with objects.*

The cost function defining the actuator's performance is shown in (1) and illustrated in Figure 5.

$$A_f = \frac{1}{n_a}\sum_{1}^{i=n_a}\frac{1}{t_m}\int_0^{t_m}\frac{\sqrt{(A_i - .5)^2}}{.5 - Mar}dt \quad (1)$$

Where n_a is the number of actuators, t_m is the maximum simulation time, A_i the actuator output at time t, Mar the specified margin of error, and dt the time step of the simulation.

Here, the zero point for the actuator is 50%. The function is, in essence, a time average of the deviation from the neutral point normalised by the margin of error. The performance of all the actuators is averaged over time and over the number of actuators.

This function aims to create a single measure for all the actuators over the time period of operation between 0 and 1. The cost function gives a gradual increase in the failure. If an actuator reaches either 100% or 0%, this results in the failure of the system being set to 1. This can be considered a critical failure, as would a collision, since the system would very likely become unsafe.

The controller's performance is defined in (2) and shown in Figure 6.

$$C_f = \frac{1}{n_s}\sum_{i=0}^{i=n_s}\frac{1}{t_m}\int_0^{t_m}\frac{\sqrt{(R_i - u_i)^2}}{Dif_i}dt \quad (2)$$

Where n_s is the number of controlled states, R_i is the command reference, u_i the measured state of the system, and Dif_i the specified max difference between the actual and reference values.

It is essentially the same as the cost function used in Linear Quadratic Regulator controllers. The difference between the reference and controlled state is normalised by a desired maximum distance. It is then averaged over both time and the number of controlled states. A discontinuity exists when the system becomes unstable.

The guidance performance is defined by both in (3) and Figure 7.

$$G_f = \frac{1}{t_m}\int_0^{t_m}\frac{\sqrt{(\delta_x + \delta_y + \delta_z)^2}}{Div}dt \quad (3)$$

Where δ_x, δ_y, and δ_z are the orthogonal difference between the actual position and the desired path and Div is the specified maximum deviation from the path.

It is the length of the vector perpendicular to the nearest point on the desired path from the system's current location. It is then normalised by the desired maximum deviation from the path. A discontinuity does not explicitly exist with this function, however the discontinuities are handled by the mission manager's performance, see Criteria Analysis section later.

The navigation's performance is defined by (4) and by Figure 8.

$$N_f = \frac{1}{t_m}\int_0^{t_m}\frac{Prox}{P}dt \quad (4)$$

Where P_n is the planned proximity at the point on the path perpendicular to the current position, P the proximity to the nearest object, and $Prox$ is the specified maximum proximity to an object.

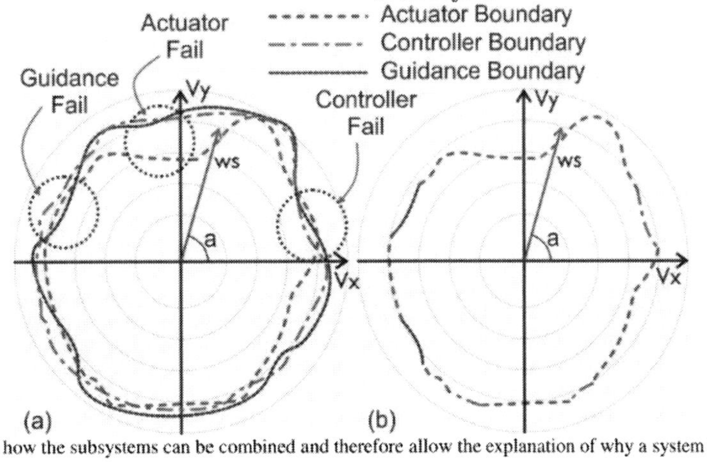

Figure 4. Illustration of how the subsystems can be combined and therefore allow the explanation of why a system failed to operate safely

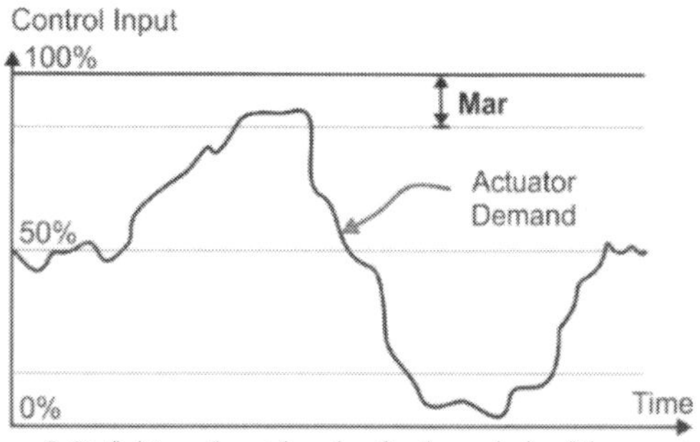

Figure 5. Definition of cost function for the analysis of the actuator's performance

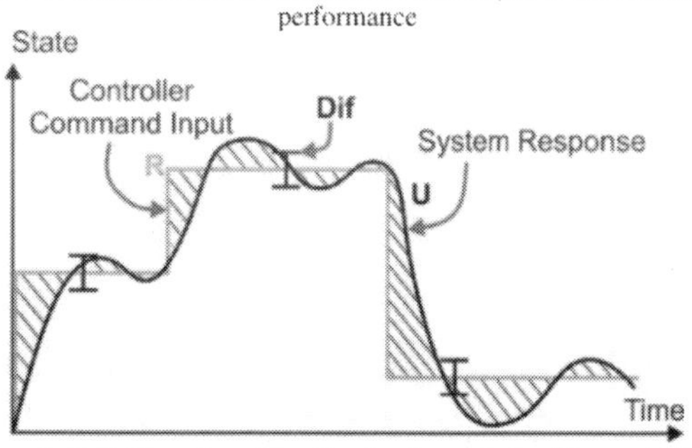

Figure 6. Definition of cost function for the analysis of the controller's performance

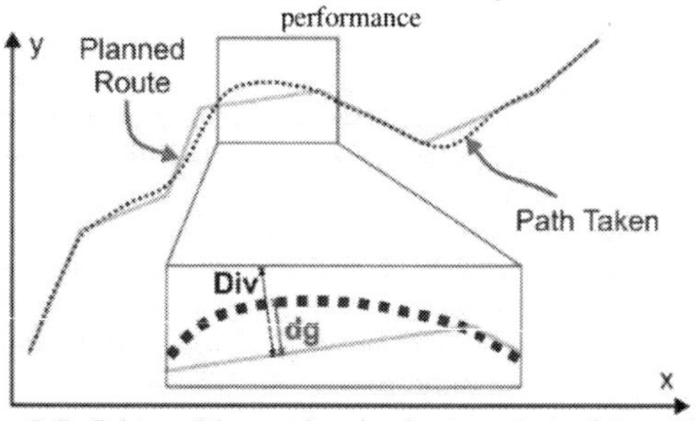

Figure 7. Definition of the cost function for the analysis of the guidance performance

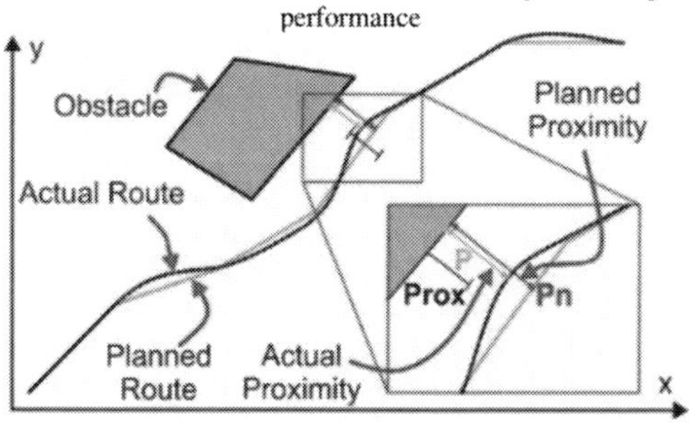

Figure 8. Definition of the cost function for the analysis of the navigation performance

B. Simulation Environment

A simple simulation environment of a helicopter moving around the legs of an oil rig is used to generate the data required to test the above cost functions, see Figure 9.

It consists of a series of linearized state space flight dynamics models identified from a non-linear simulation model. The models are then scheduled based on the forward flight speed of the UAV, to account for the changing dynamics.

To control the helicopter a PI controller [11] is gain scheduled and a waypoint following with cross tracking error is used as the guidance method [12]. A simple A* route finding algorithms is used for the navigation [13], where a simple hazard model is used to allow the planner to plan a route around the wakes of the oil rig legs.

A sample data set is taken from the simulation environment and presented in the next section. The cost functions are then applied to the output of the simulator.

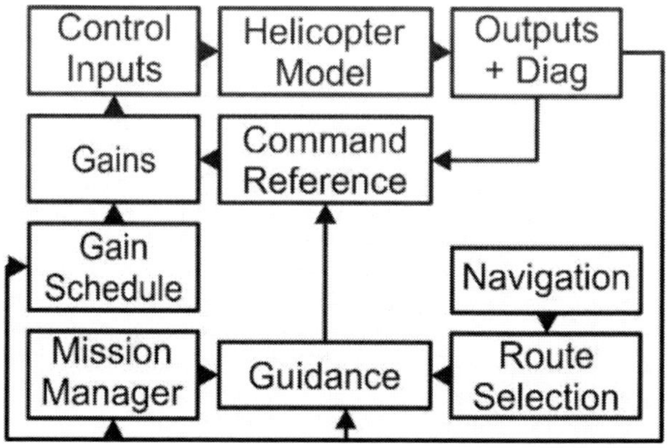

Figure 9. Systems diagram for the simulator

IV. RESULTS

When testing and analysing an autonomous system's performance, a designer may be presented with the output shown in Figure 10 to Figure 12. From this the designer would be able to determine whether the UAV was able to carry out the task assigned to it. In this case, simply move from bottom left to the right of the top right leg.

However, some of the routes come very close to the legs, to the point where a collision is very likely. This is also for only a single set of conditions, but can only be interpreted visually. If the conditions change, will the UAV be able to still carry out the task? How does this compare to other UAVs or settings/weightings within the autonomous components of the UAV?

A closer inspection of the least risky plan's response of the UAV can be seen in Figure 13, Figure 14, and Figure 15. From this, it can be determined that the control input is not exceeded, the body velocities follow the reference values and the UAV follows the desired path reasonably well. However, again this does not allow an easy comparison to other UAVs or settings. The interpretation is also abstract and not quantified.

Further detail can be determined from Figure 16 and Figure 17, where how well the UAV followed the planned path and how well the plan enabled the UAV to avoid collisions with its surroundings is shown. The actuator cost function can be applied to the results in Figure 13, the controller function to Figure 14, the guidance function to Figure 16 and the navigation function to Figure 17.

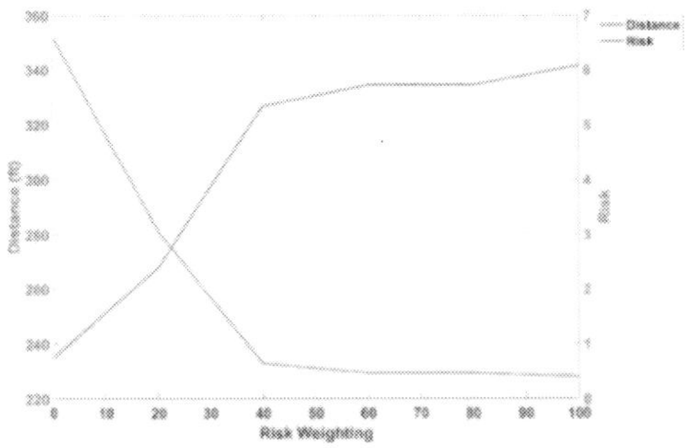

Figure 10. Balance between a route's total distance and the risk associated with it

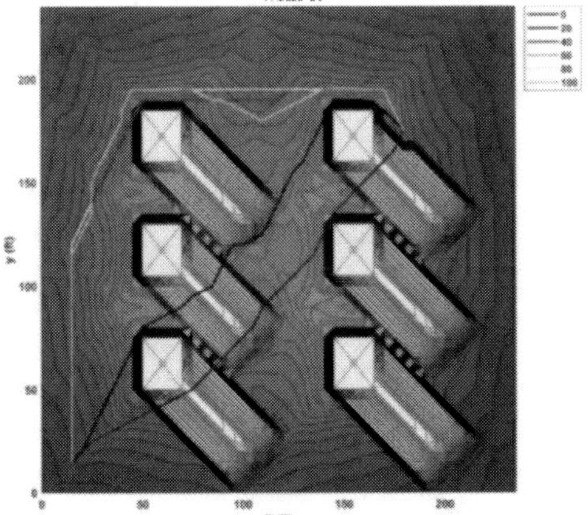

Figure 11. Planned routes for a range of risk weightings

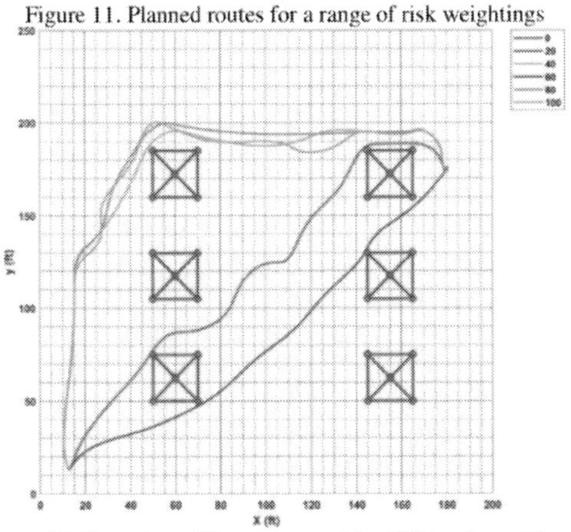

Figure 12. Plan view of the response of the UAV as the guidance, controller and model tries to follow the planned route

This allows a simple metric to be applied to the UAV's response, reducing the interpretation of the performance down to a single number, thus allowing easier comparisons and optimisations of the UAV's settings to be made.

Figure 18 to Figure 21 show the cost functions of the UAV response for a range of different performance specifications.

Figure 18 shows that, as the specification is made more demanding, the cost increases, as would be expected. It also illustrates the control that is closest to failure, in this case the collective.

Figure 19 shows the performance of the flight controller. It can be seen that the u and v velocities are by far the most difficult for the controller to follow; also that unless very strict limits on the deviation of the actual from the command reference values are imposed, the performance is good. A similar story can be seen in Figure 20, where only very small allowed deviations from the desired direction will result in the system's failure.

Figure 20 shows that, on average, the guidance system allows the UAV to follow the desired path well. Only when the allowable deviation from the desired path is below 4 ft will the system fail. Therefore, showing that the guidance is able to perform correctly, unless under tight restrictions.

The navigation performance is shown in Figure 21, where the performance decreases as the closest allowable proximity of the UAV to an object is increased. It can be seen that only small allowable proximities result in the system being safe.

Taking Figure 18 to Figure 21 together, it can be seen that the actuators and controller are performing well, even under tight requirements. Guidance performs well, but the navigation component is the likely cause of the systems to be unable to carry out its assigned task. This is in contrast to the interpretation of Figure 10 to Figure 12, where such conclusions are harder to draw, as the performance of the system is not quantified.

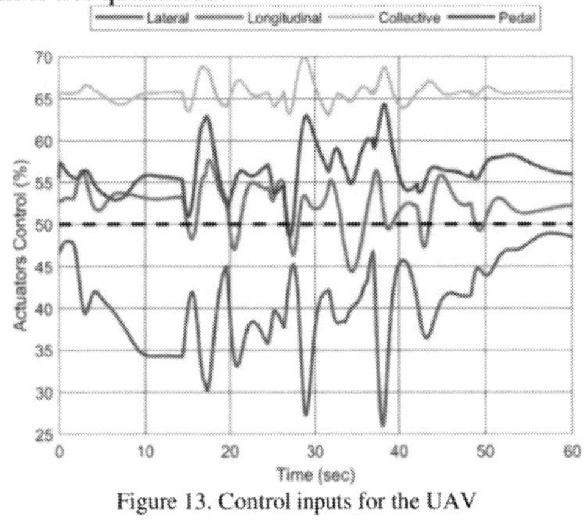

Figure 13. Control inputs for the UAV

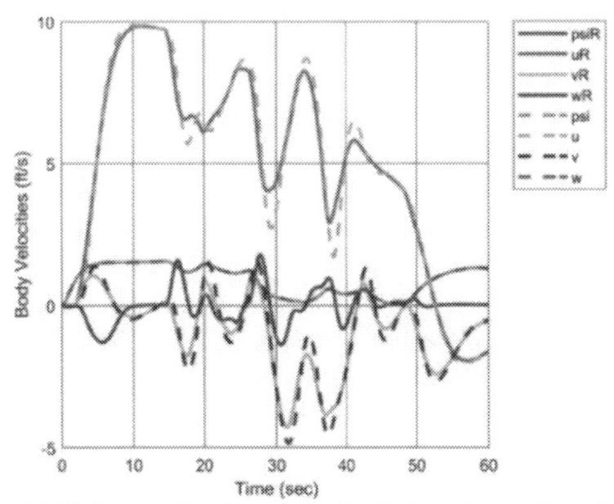

Figure 14. Body velocities (u,v,w)/heading (psi) and controller reference velocities (uR, vR, wR, psiR)

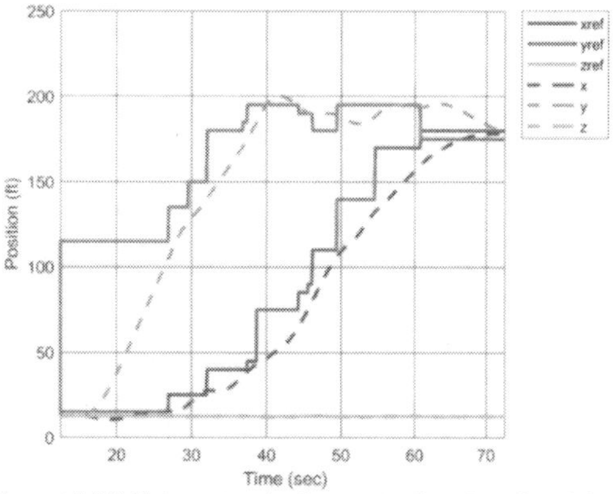

Figure 15. UAV (x, y, z) and reference (xref, yref, zref) positions

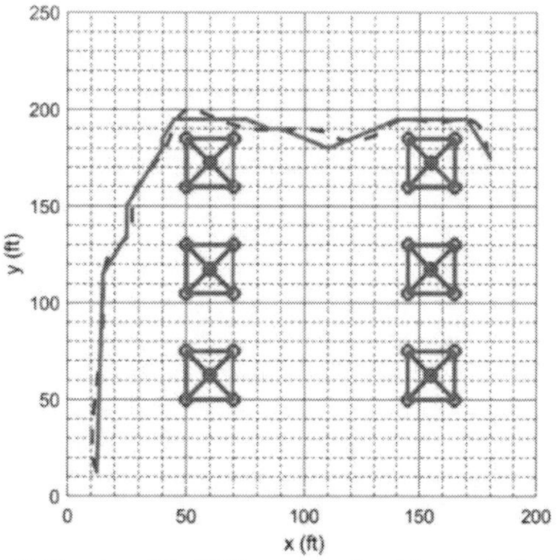

Figure 16. Plan view of the UAVs response when following the least risky planned route. Solid line = planned route. Dashed line = path taken

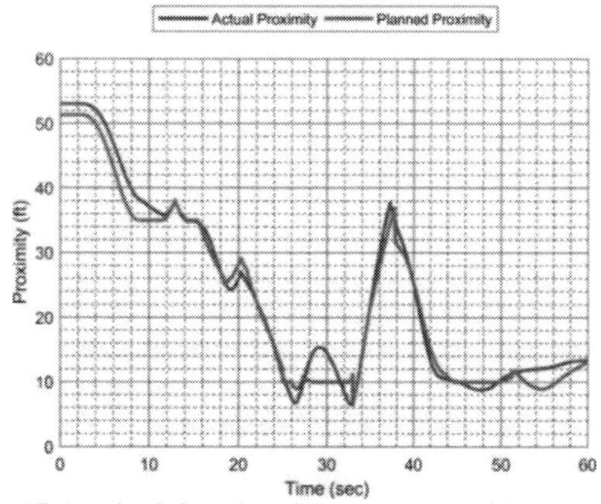

Figure 17. Actual and planned proximity to the nearest object at a point in time in the UAV's response

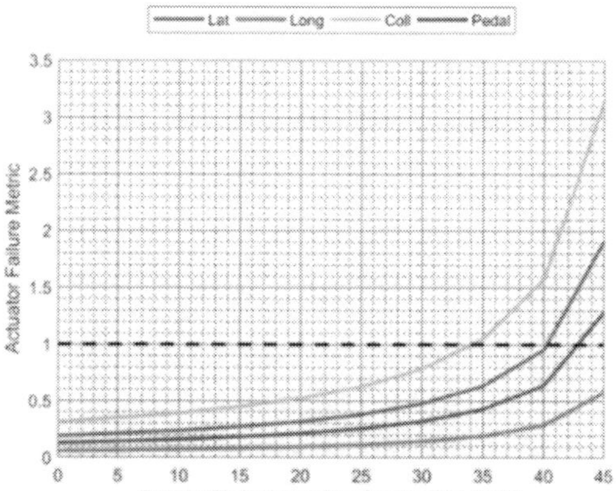

Figure 18. Performance metric for the actuator when applied to the UAV's response for a range of specifications

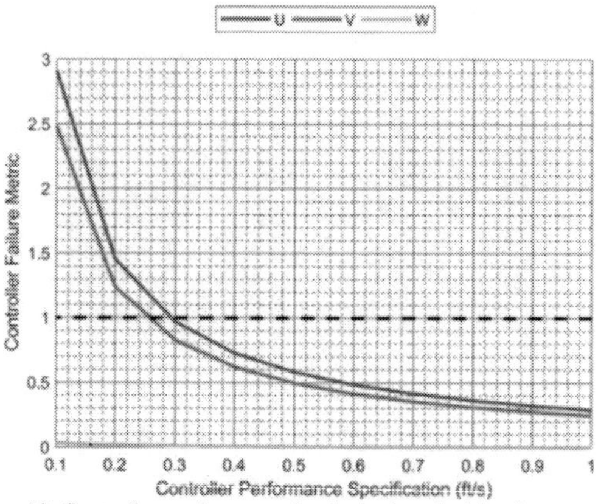

Figure 19. Controller performance for the body velocities for a range of specifications

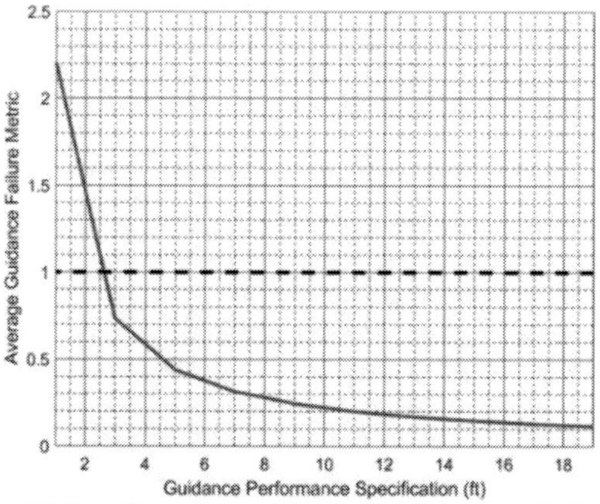

Figure 20. Controller performance for the direction command reference

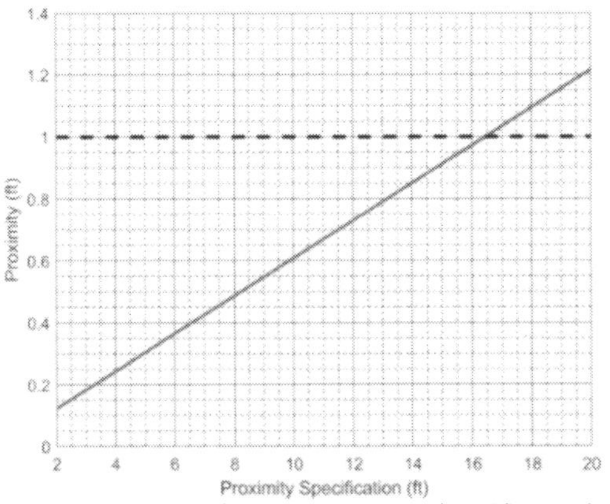

Figure 21. Navigation performance for a range of specified proximity specifications

V. CONCLUSION AND FUTURE WORK

A. *Conclusion*

A method for the analysis of the continuous autonomous components of a system has been reported. Results from a scenario where a UAV moves around an oil rig's legs have been presented.

The need to certify an autonomous systems operating in hazardous environments by V&V methods was discussed and the need to separate the failure of subsystems outlined.

It was found that by applying the presented methodology, the performance of the system can be quantified; also, that the component that is likely to cause the system to fail can be found, and therefore focused on by the system's designer. Thus, the first stages of a method to analyse a system to determine when a system fails and why was successfully demonstrated.

B. *Future Work*

Having a quantifiable metric of a systems performance allows two follow up pieces of work. First, it allows the generation of operating envelopes, which can then be used by a systems user or by the system itself as safety run time errors. Second, it allows the performance of the system to be optimised by wrapping the simulation and analyse method in an optimiser, where the bias, weightings and settings of the system are the independent variables and the outputs of the presented cost functions can be used to form a cost function of an optimiser.

To achieve both of these, a third and final follow up task is required, where an algorithm to search all the variables that can influence the system's performance is needed. The algorithm will be required to move through both continuous and discrete parameter space. A hybrid evolutionary/genetic algorithm or a modified Particle Swarm Optimisation method is a likely solution to meet this requirement.

ACKNOWLEDGEMENTS

Authors acknowledge funding for this work in the UK by EPSRC through the ORCA [EP/R026173] Robotics and Artificial Intelligence Hub.

ORCA HUB
Offshore Robotics for Certification of Assets
Remote Safety and Integrity

REFERENCES

[1] UK-RAS Network. "White Paper: Robotics & Autonomous systems: Challenges and Opportunities for the UK", ISSN 2398-4414, 2018.

[2] M. Wooldridge "An Introduction to Multiagent Systems" John Wiley & Sons, 2002.

[3] UK Civil Aviaton Authority (CAA), "CAP 722 Unmanned Aircraft System Operations in UK Airspace: Guidance".

[4] I. Owen, M. D. White, G. D. Padfield, and S. J. Hodge "A virtual engineering approach to the ship-helicopter dynamics interface - A decade of modelling and simulation reserach at the University of Liverpool", The Aeronautical Journal, vol. 121 , no. 1246 , pp. 1833-1857, 2017.

[5] M. Fisher et al. "Verifiable Self-Certifiying Autonomous Systems", International Symposium on Software Reliability Engineering Workshops (ISSREW), pp. 241-348, 2018.

[6] M. Webster, N. Cameron, M. Fisher, and M. Jump "Generating Certification Evidence for Autonomous Unmanned Aircraft Using Model Checking and Simulation", Journal of Aerospace Information Systems, vol. 11, no. 5, pp. 258-278, 2014.

[7] M. Webster et al. "A Corroborative Approach to Verification and Validation of Human-Robot Teams". arXiv:1608.07403v2, 2016.

[8] M. Fisher, "An Introduction to Practical Formal Methods Using Temporal Logic", Wiley, 2011.

[9] D. M. Lane, G. J Falconer, G. Randall, and I. Edwards, "Interoperability and synchronisation of distributed hardware-in-the-loop simulation for underwater robot development: issues and experiments" IEEE Iternational Conference on Robotics and Automation, vol. 1, pp. 909-914, 2001.

[10] J. Saunders, D. S. Syrdal, K. L. Koay, N. Burke, and K. Dautenhahn, "Teach Me - Show Me- End-User Personalisation of a Smart Home and Compansion Robot" IEEE Transactions on Human-Machine Systems, vol. 46, no. 1, pp. 27-40, 2016.

[11] H. Purnawan, M. Mardlijah, and E.B. Purwanto, "Design of linear quadratic regulator (LQR) control system for flight stability of LSU-05" Journal of Physics: Conference Series 890, 2017.

[12] T. Shima and S. Rasmussen, "UAV Cooperative Decision and Control: Challenges and Practical Approaches" Society for Industrial and Applied Mathematics, 2009.

[13] D. Ferguson, M. Likhachev, and A. Stentz, "A guide to heuristic-based Path Planning" American Association for Artificial Intelligence, 2005.

Design of Autonomous Systems for Cybersecurity Threat Detection Using Deep Learning

Strahil Sokolov
University of Telecommunications and Post
Department of Information Technologies
Sofia, Bulgaria
e-mail: strahil.sokolov@gmail.com

***Abstract*—In this paper, an approach is proposed for designing autonomous systems featuring machine learning and neural networks for cybersecurity threat detection. It is proposed that neural models are trained on monitoring data obtained from cloud environments that service enterprise applications. Cybersecurity is a hot topic and a broad field of science that spreads over activities, such as protecting infrastructure, computers and servers, industrial and telecommunications equipment, applications and data. All modern networks are capable of substantial throughput due to enormous volumes of generated traffic. A design is proposed for autonomous threat detection systems, which is based on combining traditional and deep neural networks for cloud monitoring data analysis and an algorithm for combining classifier results. The proposed autonomous system design delivers promising results that are comparable to existing approaches and can become useful in enterprise cloud applications.**

Keywords-cybersecurity; autonomous threat detection; deep learning.

I. INTRODUCTION

Research in the field of cybersecurity has been ongoing for decades. With the continual increase of data volumes, protecting computer and telecommunication systems has become a primary concern. There are several approaches which are currently in use: traffic analysis, content analysis, application and user behavior analysis.

There exist a number of layers with common groups of threats, existing protection capabilities and Information and Communication Technology (ICT) resources that are under constant attack nowadays. The most popular applications based on traffic analysis [1] can be grouped into the fields of: network intrusion detection, botnet detection and malware detection. Over the recent years, approaches emerged based on machine learning algorithms for each of these fields. Some of the Intrusion Detection and Protection Systems (IDPS) are trained to recognize abnormalities in traffic, e.g., in peer-to-peer applications. There are Intrusion Detection Systems (IDS) for protecting against Distributed Denial-Of-Service (DDoS) attacks. There are e-mail protection services, which are able to detect harmful applications that steal information; mobile malware applications are also widespread [2]. Malware application behaviours are analyzed and detectors are trained to classify an application or part of it as harmful [2]. Another type of threat is the botnet: many compromised devices or hosts, infected with malware and connected to the Internet, that are controlled and manipulated by botmasters [3]. Botnets are mainly used for sending spam emails, DDoS attacks, identity thefts or just making use of the victim's computational resources for purposes of, e.g., tunnelling, proxying or even cryptocurrency mining.

There are several modern proposals that have appeared on the usage of advanced techniques for intrusion detection [4]. The authors propose a cybersecurity framework based on two-stage Markov model for early prediction of malicious edge devices as well as legitimate edge devices in fog computing.

In [5], focus has been given to the recent rise of security incidents affecting critical infrastructure, such as power grids and water suppliers. The German cybersecurity office - Bundesamt für Sicherheit in der Informationstechnik (BSI) - reported that not all of the incidents were due to hacking. Another recent publication [6] shows flaws and vulnerabilities in an entire European country. The author shows how vulnerability scanning can be organized by a single person and justifies the importance of cybersecurity threat detection software.

This paper is organized as follows: in Section 2, an overview is given on existing techniques for cyberthreat detection based on network traffic analysis. In Section 3, the proposed approach for design of autonomous threat detection techniques is described. Section 4 describes the technique for combining classifier results. The paper's conclusion is in Section 5.

II. THREAT DETECTION TECHNIQUES BASED ON NETWORK TRAFFIC ANALYSIS

A. Intrusion Detection Systems (IDS) and Intrusion Prevention (IPS) Systems

Both IDS and IPS are entitled to try and recognize malicious traffic from normal traffic. There are Host-Based Intrusion Detection Systems (HIDS) and Network Intrusion Detection systems (NIDS) [7]. To achieve this goal, both IDS and IPS rely on network traffic analysis. Most of the existing systems rely on rule-based classification to detect the nature of the attacks; the malicious traffic is often concealed within botnet, DDoS attack traffic or spam traffic. It can be expected that the accuracy of such systems is relatively low [8], due to the limits of their operation modes: signature based and anomaly-based [7]. Signature based threat detection uses a set of predetermined rules that are available from the community or vendors. These rules contain signature patterns of threats similar to antivirus software. The anomaly based detection function is to detect abnormalities in the current network traffic or states of services in logs.

The big manufacturers of network equipment offer bundles of IDS/IPS systems, which claim high accuracy and machine learning capabilities. It is worth exploring some of the open source available systems.

- OSSEC [9] stands for Open Source Security. It is an open source host intrusion detection system owned by Trend Micro, one of the leading names in IT security.
- SNORT [10] is an open source intrusion prevention system capable of real-time traffic analysis and packet logging.
- Suricata [11] is a free and open source, mature, fast and robust network threat detection engine. The Suricata engine is capable of Real Time Intrusion Detection (RTID), Inline Intrusion Prevention (IIP), Network Security Monitoring (NSM) and offline pcap processing.
- Zeek [12] (ex. Bro) is a powerful network analysis framework that consists of event engine and policy scripts.
- The Samhain [13] Host-based Intrusion Detection System (HIDS) provides file integrity checking and log file monitoring/analysis, as well as rootkit detection, port monitoring, detection of rogue Set User ID (SUID) executables, and hidden processes.
- Fail2ban [14] scans log files (e.g. /var/log/apache/error_log) and bans IPs that show the malicious signs – too many password failures, seeking for exploits, etc.
- Security Onion [15] is a free and open source Linux distribution for intrusion detection, enterprise security monitoring, and log management. It includes Elasticsearch, Logstash, Kibana, Snort, Suricata, Bro, Wazuh, Sguil, Squert, CyberChef, NetworkMiner, and many other security tools.

B. *Malware analysis*

Malware detection has been a field of interest for computer virologists for a long time. In order to address the automated classification of malware based on behavioral analysis, the researchers usually need a virtual machine where they can start and analyze the malware behaviour in all of it aspects , such as function calls [2].

According [8], there is a growing number of malware threats worldwide and also the level of technological sophistication of malicious software is increasing mainly due to the popularity of smartphones. This is what makes malware analysis an important task in cybersecurity. Malware detection systems which detect malicious traffic are usually able to classify threads in the following categories: unclassified (0-day), misc-attack, Trojan-activity, not-suspicious, and misc-activity.

Among the most wide-spread malwares on the Internet as of November 2018 according to [16], the following are listed: *Coinhive; Cryptoloot; Andromeda; Roughted; Dorkbot; Jsecoin; Emotet; Conficker; XMRig* and *Nivdort*.

Among the mobile devices, [16] reports the following threats: *Triada; Hiddad* and *Lokibot*. The three most exploited Common Vulnerability Exposures (CVE) are reported as:

- Microsoft IIS WebDAV ScStoragePathFromUrl Buffer Overflow (CVE-2017-7269) - 48% of organizations have dealt with this threat;
- OpenSSL TLS DTLS Heartbeat Information Disclosure (CVE-2014-0160; CVE-2014-0346) – An attacker can leverage this vulnerability to disclose memory contents of a connected client or serve that had global impact of 44%.
- OpenSSL tls_get_message_body Function init_msg Structure Use After Free (CVE-2016-6309) – A remote, unauthenticated attacker could exploit this vulnerability by sending a crafted message to the vulnerable server. Successful exploitation allows the attacker to execute arbitrary code on the system impacting 42% of organizations.

C. *Botnet detection*

Compromised devices in botnets provide attackers with means to send spams, launch DDoS attacks, run brute-force password cracking, steal private information, and hide the origin of cyber attacks [3][17]. Malware network traffic can spread rapidly through various platforms and this is what makes botnet detection an important part in cybersecurity. According to the structure of botnets, two categories exist: Peer-to-Peer (P2P) and centralized botnet [8]. In a P2P botnet, the botmaster can control each bot with distributed commands sent from peers; whereas in a centralized botnet, the centralized Command & Control (C&C) architecture is formed with protocols like Internet Relay-Chat (IRC) and HTTP.

Network traffic analysis serves for detection of the botnets. The typical approach to detect compromised hosts on the network and filter botnet traffic is to maintain a blacklist of openly available C&C domains. The efficiency is poor because the blacklist has to be updated manually. There are botmasters who often use unchanged P2P-based C&C structures with pseudo random domain generation algorithms to evade the detection by blacklisting and to increase the reliability of the botnet. That is, the bots search for working C&C servers by periodically generating a set of pseudo-random domain names and resolving the generated domain names to IP addresses through DNS queries [18]. Therefore, these botnets can still survive even after some C&C servers are detected and blocked.

Machine Learning (ML) techniques are vital for the statistical based traffic classification [19]. The traffic can be processed by supervised learning, also known as classification, or by unsupervised learning, also known as clustering [20][21]. The disadvantage of the ML approaches for network traffic analysis comes mainly from the lack of online (or as some authors refer to it: real-time) detection capabilities [22]. There are many prerequisites for the successful application of supervised learning [23] with – the most important of which is the annotation of the dataset. This is what makes the unsupervised clustering ML techniques, rule-based and anomaly-based approaches preferable in these scenarios.

III. AUTONOMOUS SYSTEMS FOR CYBERSECURITY THREAT DETECTION BASED ON DEEP LEARNING TECHNIQUES

The main idea of this work is to present a linear autonomous system for prepossessing of incoming traffic. The proposed system has the capability for file content analysis and is targeted towards cloud applications, which serve multimedia (Figure 1). The incoming traffic is analyzed in an IDS; cyberthreats are blocked based on rules, anomaly detection and correlation analysis.

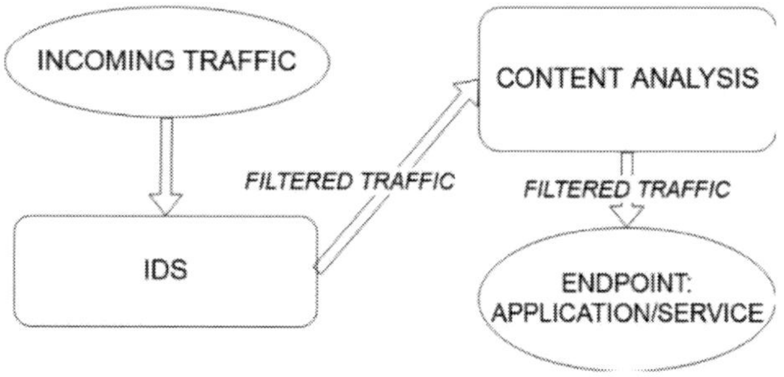

Figure 1. Workflow of the proposed protection cybersecurity protection system for cloud applications.

In the experiments, Suricata was used as well as a Surricata module based on the Google TensorFlow framework for Deep Learning [24]. The IDS filtered traffic was then subjected to content analysis where the traffic is decoded in a proxy server and the incoming text, video and images were analyzed with deep neural network classifiers (Figure 2) [25].

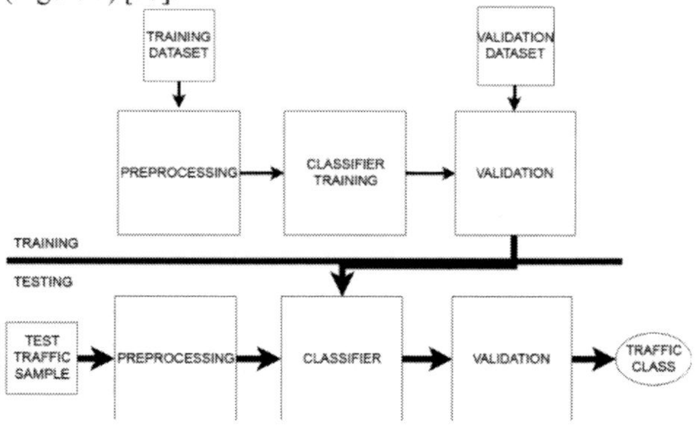

Figure 2. Classifier for network traffic analysis

With the appearance of large quantities of unstructured (or partially structured data) – the so called Big Data – and the improvement of computing power, deep learning has become extremely popular both for research and commercial purposes. ML algorithms are highly dependent on the choice of features. There are described cases with Bayesian classifiers where feature selection can greatly improve classification accuracy [25]. Deep learning techniques solve some of these challenges by automatically combining low-order features of the input, transforming and arranging them in order to calculate high-order features. In such scenario, it is not needed to add a manual step to eliminate for calculation of higher-order features of the training set. To an extent, the deep neural network structure is similar to the multi-layer neural network which includes input layer, hidden layer and output layer (Figure 3).

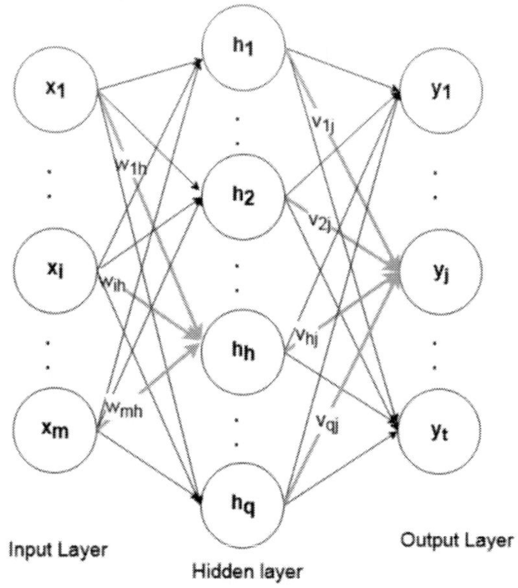

Figure 3. Multi-layer neural network general structure

The network parameters are initialized with random values, and the neuron weights are updated using the Back Propagation (BP) algorithm. In the standard neural network schema (Figure 2), the input for the of the j-th neuron from the output layer is calculated as follows:

$$o_j = \sum_{h=1}^{q} v_{hj} h_h \quad (1)$$

where v_{hj} is the weight of the connection of the hidden neuron *h* to the output neuron *j* and h_h is the output from the *h-th* hidden neuron. For the input of the *h-th* hidden neuron, the following is calculated:

$$\sigma_h = \sum_{i=1}^{q} w_{ih} x_i \quad (2)$$

where w_{hj} is the weight of the connection of the input neuron *i* to the hidden neuron *h* and x_i is the *i-th* input. For the k-th training sample (x_k, y_k), the output of the neural network is $\hat{y}_k = (\hat{y}_1^k, \hat{y}_2^k, \ldots, \hat{y}_l^k)$. With another representation known as offset term ϵ_j, it is given as $\hat{y}_l^k = f(o_j - \epsilon_j)$. The aim of the back-propagation training algorithm is to minimize the mean square error of the network on the k-th training sample. It is used for automatic update of the weights of the neural network. The regular multi-layer neural network carries the pitfalls of the disappearing gradient. With the increase in the number of layers, the number of weight parameters correspondingly grows, leading to a more complex model which can overfit [25]. Deep learning introduced the ReLU activation function, a new weight initialization method, a new loss function and new anti-fitting method (Dropout, regularization) to solve the traditional multi-layer perceptron disadvantages in terms of network structure and training capabilities.

IV. Combination of Classifier Results

The classifier combination in the proposed approach depends on the modality of the cyberthreat in each classifier. The final score is given through:

$$C_{out} = \text{argmax}(C_i) \tag{3}$$

where C_{out} is the final class label and C_i is the output from the i-th classifier. The final score represents the most certain classifier [26] out of several classifiers which use different modalities and learning algorithms.

V. Experimental Results

The Pytbull framework was used [27] to test the rules in Suricata. The accuracy of the detection with the most current rule sets was about 85%. The test setup included 4 virtual machines in private cloud infrastructure at the University of Telecommunications and Post, Sofia, Bulgaria.

A neural classifier was created using datasets obtained from [28][29] and modeled a neural network in the Weka [30] tool. The model delivered the highest accuracy of about 83% with 115 inputs four hidden neuron layers and 11 output neurons. The used dataset was derived from [23] containing 10 types of data with 249 attributes. Some of the classes contain fewer training samples and it was observed that other researches have excluded them from their training set.

Content analysis in terms of Spam detection was realized with a Convolutional Neural Network (CNN) trained in the Weka tool. The model was tested on the dataset [31] and the achieved accuracy in two classes was about 70%. Image classification was based on previous work [26] on human emotion analysis and is intended to be used on image data uploaded to a transparent proxy on the system. The achieved classification accuracy in 5 classes is about 73%.

VI. Conclusion and Future Work

In this paper, an approach was presented based on deep neural networks for design of autonomous cybersecurity threat detection systems in cloud applications. The proposed system uses 4 neural classifiers for network traffic, spam comments, spam email and images. The achieved results are comparable with contemporary approaches. The achieved accuracy for the individual components is comparable to other authors. The next steps will include expanding this framework and adopting it at the University of Telecommunications and Post, Sofia, Bulgaria.

Acknowledgment

This work is supported by the University of Telecommunications and Post (UTP), Sofia, Bulgaria, internal research grant Nr. NID16/03.04.2018 - "UNICLOUD2.0: Development and integration of cloud services in the learning process of UTP".

References

[1] J. Zhang, X. Chen, Y. Xiang, W. Zhou, and J. Wu, "Robust network traffic classification." IEEE/ACM Transactions on Networking 23, no. 4, 2015, pp. 1257-1270.

[2] G. Wagener, R. State and A. Dulaunoy, "Malware behaviour analysis". Journal in Computer Virology. Vol.4., 2013, pp.279-287.

[3] F. Haddadi et al., "Botnet Behaviour Analysis using IP Flows With HTTP filters using classifiers", Proceedings of the 28th International Conference on Advanced Information Networking and Applications Workshops, 2014, pp. 7-12

[4] A. S. Sohal, R. Sandhu, S. K. Sood, and V. Chang, "A cybersecurity framework to identify malicious edge device in fog computing and cloud-of-things environments." Computers & Security 74, 2018, pp. 340-354.

[5] M. Chambers, Reuters [retrieved: May 2019], "Germany sees big rise in security problems affecting infrastructure", https://www.reuters.com/article/us-germany-cybersecurity-idUSKCN1Q60CS

[6] C. Haschek [retrieved: May 2019], "I scanned the whole country of Austria and this is what I've found", https://blog.haschek.at/2019/i-scanned-austria.html

[7] R. L.-Langlois, [retrieved: May 2019], "Top 10 Intrusion Detection Tools: Your Best Free Options for 2019", https://www.addictivetips.com/net-admin/intrusion-detection-tools/

[8] Y. Miao et al., "Automated Big Traffic Analytics for Cyber Security." arXiv preprint arXiv:1804.09023, 2018.

[9] Open Source Host-based Intrusion Detection System, [retrieved: May 2019], http://www.ossec.net/

[10] M. Roesch, "Snort - lightweight intrusion detection for networks," inProceedings of the 13th USENIX conference on System administration, LISA '99, 1999, pp. 229–238

[11] "Suricata, open source ids/ips/nsm engine." [retrieved: May 2019], https://suricata-ids.org/

[12] "The Zeek Network Security Monitor", [retrieved: May 2019], https://www.zeek.org/

[13] "The SAMHAIN file integrity / host-based intrusion detection system", [retrieved: May 2019], https://www.la-samhna.de/samhain/

[14] "Fail2Ban – an intrusion prevention software (IPS) framework that protects computer servers from brute-force attacks", [retrieved: May 2019], http://www.fail2ban.org

[15] "Security Onion – a free and open source Linux distribution for intrusion detection, enterprise security monitoring, and log management", [retrieved: May 2019], https://securityonion.net/

[16] Check Point Software: Latest Global Threat Index November 2018's Most Wanted Malware: The Rise of the Thanksgiving Day Botnet, [retrieved: May 2019] https://blog.checkpoint.com/2018/12/11/november-2018s-most-wanted-malware-the-rise-of-the-thanksgiving-day-botnet/

[17] Kaspersky Labs Technical Report, [retrieved: May 2019], "Botnet activity in H1 2018: Multifunctional bots becoming more widespread", https://www.kaspersky.com/about/press-releases/2018_botnet-activity-in-h1-2018-multifunctional-bots-becoming-more-widespread

[18] DNS-BH- Malware Domain Blocklist, [retrieved: May 2019]. Available: http://www.malwaredomains.com/

[19] T. Nguyen and G. Armitage, "A survey of techniques for internet traffic classification using machine learning." IEEE Communications Surveys & Tutorials 10, no. 4, 2008, pp.56-76.

[20] D. Zhao et al., „Botnet detection based on traffic behavior analysis and flow intervals", Computers & Security,Vol. 39, 2013, pp. 2-16

[21] S. García, A. Zunino, and M. Campo, "Botnet behavior detection using network synchronism.", In Privacy, Intrusion Detection and Response: Technologies for Protecting Networks, IGI Global, 2012, pp. 122-144.

[22] S. Keshapagu and S. Suthaharan, "Analysis of datasets for network traffic classification.", In Topics from the 8th Annual UNCG Regional Mathematics and Statistics Conference, Springer, New York, NY, 2013, pp. 155-168.

[23] A. K. J. Michael, E. Valla, N. S. Neggatu, and A. W. Moore. "Network traffic classification via neural networks", No. UCAM-CL-TR-912. University of Cambridge, Computer Laboratory, 2017.

[24] M. Abadi, P. Barham, J. Chen, Z. Chen, A. Davis, J. Dean, M. Devin et al. "Tensorflow: a system for large-scale machine learning." In OSDI, vol. 16, 2016, pp. 265-283.

[25] J. H. Shu, J. Jiang, and J. X. Sun. "Network Traffic Classification Based on Deep Learning." Journal of Physics: Conference Series, vol. 1087, no. 6, 2018, p. 062021.

[26] S. Sokolov. "Neural Network Based Multimodal Emotion Estimation." ICAS 2018 vol 12, 2018, pp 4-7.

[27] Pytbull IDS/IPS testing framework, [retrieved: May 2019], http://pytbull.sourceforge.net/index.php?page=home

[28] D. Duaand and E. K. Taniskidou, "UCI Machine Learning Repository", Irvine, CA: University of California, School of Information and Computer Science, 2017.

[29] Y. Meidan et al., "N-BaIoT—Network-Based Detection of IoT Botnet Attacks Using Deep Autoencoders." IEEE Pervasive Computing 17, no. 3, 2018, pp: 12-22.

[30] F. Eibe, M. A. Hall, and I. H. Witten, "The WEKA Workbench. Online Appendix for Data Mining: Practical Machine Learning Tools and Techniques." Morgan Kaufmann 2016.

[31] A. L. Maas et al., "Learning word vectors for sentiment analysis." In Proceedings of the 49th annual meeting of the association for computational linguistics: Human language technologies-volume 1, Association for Computational Linguistics, 2011, pp. 142-150.

Transfer Learning Approach for Autonomous Agents in Collective Games

Ventseslav Shopov, Vanya Markova

Institute of Robotics
Bulgarian Academy of Sciences
Bulgaria
Email: vkshopov@yahoo.com, markovavanya@yahoo.com

Abstract—**The aim of this study is to present a new approach for Transfer Learning in collective games. This framework is a set of methods for transferring accumulated knowledge. In this way, autonomous agents share their knowledge in order to achieve better performance. The main hypothesis in the study is that the group of agents who exchange knowledge performs better than the same group without Transfer Knowledge, under the same conditions.**

Keywords–autonomous agents; reinforcement learning; transfer learning.

I. Introduction

The subject of the study is the transfer of knowledge in training and decision-making for autonomous agents. In this study, we look at the environment as collective sequential games. Our goal is to clarify whether Markov Decision Process (MDP) solving methods can be applied to collective games with partially observable goals and partially dynamic environments.

In addition, we raise the question of how effective transfer of knowledge in training and decision-making by autonomous agents in collective games is.

Exploring these issues is important for the development of training with support in general, and in particular for the transfer of knowledge between agents in partially observable and dynamic environments. Knowledge transfer can significantly speed up training and decision-making by autonomous agents. Such research can be found in machine learning, the video game industry, and robotics.

In this study, we build upon a recent method for knowledge transfer, which formulates the sequencing problem as a Markov Decision Process. Recently, various representations that make such knowledge transfer possible for multiple agents in different domains have been explored [1]. In addition, some generalisation of curriculum MDP model have been proposed [2] to handle different kinds of transfer learning algorithms. Another approach formulates the design of a curriculum as a Markov Decision Process, which directly models the accumulation of knowledge as an agent interacts with tasks to produce an agent-specific curriculum [2] such that overall performance or learning speed is improved [3].

There are several studies that introduce methods to generate a curriculum based on task descriptors [4], or by data-driven automated similarity measures [5]. Other methods combine feature-based control in a non-rewarding discrete environment, and imitation learning applied to an ambiguous and unconstrained third party agent [6].

Some recent studies have been performed in regard of creating frameworks for selecting source tasks in the absence of a known model or target task samples based on meta-data [7] or guided by policy sketches. [8]

In our study, we make an effort to allow the application of already developed and tested methods and algorithms to solve MDP in fields such as multi-agent systems and collective games. TL can also accelerate the learning process in various areas of machine learning, the video game and robotics industries. Given certain limitations, it is possible to use solutions that have already been tested, which may lead to a reduction in time of developing new applications.

The main hypothesis of this study is that, subject to certain limitations, it is possible to use classical MDP solving methods for partially observable and dynamic environments. It is also possible to apply knowledge transfer to groups of autonomous agents. Such a transfer leads to acceleration of training and decision-making in collective games.

The article is organised as follows: In Section 2, we briefly look at the theory underlying the proposed solutions, and then we describe the theoretical limitations of our approach and the respective implementation. In Section 3, we experimentally examine the applicability and effectiveness of our approach. In the last part, we describe our findings.

II. Methods and Materials

A. Theory

1) Sequential games: We consider sequential games, which are n-player non-zero sum games played on finite trees. Each node of the tree is controlled by either of the players, and the game is played by moving a token along the branches of the tree, from the root node, up to the leaves, which are libelled by a payoff. We also associate a preference relation with each player that indicates how he ranks the payoffs. Let us now formalise the basic notions about these games. The definitions and notations of this section are inspired from [9].

Definition 1. A sequential or extensive form game G is a tuple $(N; A; H; O; d; p; (\prec_i)$ where:

N is a non-empty finite set of players;

A is a non-empty finite set of actions;

H is a finite set of finite sequences of A which is prefix-closed. That is, the empty sequence ϵ is a member of H; and $h = a^1, ..., a^k \in H$ implies that $h^l = a^1, ..., a^l \in H$ for all $l < k$. Each member of $H$is called a node. A node $h = a^1, ..., a^k \in H$ is terminal if $\forall a \in A, a^1, ..., a^k, a \notin H$. The set of terminal nodes is denoted by Z.

O is the non-empty set of outcomes, $d : H \setminus Z \to N$ associates a player with each non-terminal node;

$p : Z \to O$ associates an outcome with each terminal node;

For all $i \in N : \prec_i$ is a binary relation over O, modelling the preferences of player i.

From now on, we fix a sequential game $G = (N, A, H, O, d, p, (\prec_i)_{i \in N})$.

Then, we let $H_i = (h \in H \setminus Z \mid d(h) = i)$ be the set of nodes belonging to player i. A strategy $s_i : H_i \to A$ of player i is a function associating an action with all nodes belonging to player i, s.t. for all

$h \in H_i : hs_i(h) \in H$, i.e., $s_i(h)$ is a legal action from h. Then, a tuple $s = (s_i) \in N$ associating one strategy with each player is called a strategy profile. For all strategy profiles s, we denote by (s) the outcome of s, which is the outcome of the terminal node obtained when all players play according to s. Single-agent Reinforcement Learning (RL) concepts are given first, followed by their extension to the multi-agent case.

2) Markov Decision Process: We formulate the transfer learning problem in sequential decision making domains using the following framework of Markov Decision Process. We use the following definition of MDP as a 5-tuple

$$< S, A, P, R, \gamma > \quad (1)$$

where the set of states, set of actions, transition function and reward function are described. And

$$P : S \times A \to \Pi(S) \quad (2)$$

is a transition function that maps the probability of moving to a new state given an action and the current state,

$$R : S \times A \to R \quad (3)$$

is a reward function. that gives the immediate reward of taking an action in a state.

And

$$\gamma \in [0, 1] \quad (4)$$

is the discount factor. The gradient formula can be written as [10]. So the MDP of the agent is described in (1), where s is the set of states, a is the set of actions, p is the transition function and r is a reward function. The transition function p maps the the probability of moving to a new state given an action and the current states and is shown in (2). The reward functions r that gives the immediate reward of taking an action is described in (3). The discount factor γ is bounded as is shown in 4.

Multi-agent Markov games can be defined by N agents with a set of global or local observations $O_1, ..., O_N$, a set of actions $A_1, ..., A_N$, a set of states S and a state transition function

$$T : S \times A_1 \times A_2 \times ... \times A_N \to S \quad (5)$$

which determines the Markov process. For each agent i, it interacts with the environment by taking actions following its policy $\pi_{Q_i} : A_i \to [0, 1]$ transformed into the next state and gets a reward $r_i : S \times A_i \to R$ to judge the policy's performance. Each agent tries to maximise the accumulated discount return

$$R = \sum t = 0^T \gamma^t r^t \quad (6)$$

and T is the expect time horizon and γ is the discount parameter. In this paper, only local observations are available for all games.

3) Reinforcement Learning: To solve sequential decision-making problems, the agent should learn about the optimal value of each action, defined as the expected amount of future rewards when taking this action and following the optimal policy afterwards. Under a given policy π , the true value of an action a in a state s is

$$Q_\pi(s; a) = E[R_1 + \gamma R_2 + \dots | S_0 = s; A_0 = a;] \quad (7)$$

where $r \in [0; 1]$ is a discount factor which trades off the importance of immediate and later rewards. The optimal value is then $Q_{\pi*}(s; a) = maxQ(s; a)$. An optimal policy can be easily learned from the optimal values by selecting in every state the highest valued action.

4) Q-Learning: The optimal action values can be derived through Q-learning [11] [12], a form of time learning. The real problems are too large to learn all the action values in all states separately. Instead, we can learn a parametric value $Q(s; a; q_t)$. In this way, Q-learning values update the parameters after taking action A_t at S_t and observe the immediate reward R_{t+1} so that the resulting state S_{t+1} is then

$$q_{t+1} = q_t + \alpha(Y_t^Q - Q(S_t; A_t; q_t))\nabla_{q_t} Q(S_t; A_t; q_t) \quad (8)$$

where q is a scalar value and the target Y_t^Q is defined as

$$Y_t^Q = R_{t+1} + \gamma \max_a Q(S_{t+1}; a; q_t) \quad (9)$$

In order to update the current value $Q(S_t; A_t; q_t)$ towards a target value Y_t^Q the agent applies stochastic gradient descent approach.

5) Deep Q Networks: Deep Q networks (DQN) are multi-layered neural networks. These networks, for a given state s, output a vector of action values $Q_{theta}(s; a; q)$, where θ are the parameters of the network. If an action space contains m actions and state space is a n-dimensional vector, the neural network maps R^n to R^m. In addition, in Deep Q Network there is target network [13], with parameters θ^-. This additional network is the same as the original network except that its parameters are copied every τ steps from the online network, so that $\theta_t^- = t$, and are not changed on all other steps. So, the target used by DQN is then

$$Y_t^{DQN} = R_{t+1} + \gamma \max_a Q(S_{t+1}; a; \theta_t) \quad (10)$$

6) Double Q-learning: To prevent overoptimistic value estimation, we can decouple the selection from the evaluation. This is the idea behind Double Q-learning [14]. In the original Double Q-learning algorithm, two value functions are learned by assigning each experience randomly to update one of the two value functions, such that there are two sets of weights, and 0. For each update, one set of weights is used to determine the greedy policy and the other to determine its value. For a clear comparison, we can first untangle the selection and evaluation in Q-learning and rewrite its target 10 as

$$Y_t^Q = R_{t+1} + \gamma Q(S_{t+1}, max_a Q(S_{t+1}; a; q_t); q_t) \quad (11)$$

The Double Q-learning error can then be written as

$$Y_t^{DoubleQ} = R_{t+1} + \gamma Q(S_{t+1}, max_a Q(S_{t+1}; a; q_t); q_t) \quad (12)$$

7) Autonomous agents: the autonomous agent in our approach has the following main features: - Autonomy - Reactivity - Proactivity - Communicativeness It is important to emphasise that our agents are autonomous not only during decision-making but also during training. This means that agents are able to learn and adapt to changes in the environment without the need for external training.

B. Implementation

To enable the MDP agent to work in Partially Observed Markov Decision Process (POMDP), its learning algorithm and decision-making algorithm must be expanded. The drawback of this approach is that already trained agents and knowledge gained in the MDP training process can not be reused.

The environment for partially observable dynamic collective games in the MDP environment is important due to two reasons: to be able to apply methods and algorithms developed for classic MDP cases of partially observable dynamic collective games; and it allows to transfer knowledge between agents trained in MDP and POMDP.

In this study, we describe the agent environment as MDP. We are driven by the desire to present the various properties of the autonomous agent so that the agent is compatible with the MDP constraints. Moreover, we strive for a generalised approach to the training of our autonomous agents.

By expanding agents' space, we present POMDP as MDP. Such representation is only possible if the following limitations are met: Partial environmental observability can be eliminated through communication between agents; dynamic changes in the environment are reflected by expanding the transition function.

Our goal is not to expand the environmental model. In addition, environments represented by POMDP can describe significantly complex systems of interactions with those described with classic MDP. Thus, by expanding the agent's state space by adding global states of the medium, the agent is compatible with the classical MDP environments.

But the extension of the MDP notation leads to some drawbacks: such as the need to modify learning algorithms s that the incompatibility of policies resulting from such training has made the transfer of knowledge between MDP trained agents enriched by such trainees POMDP environments. In the case of sequential collective games, describing the environment as partially observable does not necessarily have to be achieved by introducing POMDP. The agents themselves are able to change the environment, but by clearly announcing the changes in the environment, the agents through communication are able to bypass the limit of partial observability.

The imposition of restrictions and the expansion of the state space takes place in two stages:

a set pair $< s_{agent}, s_{env} >$ is created. The so-called pair is used for a generalised representation of agent states in a partially observed collective game environment. By imposing these limitations, we allow the use of MDP solving methods to be applied in the field of collective games with a dynamic environment.

We start with expansion of the state space, where state space is:

$$S = \{s_i\}, i = 1, ..N \tag{13}$$

so we expand space of agent s_{agent} with the space of the environment s_{env}a: so we form a tuple:

$$s_i =< s_{agent}, s_{env} > \tag{14}$$

where s_{agent} as a result of agent's actions and s_{env} as a result of environment changes.

However, to incorporate in natural manner the changes in environment we also have to expand the transition function:

$$< s'_{agent}, s'_{env} >= T(s_i) = T(s_{agent}, s_{env}) \tag{15}$$

so that the agents state is defined as follow:

$$s'_{agent} = Pr[s_{agent}(t+1) = s'_{agent}(t) = s, a_t = a] \tag{16}$$

and the environment changes reflect in environment state:

$$s'_{env} = Te[s_{env}(t+1) = s'_{env}(t) = s, a_t = a] \tag{17}$$

Thus, by expanding the state space and the transition function we map the constrained unobservables and dynamic of the environment into combined state space and extended transition function.

Each agent may have an individual transition function, so different agents can interact in a team, but the degree of knowledge transfer depends on how different the transition function differs between agents. So, to achieve full portability of the methods, as well as knowledge transfer between individual agents the function of the transition of the environment is have to be the same for all agents.

III. Experiments and Results

We gather evidence to support the hypothesis that we will speed up the learning process for knowledge transfer. It performs the following experiments: for a given map several combinations of autonomous agents should be generated. These agents should be grouped in three main parts: competitive, cooperative and neutral.

The map is described by its size $n \times n$ and the complexity factor R_c. The map generates random k treasure chests with treasure. The treasure value is 100. Additionally, k traps are generated. These pits can not be set right beside the treasures. If an agent gets into a pit, a -100 prize is generated. As a result of the complexity factor R_c, obstacles are generated. If an agent hits an obstacle, he returns to the starting position. The obstruction generation algorithm does not allow the creation of a closed area. We only issue instances when the number of agents is equal to the number of treasures. A game ends when the agent finds the treasure and takes it, falls in a trap or makes more than n^2 moves. For each move, except the last agency, agent get a small negative reward (for example -1).

Once the agent starts to learn it use a Reinforcement Learning approach. As a base algorithm, we use SARSA. For one agent, we have one pit and one treasure. Solving this problem is trivial.

If we put one agent in map with one treasure then agent quickly learns how to get the treasure. A problem arises when there are two agents and two treasures. Once the first agent reaches his treasure and takes it then in the map will remain an "empty" chest. The second agent, if closer to a treasure already taken, will try to take it, but the chest is now empty. So the second agent will go down to a local minimum and end the game with negative reward.

If the agency is a cooperative then when the first agent gets its treasure it reports to others that treasure is already

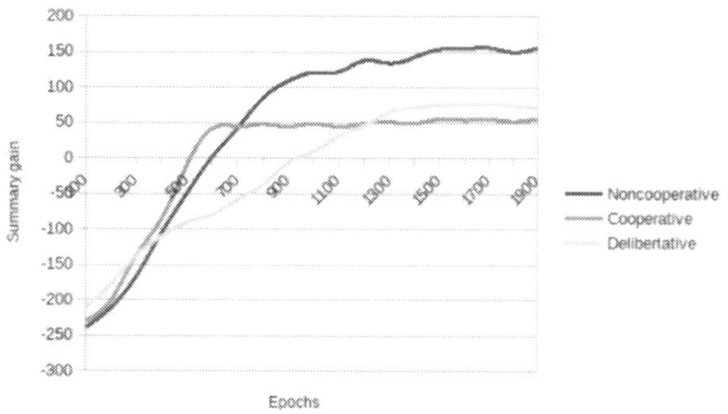

Figure 1. We compare cooperative and competitive strategies in simple one-goal map. In this map there are only one trap and relatively small amount of obstacles.

taken. There are several ways to address this issue, so we need to expand the MDP model. In order to stay in place, the agent should initially "change" the environment so that the "changed" environment is in consistency with a policy that will lead to the treasure.

We compare three approaches:

- Non-cooperative game with non-cooperative learning: where the first one has reached treasure ends the game with a 100 prize, and the next may fall to the local minimum.
- Cooperative Game with Deliberative Cooperative Learning: A binary vector for treasure is generated at the coordinator. In practice, the number of states in which there is a permanent effect on all possible treasure states is increased. If only the positive reward of the training process are combined against a sufficiently high level.

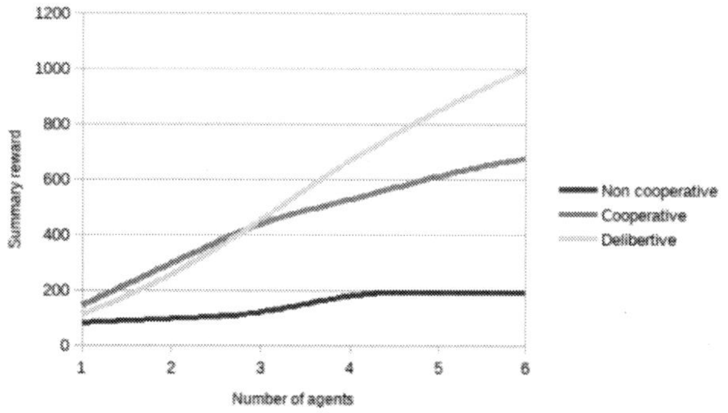

Figure 2. We compare competitive, cooperative and deliberative strategies in complex multi-goal map. In this map there are plenty of traps and relatively big amount of obstacles.

As can be seen in Figure 1, if we have only one prize, then cooperative behaviour has no advantage over competitive behaviour. In Figure 2 one can see that with the growing number of agents in the team, the use of the deliberate approach is better than the rest of the algorithms.

IV. Conclusion

A new approach is proposed to transfer knowledge among agents in collective games.The approach suggested in this article allows knowledge from pre-trained agent for pre-defined environments to be used. Our approach allows to speed up the training of agents. Instead of random values initialisation of utility or quality function, we can take such values from an already trained agent. By expanding the state space and transition function in MDP classes, we allow, subject to certain limitations, that MDP solving methods be applied to partially observable and partially dynamic environments. In addition, it is possible to transfer knowledge into collective applications.

From the results of our research it follows that in the case of only one treasure, complex cooperative interaction has no advantages over competitive approaches. In other words, the use of deliberative techniques in simple systems is over-engineering. And only with the increasing complexity of the choice between individual goals, the cooperative behaviour demonstrates the advantages of the deliberative approach.

References

[1] S. Narvekar and P. Stone, "Learning curriculum policies for reinforcement learning," arXiv preprint arXiv:1812.00285, 2018.

[2] S. Narvekar, J. Sinapov, and P. Stone, "Autonomous task sequencing for customized curriculum design in reinforcement learning." in IJCAI, 2017, pp. 2536–2542.

[3] S. Narvekar, J. Sinapov, M. Leonetti, and P. Stone, "Source task creation for curriculum learning," in Proceedings of the 2016 International Conference on Autonomous Agents & Multiagent Systems. International Foundation for Autonomous Agents and Multiagent Systems, 2016, pp. 566–574.

[4] M. Svetlik et al., "Automatic curriculum graph generation for reinforcement learning agents," in Thirty-First AAAI Conference on Artificial Intelligence, 2017, pp. 2590–2596.

[5] H. B. Ammar et al., "An automated measure of mdp similarity for transfer in reinforcement learning," in Workshops at the Twenty-Eighth AAAI Conference on Artificial Intelligence, 2014.

[6] P. Fournier, O. Sigaud, M. Chetouani, and C. Colas, "Clic: Curriculum learning and imitation for feature control in non-rewarding environments," arXiv preprint arXiv:1901.09720, 2019.

[7] J. Sinapov, S. Narvekar, M. Leonetti, and P. Stone, "Learning inter-task transferability in the absence of target task samples," in Proceedings of the 2015 International Conference on Autonomous Agents and Multiagent Systems. International Foundation for Autonomous Agents and Multiagent Systems, 2015, pp. 725–733.

[8] J. Andreas, D. Klein, and S. Levine, "Modular multitask reinforcement learning with policy sketches," in Proceedings of the 34th International Conference on Machine Learning-Volume 70. JMLR. org, 2017, pp. 166–175.

[9] M. J. Osborne et al., An introduction to game theory. Oxford university press New York, 2004, vol. 3, no. 3.

[10] R. S. Sutton and A. G. Barto, Reinforcement learning: An introduction. MIT press Cambridge, 1998, vol. 1, no. 1.

[11] C. J. Watkins and P. Dayan, "Q-learning," Machine learning, vol. 8, no. 3-4, 1992, pp. 279–292.

[12] C. J. C. H. Watkins, "Learning from delayed rewards," Ph.D. dissertation, King's College, Cambridge, 1989.

[13] V. e. a. Mnih, "Human-level control through deep reinforcement learning," Nature, vol. 518, no. 7540, 2015, pp. 529–538.

[14] H. Van Hasselt, A. Guez, and D. Silver, "Deep reinforcement learning with double q-learning." in AAAI, vol. 16, 2016, pp. 2094–2100.

Deep Learning with Evolutionary Strategies for Building Autonomous Agents Behaviour

Ventseslav Shopov, Vanya Markova

Institute of Robotics
Bulgarian Academy of Sciences
Bulgaria
Email: vkshopov@yahoo.com, markovavanya@yahoo.com

Abstract—**In this study, we will consider the construction of the behaviour of an autonomous agent in an environment that has many traps and a large number of obstacles. Such environments require the agent to build a policy that will lead them to the goal as quickly as possible. As a working basis, we use Reinforcement Learning and apply approaches from the field of random search and Evolutionary Strategies.**

Keywords–Autonomous Agents; Reinforcement Learning; Evolutionary Strategies.

I. INTRODUCTION

Reinforcement Learning (RL) is a scientific area where the main topics is agent training without supervision. Thus, an agent is an autonomous subject who learns and makes decisions independently. Such an agent, through interactions with the environment, finds the optimal policy for consistent decision making [1]–[3].

Deep learning prevails in the areas of studying natural language, recognising objects in the pictures of classification in multidimensional cases. Q-nets, AlphaGo, asynchronous methods and many others are examples of successful Deep Learning applications [4]–[8]. Deep learning leads to great benefits in areas of big data and data science. However, there are cases in which employing greedy optimisation for a reward can lead to sticking to a local minimum or suffer of slow converging [9].

Evolutionary Strategies (ES) are an approach that helps to find global minimums. A comprehensive overview of different ES techniques in the field of machine learning is given in [10]. Several studies have been done so far [11] [12], however most of them consider the ES as an alternative to RL.

In our study, we combine ES as they were described in [10] and Deep Q-Networks [4]–[6] in Reinforcement Learning to explore the applicability and effectiveness of the agent learning in the field of Sequential Games. At the moment, many specific methods of gradient descent have been proposed, but they all assume that the gradient behaves well: there are no cliffs where it increases abruptly, or a plateau where it vanishes. The first problem can be dealt with using the gradient clipping, but the second is more challenging.

The main objective of this study is to compare the performance of classical optimisation methods and ES as well as to verify how these algorithms affect learning speed. Thus, the hypothesis in this study is to compare the behaviour of gradient optimisation algorithms and algorithms for ES.

This paper is organised as follows: in Section 2, we briefly describe some basic theories of learning in the field of reinforcement, Deep Learning, and ES. In addition, we present the implementation of our approach. In Section 3 of our article, we describe the experiments and collect evidence to support our hypothesis. We conclude the work in Section 4.

II. METHODS AND MATERIALS

A. Theory

1) Autonomous Agent Behaviour: Information about past and current states of the agent and environment allows agents to evaluate their own progress. In reinforcement training, an agent builds up policies based on progress. The policy determines the reaction of the agent to the state of the environment. Through RL, the agent builds such policies that will achieve the goal with the maximum benefit for the agent.

So, if we describe the states of the agent and environment as a time series, then the task of making efficient plans will be significantly aided if the agent could forecast the future with desirable accuracy. An n-tipple (vector) is a result of one cycle of the work of the agent. It consists of the parameters of the behaviour of the agent: $b(b1, b2, \ldots, bn)$. The data from environment are collected and transformed into time series in the knowledge base of the agent.

2) Markov Decision Process: We formulate the transfer learning problem in sequential decision making domains using the following framework of Markov Decision Process. We use the following definition of Markov Decision Process (MDP) as a 5-tuple

$$< S, A, P, R, \gamma > \quad (1)$$

where the set of states, set of actions, transition function and reward function are described. $P : S \times A \rightarrow \Pi(S)$ is a transition function that maps the probability of moving to a new state given an action and the current state,

$$R : S \times A \rightarrow R \quad (2)$$

is a reward function that gives the immediate reward of taking an action in a given state. $\gamma \in [0, 1)$ is the discount factor. The MDP of the agent is described in (1), where S is the set of states, A is the set of actions, P is transition function and R is a reward function.

3) Reinforcement Learning: To solve sequential decision-making problems, the agent should learn about the optimal value of each action, defined as the expected amount of future rewards when taking this action and following the optimal policy afterwards. Under a given policy π , the true value of an action a in a state s is

$$Q_\pi(s;a) = E[R_1 + \gamma R_2 + \ldots | S_0 = s; A_0 = a;] \quad (3)$$

where $r \in [0;1]$ is a discount factor which trades off the importance of immediate and later rewards. The optimal value is then $Q_{\pi*}(s;a) = maxQ(s;a)$. An optimal policy can be easily learned from the optimal values by selecting in every state the highest valued action.

4) Q-Learning: The optimal action values can be derived through Q-learning [13] [14], a form of time learning. The real problems are too large to learn all the values of action in all states separately. Instead, we can learn a parametric value $Q(s;a;q_t)$. In this way, Q-learning values update the parameters after taking action A_t at S_t and observe the immediate reward R_{t+1} so that the resulting state S_{t+1} is then

$$q_{t+1} = q_t + \alpha(Y_t^Q - Q(S_t;A_t;q_t))\nabla_{q_t} Q(S_t;A_t;q_t) \quad (4)$$

where q is a scalar value and the target Y_t^Q is defined as

$$Y_t^Q = R_{t+1} + \gamma \max_a Q(S_{t+1};a;q_t) \quad (5)$$

Updating the current value $Q(S_t;A_t;q_t)$ towards a target value Y_t^Q the agent applies stochastic gradient descent approach.

5) Deep Q Networks: Deep Q Networks (DQN) are multi-layered neural networks.These networks for a given state s outputs not a single action but a vector of action values $Q(s;a;q)$, where θ are the parameters of the network. If an action space containing m actions and state space is a n-dimensional vector, the neural network maps R^n to R^m. In addition in Deep Q Networks, there are target network [5], with parameters θ^-. This additional network is the same as the original network except that its parameters are copied every τ steps from the online network, so that then $\theta_t^- = t$, and are not changed on all other steps. So, the target used by DQN is then

$$Y_t^{DQN} = R_{t+1} + \gamma \max_a Q(S_{t+1};a;\theta_t) \quad (6)$$

6) Double Q-learning: The max operator in standard Q-learning and DQN, in 4 and 6, uses the same values both to select and to evaluate an action. To prevent this overoptimistic value estimation we can decouple the selection from the evaluation. This is the idea behind Double Q-learning [15]. In the original Double Q-learning algorithm, two value functions are learned by assigning each experience randomly to update one of the two value functions, such that there are two sets of weights, and 0. For each update, one set of weights is used to determine the greedy policy and the other to determine its value. For a clear comparison, we can first untangle the selection and evaluation in Q-learning and rewrite its target as

$$Y_t^Q = R_{t+1} + \gamma Q(S_{t+1}, max_a Q(S_{t+1};a;q_t);q_t) \quad (7)$$

The Double Q-learning error can then be written as

$$Y_t^{DoubleQ} = R_{t+1} + \gamma Q(S_{t+1}, max_a Q(S_{t+1};a;q_t);q_t) \quad (8)$$

7) Evolution Strategies: If the action values contain random errors uniformly distributed in an interval $[-\epsilon, epsilon]$ then each target is overestimated up to $\gamma\epsilon\frac{m-1}{m+1}$, where m is the number of actions [16]. This could leads to local optima. So, we need a new approach for achieving the exploration strategy that will lead us to a global optima. Such kind of algorithms are ES.

ES are a class of black box optimisation algorithms inspired by natural evolution [17]. At every iteration (generation), a population of parameter vectors (genomes) is perturbed (mutated) and, optionally, recombined (merged) via crossover. The reward (fitness) of each resultant offspring is then evaluated according to some objective function. Some form of selection then ensures that individuals with higher reward tend to produce the individuals in the next generation, and the cycle repeats.

Recent work from OpenAI outlines a version of NES applied to standard RL benchmark problems [11]. We will refer to this variant simply as ES going forward. In their work, a fitness function $f()$ represents the stochastic reward experienced over a full episode of agent interaction, where θ is the parameters of a policy π.

$$\nabla_\phi E_{\theta\sim\phi}[f(\theta)] = \frac{1}{n}\sum_{i=1}^{n} f(\theta_t^i)\nabla_\phi \log p_\phi(\theta_t^i) \quad (9)$$

where n is the number of samples estimated per generation. The sample parameters in the neighbourhood of t and determines the direction in which t must move to improve the expected reward. Instead of the baseline, the ES relies on a large number of samples n to reduce the variance of the gradient estimate. To avoid bias in the optimisation process due to large scale of reward between domains, we follow the approach of [11] and rank-normalise $f(\theta_t^i)$ before taking the weighted sum.

B. Implementation

The idea is quite simple. With a standard gradient descent, at each step we look at the inclination of the surface on which we are located and move in the direction of the greatest gradient. In ES, we fire a nearby neighbourhood with points where we can supposedly move, and move in the direction where most points with the greatest height difference fall (and the farther the point, the more weight is attached to it).

In the case of a piecewise-step function, the resulting estimate will represent the gradient of the smoothed function without having to calculate the specific values of this function at each point. Also in the case when the loss function depends on the discrete parameters, it can be shown that the estimate remains valid, since in the proof one can interchange the order of taking the expectation. Which is often not possible for ordinary Stochastic Gradient Descent (SGD).

$$\mathbb{E}_\epsilon \epsilon E(\theta + \epsilon) = \mathbb{E}_\epsilon \epsilon \mathbb{E}_x E(\theta + \epsilon, x) = \mathbb{E}_x \mathbb{E}_\epsilon \epsilon E(\theta + \epsilon, x) \quad (10)$$

The greater the sigma distribution, the less the local structure of the function manifests itself. When the sampling algorithm is too large, the optimisation algorithm does not show narrow minima and hollows, from which one can go from one good state to another. If it is too small, the gradient descent may not start if the initialisation point was chosen unsuccessfully.

Sampling makes noise in the gradient calculation, which makes learning more sustainable. Just like dropout in learning neural networks in the usual way. ES does not depend on frame-skip with RL. Also ES allow learning more easily than regular SGD, when a large amount of time can pass between an action in RL and a positive response, and in noisy conditions, when it is not clear which change helped improve the result. What are the disadvantages? The computation per episode is slower than in SGD. And the final results are not significantly better. Noise in gradients - even with one-dimensional optimisation, are slightly unstable.

The RL algorithm can query the environment by sending it the suggested policy π. The model then selects a random variable e, independent of the past, and generates a vector from the system in accordance with the policy π and randomness e.And then the model returns to the our algorithm a sequence of states, actions, and rewards (s, a, r), which represent a vector generated from the system in accordance with the policy π. In this scheme, one request is called an episode. The purpose of the RL algorithms is to approximate the solution of problem by making as few calls as possible to the medium.

III. EXPERIMENTS AND RESULTS

For the purposes of our research, we do the following : we look at a stochastic single player game that strives to maximise its winnings. The game is a 2d map in which the player must reach a certain goal by avoiding certain traps. The reward in the target is 100 and the reward in the trap is -100. For each idling, the player receives a -5. The game has a stochastic policy because the probability of going to the next scheduled state is 0.9 and with probability 0.025 the agent will either end up in one of the neighbours to the current state or will remain in the current state. In this way, an odometric error or a real agent monitoring error is modelled. If the agent made a transition to an obstacle or out of the map, we see this as a "collision". Upon collision, the agent returns, returning to the current state and receiving a -10 reward. The agent performs one episode until it reaches a terminal state or by making a number of steps larger than the size of the environment.

Maps are rated by many parameters as: size, size of hurdles, trap to size ratios, and reward ratios to size. The latter is always inversely proportional to the size of the map. We are looking at a couple of specially made maps:

- map with minimal obstacles and traps. This map is a virtually ideal playing field. The likelihood of collision or the agent becoming trapped is minimal. Depending on the ratio of the reward to the size, the agent is favourably trained in small-sized maps.
- map with a significant number of obstacles and traps. In this case, we have an obstacle to size ratio of 0.2 and trap ratios to the size of 0.2. On this map, the total return is less than the first. However, obstacles and traps are selected so that there are no conditions for occurrence of local minima.
- map with a significant number of obstacles and traps designed to generate a local minimum. This map has the same ratio of obstacles and traps as in the previous case, but here the goal is surrounded by traps and obstacles. We have done this arbitrarily in order to check how our policy optimisation methods will behave in such a situation.

We create a model of the RL problem in a way similar to the one in [18]. This model allows us to get an estimate of the information our agent can extract from the environment. The training agent generates policy and applies it to the environment. In fact, the agent uses this policy for an episode. In addition, the agent generates a random magnitude that I apply to policy parameters. This magnitude is different and independent for each step. In this way, the environment generates a vector with the responses to the proposed policy for each step.

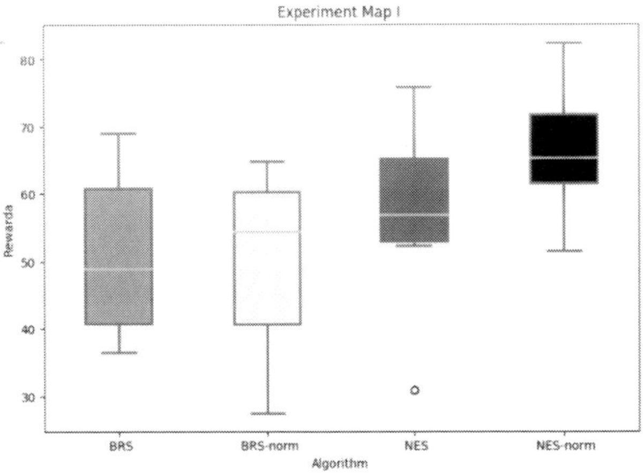

Figure 1. We study the performance of the algorithms in simple map.

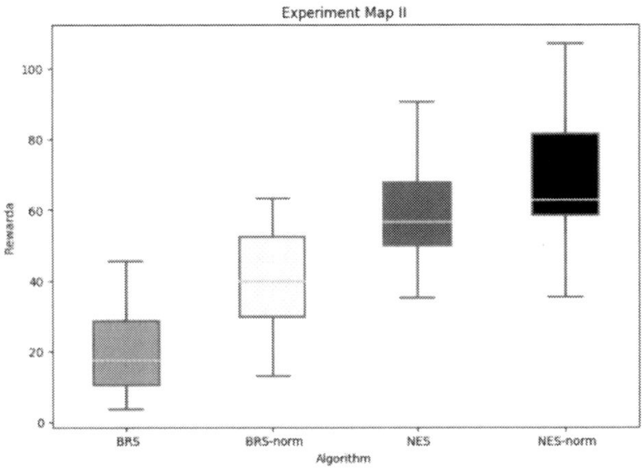

Figure 2. We study the impact of higher number of obstacles and traps.

This vector has the form $< s, a, r >$ where c is the current state, and the action a r is the reward. This vector is recorded for each episode. The optimisation method should change the policy parameters depending on what reward is awarded at each episode step. Through this model, we get the opportunity to generate queries to the environment and get vectors with all of the agent's trajectories for each episode.

From a practical point of view, the agent strives to obtain a policy whereby the overall return is maximum. Creating a stop criterion is not a trivial task especially if we have a stochastic pattern of behaviour. Fluctuations in rewards as a result of unfavourable coincidence of random events lead to a significant volatility of the overall return. However, in our research we are are primarily interested in the comparative characteristics of the two policy optimisation approaches. Therefore, we will ignore the convergence criterion and set a final number of epochs as a measure of completing the training.

We compare the following four algorithms: BRS, BRS-norm, Natural Evolutionary Strategies (NES) and NES-norm. BRS and BRS-norm differ only in that the initial initialisation of the BRS-norm parameters is normalised according to the maximum and minimum reward. The same applies to NES and NES-norm.

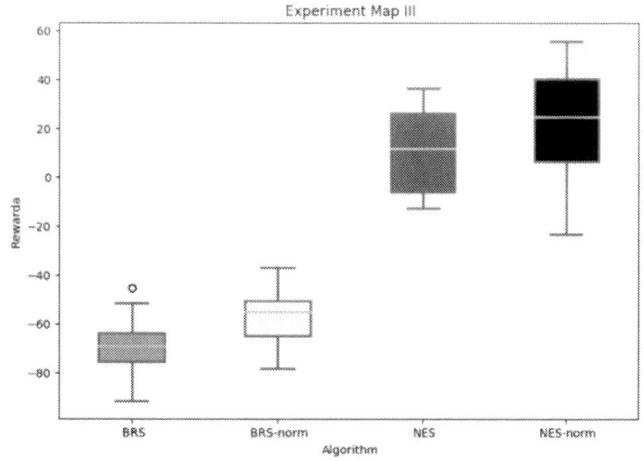

Figure 3. We see the impact of "local minima" environment.

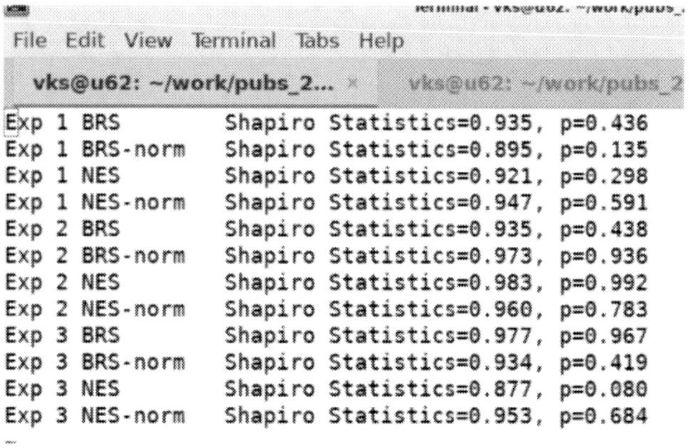


```
Exp 1 BRS        Shapiro Statistics=0.935, p=0.436
Exp 1 BRS-norm   Shapiro Statistics=0.895, p=0.135
Exp 1 NES        Shapiro Statistics=0.921, p=0.298
Exp 1 NES-norm   Shapiro Statistics=0.947, p=0.591
Exp 2 BRS        Shapiro Statistics=0.935, p=0.438
Exp 2 BRS-norm   Shapiro Statistics=0.973, p=0.936
Exp 2 NES        Shapiro Statistics=0.983, p=0.992
Exp 2 NES-norm   Shapiro Statistics=0.960, p=0.783
Exp 3 BRS        Shapiro Statistics=0.977, p=0.967
Exp 3 BRS-norm   Shapiro Statistics=0.934, p=0.419
Exp 3 NES        Shapiro Statistics=0.877, p=0.080
Exp 3 NES-norm   Shapiro Statistics=0.953, p=0.684
```

Figure 4. The Shapiro tests shows that all results have normal distribution.

The results of first experiment can be seen in Figure 1. One can see that under favourable conditions the cumulative reward after training does not differ significantly. The results of second experiment are shown in Figure 2. Here we can see that NES and NES-norm have a higher median reward, but their dispersion also is higher. It is only in the third experiment (Figure 3) that we see the superiority of ES. It seems that Basic Random Search (BRS) and BRS-norm are stuck in the local minima. NES algorithms perform much better although they show higher volatility.

From Shapiro's tests (result shown in Figure 4), it can be seen that as the complexity of the environment increases, the volatility of the solutions increases. BRS and BRS-norm demonstrate more stable but significantly lower performance, while NES and NES-norm achieve a higher overall return but at the expense of increased volatility.

IV. Conclusion and Future Work

In this study, we looked at building an autonomous agent's behaviour in an environment that has both rewards and traps. Such environments require agents to build a policy that leads them as quickly as possible to the goal. On the other hand, the agent should "avoid" traps especially in the case of a stochastic policy of movement.

As a working framework, we used Reinforcement Learning. We compared approaches from the field of random search and Evolutionary Strategies. Experiments have shown that methods based on an evolutionary approach show better results when the environment is more complex. Especially important is the superiority of Evolutionary Strategies in cases where the environment has local minima.

References

[1] R. S. Sutton and A. G. Barto, Reinforcement learning: An introduction. MIT press Cambridge, 1998.

[2] C. Szepesvári, "Algorithms for reinforcement learning," Synthesis lectures on artificial intelligence and machine learning, vol. 4, no. 1, 2010, pp. 1–103.

[3] D. P. Bertsekas, Dynamic programming and optimal control 3rd edition, volume II. Belmont, MA: Athena Scientific, 2011.

[4] V. Mnih et al., "Asynchronous methods for deep reinforcement learning," in International Conference on Machine Learning, 2016, pp. 1928–1937.

[5] ——, "Human-level control through deep reinforcement learning," Nature, vol. 518, no. 7540, 2015, pp. 529–538.

[6] D. Silver et al., "Mastering the game of go with deep neural networks and tree search," nature, vol. 529, no. 7587, 2016, pp. 484–489.

[7] Y. LeCun, Y. Bengio, and G. Hinton, "Deep learning," nature, vol. 521, no. 7553, 2015, pp. 436–442.

[8] I. Goodfellow, Y. Bengio, A. Courville, and Y. Bengio, Deep learning. MIT press Cambridge, 2016.

[9] J. Lehman and K. O. Stanley, "Novelty search and the problem with objectives," in Genetic programming theory and practice IX. Springer, 2011, pp. 37–56.

[10] D. E. Moriarty, A. C. Schultz, and J. J. Grefenstette, "Evolutionary algorithms for reinforcement learning," Journal of Artificial Intelligence Research, vol. 11, 1999, pp. 241–276.

[11] T. Salimans, J. Ho, X. Chen, and I. Sutskever, "Evolution strategies as a scalable alternative to reinforcement learning," arXiv preprint arXiv:1703.03864, 2017.

[12] F. P. Such et al., "Deep neuroevolution: Genetic algorithms are a competitive alternative for training deep neural networks for reinforcement learning," arXiv preprint arXiv:1712.06567, 2017.

[13] C. J. Watkins and P. Dayan, "Q-learning," Machine learning, vol. 8, no. 3-4, 1992, pp. 279–292.

[14] C. J. C. H. Watkins, "Learning from delayed rewards," Ph.D. dissertation, King's College, Cambridge, 1989.

[15] H. Van Hasselt, A. Guez, and D. Silver, "Deep reinforcement learning with double q-learning." in AAAI, vol. 16, 2016, pp. 2094–2100.

[16] S. Thrun and A. Schwartz, "Issues in using function approximation for reinforcement learning," in Proceedings of the 1993 Connectionist Models Summer School. Hillsdale, NJ. Lawrence Erlbaum, 1993, pp. 255–264.

[17] I. Rechenberg, "Evolutionsstrategien," in Simulationsmethoden in der Medizin und Biologie. Springer, 1978, pp. 83–114.

[18] H. Mania, A. Guy, and B. Recht, "Simple random search provides a competitive approach to reinforcement learning," arXiv preprint arXiv:1803.07055, 2018.

Adaptive Control of Traffic Congestion with Neuro-Fuzzy based Weighted Random Early Detection

Irina Topalova
Department of Information Technology
University of Telecommunications and Post
Technical University Sofia
Sofia, Bulgaria
email:itopalova@abv.bg

Pavlinka Radoyska
Department of Information Technology
University of Telecommunications and Post
Sofia, Bulgaria
email:pradoiska@abv.bg

Abstract— **Differentiating class-based traffic and class-based queue management is the most advanced approach for queue management in routers and switches, controlling and preventing the congestion. The combination of a mechanism for prioritizing the Internet Protocol traffic and the way to dynamically modify the parameters of the packet rejection algorithm is essential for achieving efficient and reliable traffic. In this study, a method is proposed, exploring the automatic adaptation of new users added to the backbone of the network, to the already defined weighted random early detection parameters. A neuro-fuzzy-logic network is trained to automatically adapt new end users to the quality of service policy already set in the backbone area. This network is trained with the quality of service parameters of the backbone area and serves to adapt these parameters in the newly-added routers. The results obtained are compared with those from the study of this problem by the authors, when a multilayer neural network is used.**

Keywords-traffic congestion; Quality of Service; Weighted Random Early Detection; fuzzy logic; neuro-fuzzy system.

I. Introduction

In modern Information Technology (IT) communications, the Quality of Services (QoS) is essential for traffic efficiency. The creation of queues and their inadequate management results in substantial packet delays. The QoS aims to guarantee the quality of message delivering by congestion management and congestion avoidance. Various methods are currently applied to reduce the negative effect of the problem. But more and more experimental methods of artificial intelligence are being explored, hoping for better results as given by K. Markov et al. [1], B. Deaire et al. [2].

In this study, a method is proposed, to investigate the automatic adaptation of new users added to the backbone of the network, to previously defined weighted random early detection parameters. The neuro-fuzzy logic network is trained to automatically adapt new end-users to the service quality policy already in place. This network is trained with the service quality parameters of the main zone and serves to adapt these parameters to the newly added routers. The results obtained are compared with those, from the study of this problem by the authors, when a multilayer neural network is used, as well as with results from other similar researches. The novelty of the proposed method consists in the possibility of automated adaptation of the newly added QoS parameters to an already existing communication structure without having to reconfigure these network devices. This is made possible by the proposed adaptive neuro-fuzzy system, which approximates the parameters of these devices in order to bring them closer to the one already set.

The rest of this paper is organized as follows. Section II describes the related to the research works. Section III describes methods for congestion avoidance and Weighted Random Early Detection methods. In Section IV, the proposed method for weighted random early detection parameter adjustment is presented. Section V gives the experimental results. Section VI closes the article.

II. Related Work

In the recent years, various methods have been proposed to implement fuzzy logic to optimize traffic or to create predictive models. E. Jamhoura et al. [3] propose a method for building a fuzzy predictor to model a differentiated services (DiffServ) node with two queues - for Voice over IP (VoIP) traffic and self-similar data traffic. They define the fuzzy membership functions on the base of extending the existing queue models and apply a fuzzy model to build network traffic controllers. M. Yaghmaee et al. [4] proposed a fuzzy based controller for traffic differentiated services. Their fuzzy scheduler is based on the waited fair queue mechanism, in which the significance of each queue is adjusted by the fuzzy controller. To dynamically tune the committed interface rate, the authors use a two input one output fuzzy controller. The presented results show better performance than non-fuzzy mechanisms. The researchers S. Shalinie et al. [5] describe the input and output of a queue size regulation system, by a fuzzy set. In the proposed model, they use two inputs - Traffic Intensity and Available Link Bandwidth. Output of this model is the Queue size parameter. But fuzzy logic-based Adaptive Drop Tail shows significant improvement in controlling congestion without any need for special parameterization or tuning as given by A. Mishra [7]. The outcome shows that their proposed Adaptive Drop Tail Fuzzy Logic controller has reduced packet loss when compared to traditional Drop Tail mechanisms. The simulation is designed to maintain adaptive buffer space when a sudden change in overloading occurs, which prevents Internet router buffers from becoming full when overloading occurs.

The above-mentioned methods that use fuzzy logic offer ways to reduce congestion through non-traditional queue management in network device buffers, rather than addressing the problem of adapting the new device's QoS parameters to those already set in the primary communications area.

In our study, we use fuzzy logic combined with neural network training to offer a simplified method of adjusting the QoS parameters of newly-added routers to the backbone area. The difference in the approach of this method is that the need to create an analytical model of traffic queues is eliminated. At the same time, the use of fuzzy logic in conjunction with a Nero Fuzzy System (NFS) allows the uncertainty of the average queue, to be transformed into a specific value of the Mark Denominator parameter. This parameter, obtained as a NFS solution, is fed to the newly-added routers to match this QoS parameter to those already set in the backbone area.

III. Congestion Avoidance and Weighted Random Early Detection

Network congestion occurs in two cases: when data arrive on a big pipe and get sent out a smaller pipe and when multiple input streams arrive at a router whose output capacity is less than the sum of the inputs. Congestion avoidance in network communications has two significant components: congestion management in end devices based on Transmission Control Protocol (TCP) algorithm and Active Queue Management in routers.

A. TCP congestion avoidance

The main purpose of congestion management in end devices is to adapt TCP window size to the bottleneck throughput while maintaining an optimal exchange rate. The basic congestion control algorithms, focused on end devices are implemented in TCP protocol (RFC 5681) and include: slow start, congestion avoidance, fast retransmit (TCP Tahoe) and fast recovery (TCP Reno). Different variants are compared by authors H. Kaur and G. Singh [6], A. Mishra [7], N. Parvez et al. [8].

The TCP window size is measured in bytes. The communication starts with the slow start phase (RFC5681). The sender doubles the widow size on every received TCP acknowledgement (ACK). Slow start stops when the window size reaches slow start threshold (*ssthresh*) or at the first missing ACK. The congestion avoidance phase starts after the widow size reaches *ssthresh*. The window size increments by one full size segment on any Round Trip Time (RTT). The congestion avoidance phase stops at the first missing ACK. According to the traditional TCP algorithm, the slow start phase is activated after any missing ACK. Congestion avoidance defines how to deal with lost packets. There are two indications of packet loss: (1) waiting time has expired and (2) receipt of duplicate ACKs. Retransmit Time Out (RFC 6298) is a parameter which determines the wait time for acknowledgment. The Receiver returns to the sender an ACK after every arrived segment. But it acknowledges the latest ordered segment data. The segments that arrive out of order (there is a missing segment) are buffered, but not acknowledged. This mechanism follows more than one ACK for a segment. According to the Selective Acknowledge TCP algorithm (SACK), the receiver acknowledges the last ordered segment and all buffered segments. SACKs with the same last ordered segment acknowledged, independently of acknowledged buffered segments, are considered as duplicate acknowledgements.

B. Congestion avoidance mechanisms in the routers

Random Early Detection (RED) was proposed by C. Ghazel and C. Saidane [9] in the early 1990s to address network congestion in a responsive rather than reactive manner. It aims to trigger TCP congestion avoidance in end devices before traffic congestion has occurred. As a result, the data transmission speed is reduced and congestion in the router is avoided. RED controls the average queue size in the router and compares it with the predefined threshold for the minimum (*minq*) and maximum queue (*maxq*) size. RED runs in *minq* – *maxq* range – shown in Figure 1. At an average queue size less than the *minq*, the packets are sent in pure FIFO mode. At an average queue size greater than the *maxq*, all packets are dropped. RED decides which packages to drop using probability calculations based on the minimum, maximum and average queue size, the ratio of the current packet size to the maximum one and the number of packets in the queue as is given by S. Rajput [10]. MPD (Mark Probability Denominator) is used to limit the dropped packets, according to the average queue size during the RED phase. MPD defines the number of dropped packets when average queue size is equal to *maxq*, just before full drop phase.

Some authors give a review in IEEE Transactions [11] and also X. Jiang et al. [12] consider the main problems of the RED algorithm as: 1) unpredictable queuing delay and 2) a sharp decrease in the throughput with high traffic load. Unpredictable queuing delay provokes to instability of RTT. RTT may become larger than the Recovery Time Objective (RTO) and causes retransmission of packets already received, and hence overload the network. Other authors, Cisco IOS Quality of Service Solutions [13], consider this behavior to be reasonable.

The traffic flow describes the communication between two sockets. The packets marked for dropping are selected based on the probability theory rather than on full statistics. This can cause more frequent dropping of packets from some flows than packets of other flows. Thus, the mechanism of congestion avoidance in some flows is triggered more often than others, and the speed of communication between two sockets can be drastically slow while others remain high. Furthermore, some packets carry no TCP traffic and are therefore not sensitive to the TCP congestion avoidance mechanism. These packets will not reduce their transmission rate and it is very likely, that the queue will be filled with their packets only. As a result, the router will become "impassable" for TCP communication. On the third hand, in the presence of DoS (Denial of Service) attacks, the attackers turn off the slow start and congestion avoidance mechanisms and send their packages with maximum windows size. Of course, there are serious defenses against such attacks, but with low-rate DoS attacks the most of them do not work as shown by M. Al-shaw and A. Laurent [14].

The WRED algorithm given by A. Custura et al. [15] has been developed to achieve better fairness and is implemented into the operating systems of two of the leading companies in the communications industry – Cisco and Juniper. The packages are split into flows. Flows are merged into queues. Each queue gets a specific portion of the outgoing bandwidth. Within each queue, streams get their weighting priority. Priorities are defined as: high, medium, and low. The priority determines the probability of the packets dropping. Each package is marked to determine which queue it belongs to and what its priority is. The DifServ fields in the IPv4 (RFC) and Type of Service (ToS) header in the IPv6 header (RFC) are used to classify traffic. These fields are 8 bits long. The first 6 of them are used for Differentiated Service Code Point (DSCP) (RFC2474), (RFC2475) and the last 2 bits are for experimental use. RFC5865 describes service classes, according to the traffic types. When constructing the DSCP classes, it is recommended to apply Per-Hop Behaviors (PHBs) and Active Queue Management (AQM) mechanisms. Service class applies to applications with similar characteristics and performance requirements, such as specific delay, loss and jitter. DSCPs to Service Class Mapping is shown in Table 1. The network administrator may choose to implement different service classes, or to implement different behaviors for service classes, or to aggregate different kinds of traffic into one class. Only the Default Forwarding (DF) "Standard" service class is required. All other service classes are optional. Three types of queues can be defined: priority queue, rate queue and AQM. Each defined queue gets the portion of outbound bandwidth. Cisco developments recommended by Geib, R. and D. Black [16] a bandwidth distribution by types of traffic.

Only AQM queues are based on packet dropping and RED/WRED. AQM queues define only Assured Forwarding (AF) classes and DF. Any package that is not explicitly marked belongs to DF class. DSCP bits for AF classes are depicted in Figure 2. The first 3 bits define the class number, the next two - the priority, and the last one must be 0.

Collections of packets with the same DSCP setting that are sent in a particular direction can be grouped into a Behavior Aggregate (BA). Packets from multiple sources or applications can belong to the same BA. DSCP is used to select the Per-Hop Behavior (PHB) at each interface.

PHB (RFC2475) is a mechanism that allows independent management of DSCP classes in each router. DSCP classes are queueing in the router in a locally defined manner. A portion of the output bandwidth is allocated to each queue. For example, class traffic with DSCP Af11, Af12 and Af13 is incorporated in one AQM queue with name gold (statement 1). For this queue, 35% of outbound bandwidth (statement 2) is allocated. *Minq*, *maxq*, and *MPD* are defined for DSCP classes in the queue. Let configure *minq* =20, *maxq* =40, *MPD* =10 for DCSP class *af11* (statement3).

class-map match-all *gold* ***match ip dscp*** *af11 af12 af13*
class *gold* ***bandwidth percent*** *35*
random-detect dscp *af11 20 40 10*

Based on these analyzes and research, as well as our observations, we have come to the conclusion that the most efficient action, would be the implementation of a WRED mechanism, but with the ability to transform the queue uncertainty into specific values of the rejected packets. This leads to the idea of using fuzzy logic.

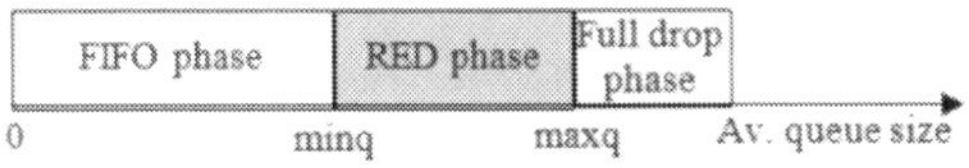

Figure 1. Queue management phases.

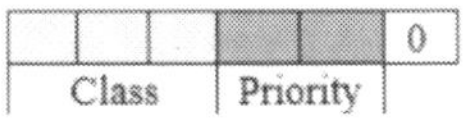

Figure 2. DSCP bits for AF classes.

TABLE I. DSCP TO SERVICE CLASS MAPPING

Service Class Name	DSCP Name	DSCP Value	Application Examples
Network Control	CS6	110000	Network routing
Telephony	EF	101110	IP Telephony bearer
Signaling	CS5	101000	IP Telephony signaling
Multimedia Conferencing	AF41, AF42, AF43	100010, 100100, 100110	H.323/V2 video conferencing (adaptive
Real-Time Interactive	CS4	100000	Video conferencing and Interactive gaming
Multimedia Streaming	AF31, AF32, AF33	011010, 011100, 011110	Streaming video and audio on demand
Broadcast Video	CS3	011000	Broadcast TV & live events
Low-Latency, Data	AF21, AF22, AF23	010010, 010100, 010110	Client/server transactions Web-based ordering
OAM	CS2	010000	OAM&P
High-Throughput Data	AF11, AF12, AF13	001010, 001100, 001110	Store and forward applications
Standard	DF (CS0)	000000	Undifferentiated applications

IV. PROPOSED METHOD FOR QOS PARAMETER ADJUSTMENT

The proposed method is based on the functional scheme shown in Figure 3. The assumption is that in the end (Remote site) routers, as well as in the Central router, the AF classes with related traffic types are already defined. We assume that WRED and differentiated services are configured in the end routers. The DSCP values and the minimum and maximum threshold range, considered for managing the average queue depth in the central router, are both configured. The Neuro-Fuzzy Device Manager

(NFDM) is trained with these two parameters and prepares in its output the calculated Mark Denominator (MD). MD defines the fraction of packets dropped when the average queue depth is at the maximum threshold. Thus, the NFDM system consists of two inputs and one output variables. As newly-added routers are connected to the Central router area, their also configured DSCP values are submitted to the already trained NFDM. According to the defined linguistic rules in the inference phase, the NFDM sends the calculated MD to the added routers. This action seems to be reasonable, because the following baseline markings with DSCP Assured Forwarding PHB are typically recommended by Cisco Systems, represented by B. Hedlund [17]:

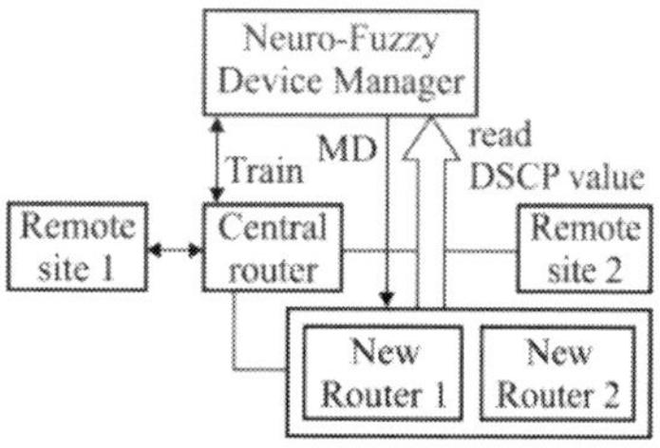

Figure 3. Functional scheme of the proposed method

- Interactive Video - AF41
- Mission Critical Data (locally defined) - AF31
- Transactional Data (dlsw, sql, sap): AF21
- Bulk Data (email, ftp, backups): AF11.

Thus, it is assumed that these classes are set by following these recommendations in the newly-added routers.

V. Experimental Results

The NFDM was trained with two input variables. The first one is represented in Figure 4 and defines the membership functions of the DSCP values - combination of traffic class and its priority. The upper angles of the trapezoidal membership functions are set to point to the exact DSCP values of the respective range of the standard AF classes. Seven ranges are defined - 10-12 and 12-14 respectively for class 1; 18-20 and 20-22 for Class 2; 26-28 and 28-30 for Class 3; 34-38 for Class 4. The overlapping areas of the trapezoidal shapes are so set, that the values of

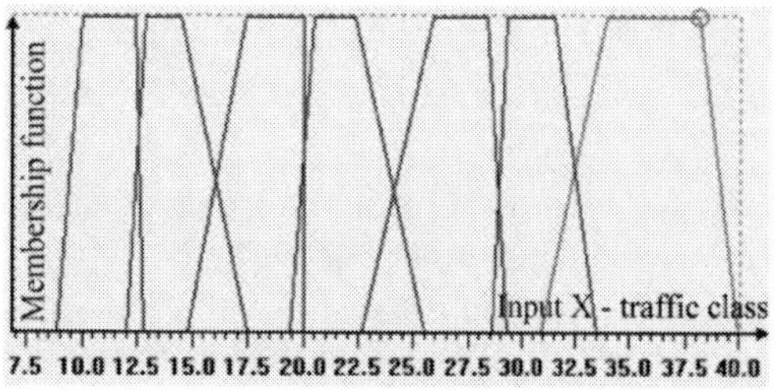

Figure 4. Membership function of DSCP values (combination of traffic class and its priority)

the membership functions are negligible, as no packets with DSCP values beyond the standard are expected. The second input variable is represented in Figure 5 and defines the four ranges are chosen as typically recommended [17]. membership function of the Min-Max threshold values. Here The defined MD as output result of the Inference and Defuzzifiction phase is shown in Figure 6. Because of its neural network structure, the system is capable of learning (an advantage of neural systems) and because of its fuzzy-like topology it is possible to recreate the processing steps. To design a system that takes advantage of neural networks and fuzzy systems in one project, we need a system that processes the fuzzy membership functions and fuzzy model rules.

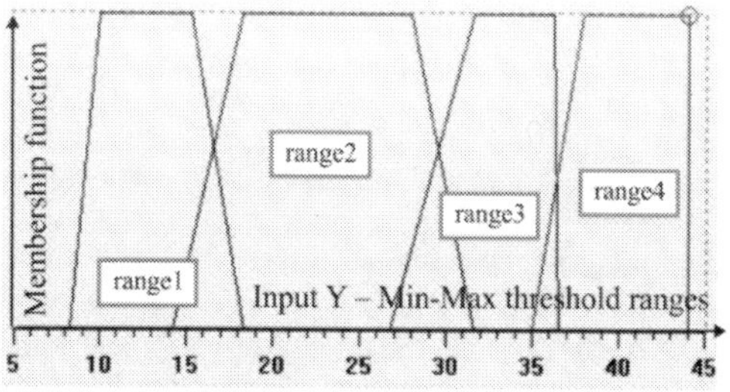

Figure 5. Membership function of the Min-Max threshold values

Thus, we can determine knowledge from the sampling data using neurons capable of learning. You can solve this problem by using a special neural network called NFN. It consists of three neural subnets (NSNs) that emulate the three sub-sequences - fuzzification, inference and defuzzification - of the fuzzy system [18].

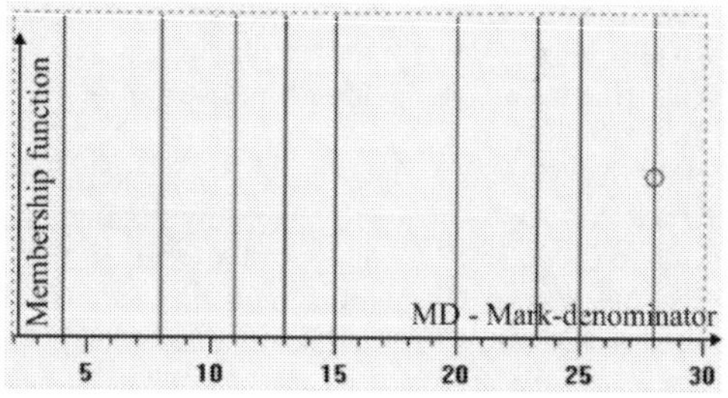

Figure 6. Membership function of MD

Thus, the fuzzification of the non-fuzzy input variables is implemented by a layer of neurons with activation functions of the both above described inputs. One neuron is assigned to each membership function of the input variables. In the second layer of the neuro-system, the rule base of the fuzzy system is applied and one neuron is assigned to each rule. The IF part of a fuzzy rules is implemented by the first neuron layer and the 2nd layer implements the THEN part of a fuzzy rule. The number of neurons in the second layer is equivalent to the number of membership functions of the output variables. The output values of the system in the 3rd neuron layer are implemented by the standard defuzzification method with MAX-PROD inference followed by centroid calculation as given in NeuroSystem, User Manual [18].

Table II demonstrates the chosen linguistic rules, which are inputs to the second layer neurons. For example, the first to third columns of Table II, set the following linguistic rules:

IF *DSCP is 10 to 12* and *Range 1* THEN MD=8;
IF *DSCP is 12 to 14* and *Range 1* THEN MD=4;
IF *DSCP is 18 to 20* and *Range 2* THEN MD=8; etc.

TABLE II. LINGUISTIC RULES OF THE NFDM

Input X: traffic class with drop preferenc	AF11-AF12 (DSCP values 10 to 12)	AF12-AF13 (DSCP values 12 to 14)	AF21-AF22 (DSCP values 18 to 20)	AF22-AF23 (DSCP values 20 to 22)	AF31-AF32 (DSCP values 26 to 28)	AF32-AF33 (DSCP values 28 to 30)	AF41-AF43 (DSCP values 34 to 38)
Input Y: Min-Max Threshold range	range 1	range 1	range 2	range 2	range 3	range 3	range 4
Output Z: MD	8	4	15	11	25	20	28

Figure 7 shows the obtained 3D surface, which illustrates the obtained dependencies between inputs X and Y and the resulting value of MD (axis Z) at the output of the NFDM. But the 3D presentation is not informative enough, when the number of input and output variables for NFDM is higher. In this case, it is better to represent the variables as it is shown in Figure 8 and Figure 9.

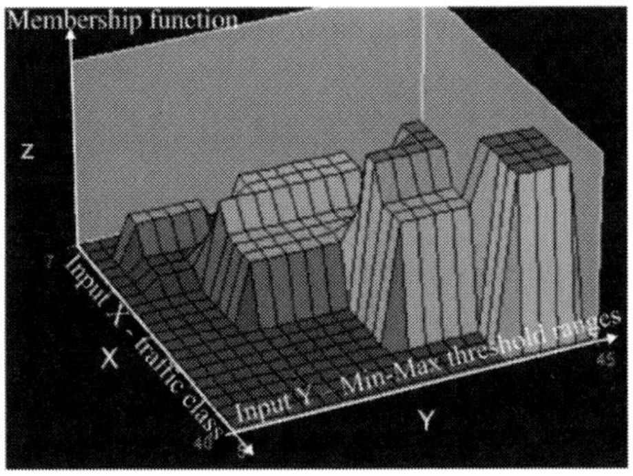

Figure 7. Membership function of MD (axis Z) according to Input X (DSCP) and Input Y (Min-Max threshold ranges)

Figure 8 shows the variations of MD (green line) according to AF12 (DSCP=12; yellow line) and all threshold ranges 1 to 4 (red line). Figure 9 shows the variations of MD (green line) according to AF32 (DSCP=28; yellow line) and all threshold ranges 1 to 4 (red line). Both figures show very well the change in the value of MD, that is submitted to the newly-added router, when its DSCP value is brought to the input of the already trained NFDM system.

VI. CONCLUSION AND FUTURE WORK

The use of fuzzy logic in conjunction with a neural network NFS in the proposed method, allows the uncertainty of the average queue to be transformed into a specific value of the Mark Denominator parameter. This parameter, obtained as a NFS solution, is fed to the newly-added routers to match this QoS parameter to those already set in the backbone area. An advantage of the method is that no any analytical model is designed, but only NFDM training is required.

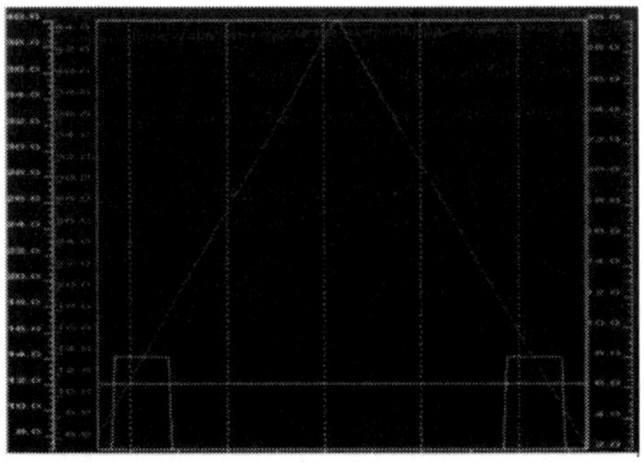

Figure 8. Variations of MD (green line) according to AF12 (DSCP=12; yellow line) and all threshold ranges 1 to 4 (red line)

The advantage is the ability of the network to learn, i.e. its ability to adapt to changed behavior and new situations. To exploit the benefits of both - the easy understandability of fuzzy systems and the ability to train neural networks - the two techniques are combined. Compared to the results of the authors' study given by I. Topalova and P. Radoyska [19], where only neural network is used to match MD, the NFDM method does not require a large volume of trained samples, as the initial uncertainty of the selected input variables. The methods discussed above use fuzzy logic and offer ways to reduce congestion through non-traditional queue management in network device buffers, rather than addressing the problem of adapting the new device's QoS parameters to those already set in the primary communications area, applying automated adaptation. In this sense, we consider the proposed method of no analogue in the scientific registers

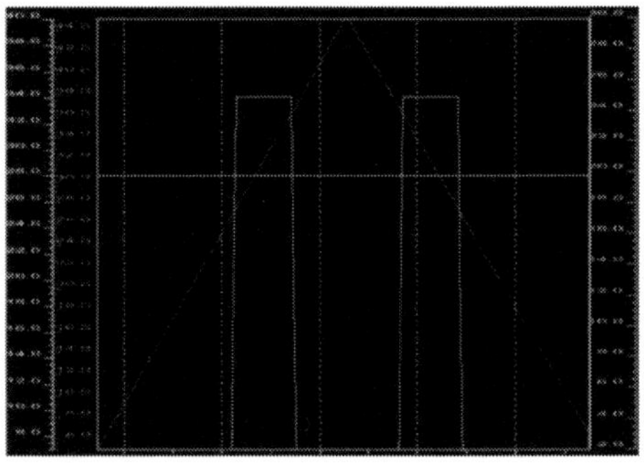

Figure 9. Variations of MD (green line) according to AF32 (DSCP=28; yellow line) and all threshold ranges 1 to 4 (red line)

As a further continuation of the study, we are testing the NFMM system with more MD values for tracking and validating the adjusted values for the newly-added routers. Different forms (for example triangular) of the Membership functions of the Min-Max threshold values and of the DSCP values will also be attempted, aiming to investigate the degree of uncertainty.

REFERENCES

[1] K. Markov, K. Ivanova, K. Vanhoof, I. Mitov, B. Depaire, V. Velychko, and V. Gladun, "Intelligent Data Processing Based on Multi-Dimensional Numbered Memory Structures," Diagnostic Test Approaches to Machine Learning and Commonsense Reasoning Systems, IGI Global, 2013, pp. 156-184, doi: 10.4018/978-1-4666-1900-5.ch007, ISBN: 978 1-4666-1900-5, EISBN: 978-1-4666-1901 2.

[2] B. Deaire, K. Ivanova, K. Markov, I. Mitov, K. Vanhoof, and V. Velychko,"Multi-dimensional Information Spaces as Memory Structures for Intelligent Data Processing in GMES," pp 347-370 In: Kr. Markov et al. Intelligent Data Processing in Global Monitoring for Environment and Security, ITHEA, 2011, Kiev, Ukraine - Sofia, Bulgaria. ISBN: 978-954-16-0045-0 (printed), ISBN: 978-954-16-0046-7 (CD/DVD), ISBN: 978-954-16-0047-4 (online). ITHEA® IBS ISC No.: 21. 410 p.

[3] E. Jamhoura, M. Pennaa, R. Nabhenb, and G. Pujolleb, " Modeling a multi-queue network node with a fuzzy predictor," Fuzzy Sets and Systems 160 (2009) 1902–1928, © 2008 Elsevier B.V., doi:10.1016/j.fss.2008.12.004.

[4] M. Yaghmaee, M. Menhaj, and H. Amintoosi, "Design and performance evaluation of a fuzzy based traffic controller for differentiated services," Computer Networks 47 (2005) 847-869, available online at www.sciencedirect.com, access date april, 2019.

[5] S. Shalinie, G. Preetha, S. Nidhya, and B. Devi, "Fuzzy Adaptive Tuning of Router Buffers for Congestion Control," International Journal of Advancements in Technology, http://ijict.org, Vol 1, No 1, © IJoAT ISSN 0976-4860, June 2010.

[6] H. Kaur and G. Singh, "TCP Congestion Control and Its Variants," Advances in Computational Sciences and Technology ISSN 0973-6107 Volume 10, Number 6 (2017) pp. 1715-1723.

[7] A. Mishra, "Performance Analysis of TCP Tahoe, Reno and New Reno for Scalable IoT Network Clusters in QualNet" ® Network Simulator, International Jpurnal of Computer Sciences and Engineering 6(8), pp:347-355, August 2018 DOI: 10.26438/ijcse/v6i8.347355.

[8] N. Parvez, A. Mahanti, and C. Williamson, "An Analytic Throughput Model for TCP NewReno," in IEEE/ACM Transactions on Networking, vol. 18, no. 2, pp. 448-461, April 2010. doi: 10.1109/TNET.2009.2030889

[9] C. Ghazel and C. Saidane, "Next generation networks dimensioning for improving and guaranteeing quality of service," The International Journal of Networks (JNW) 5 (7), pp.782-791, 2018.

[10] S. Rajput, V. Kumar, and S. Paul, "Comparative analysis of random early detection (RED) and virtual output queue (VOQ) algorithms in differentiated services network," 2014 International Conference on Signal Processing and Integrated Networks (SPIN), Noida, 2014, pp. 237-240. doi: 10.1109/SPIN.2014.6776954

[11] Learning-Automata-Like Solution, in IEEE Transactions on Systems, Man, and Cybernetics, Part B (Cybernetics), vol. 40, no. 1, pp. 66-76, Feb. 2010. doi: 10.1109/TSMCB.2009.2032363

[12] X. Jiang, J. Yang, G. Jin, and W. Wei, RED-FT: A Scalable Random Early Detection Scheme with Flow Trust against DoS Attacks, IEEE COMMUNICATIONS LETTERS, Vol. 17, No. 5, pp. 1032-1035, May 2013.

[13] Cisco IOS Quality of Service Solutions Configuration Guide, [Online] Available: https://www.cisco.com/c/en/us/td/docs/ios/12_2/qos/configuration/guide/fqos_c/qcfintro.html, access date march, 2019.

[14] M. Al-shaw and A. Laurent, QoS Design Principles and Best Practices, Cisco Press, Jan 1, 2018, [Online] Available:http://www.ciscopress.com/articles/printerfriendly/2756478, access date march, 2019.

[15] A. Custura, A. Venne, and G. Fairhurst, "Exploring DSCP modification pathologies in mobile edge networks," 2017 Network Traffic Measurement and Analysis Conference (TMA), Dublin, 2017, pp. 1-6.
doi: 10.23919/TMA.2017.8002923

[16] R. Geib and D. Black, "Diffserv-Interconnection Classes and Practice", RFC 8100, DOI 10.17487/RFC8100, March 2017, [RFC8100].

[17] B. Hedlund, "Enterprise QoS Solution Reference Network Design Guide," Cisco Systems, 2017.

[18] NeuroSystem, User Manual, Copyright © Siemens AG, 2006.

[19] I. Topalova and P. Radoyska, "Control of Traffic Congestion with Weighted Random Early Detection and Neural Network Implementation", ICAS 2018, The Fourteenth International Conference on Autonomic and Autonomous Systems, pp. 8-12, Nice, France, 20-24 May 2018.

Organic Self-Adaptable Real-Time Applications

Lial Khaluf
University of Paderborn
Computer Science
Email: lial.khaluf@googlemail.com
Düsseldorf, Germany

Franz-Josef Rammig
University of Paderborn
Computer Science
Email: franz@upb.de
Paderborn, Germany

***Abstract*—Nowadays, computing systems tend to find inspiration for their behavior in organic systems. Approaches have been published to develop a system behavior with the potential to react to environments. In the real-time domain, such approaches are still very rare and limited. In this paper, we provide an approach which is able to adapt at runtime and, at the same time, preserve all real-time constraints. In accordance to "Organic Programming", we make use of the concept of cells. A cell is an extension of a task allowing its adaptation. Cells exist by means of classes, which consist of a limited set of cell variants. All variants of a cell share the same fundamental functionality, however under different computing time demands and different costs. Our approach consists of an adaptation algorithm that behaves as a real-time cell. Under the assumption that the ecosystem of the real-time environment is given in the form of a set of real-time cells, each one with multiple variants, it provides a selection mechanism in the space of this ecosystem. The system goals aim to reduce system costs under the constraint of meeting all real-time requirements.**

Keywords–Real-time cell; variant; organic programming; optimization; self-adaptability.

I. INTRODUCTION

Turning any physical process into an online process is a current trend in many kinds of businesses. This evolution is reflected by transforming the current physical systems into Cyber Physical Systems. In such systems, the correct functionality of the system is influenced by its reaction to internal and external events. Such adaptation capabilities apply in general to control processes as, for example, in the medical or energy sectors, etc. In most cases, the nature of such processes belongs to embedded systems where timing constraints have to be achieved. Cyber Physical Systems add several advantages over traditional systems, such as self-adaptability as reaction to failures as well as unexpected conditions [1]. In this sense, such a system is evaluated by its ability to adapt itself to environmental changes in real-time. Many approaches have been proposed to solve this challenge. However, most of the existing approaches have several limitations related to the ability of reacting to unexpected events, or reacting in an undefined way. In order to overcome these deficiencies, we introduce in this paper a solution that mimics the organic behavior of objects in our real world. Real world objects have the ability to change their structure or behavior when they react to any environmental event, as cells do in an organism [2]. For this reason, our solution does not limit itself to a predefined set of events or reactions. It is assumed that the system has the ability to grow at runtime. In other words, it is assumed that the system is able to have new resources, new events and reactions at runtime. Currently, we apply our algorithm on a single node system, with the ability to import the needed information from the outside which can be considered as a remote node. This information consists of the different reactions that the system may apply in response to specific events that may result from an internal or external environmental change. The reactions are developed by external sources, and added to the system at runtime. The solution we provide applies for all kinds of real-time systems. This is done by providing the system with organic properties at the level of real-time tasks. Such tasks, in our case, are transformed into cells, called real-time cells. A real-time cell is an extension of a real-time task by mechanisms empowering it to self-adaptation. Whenever an adaptation takes place, both the adaptation and the resulting adapted system have to respect real-time restrictions. For this purpose, a selection process is part of the adaption mechanism. Its search space is restricted to a current ecosystem given by a limited number of cell classes, each one with a limited number of variants. Under the constraint that all real-time restrictions have to be satisfied, this selection process aims to minimize the overall system costs. We assume a relatively low frequency of adaptation requests. Such requests react to requested improvements or slight environmental changes. In this paper, we mostly concentrate on the central essential question: how adaptation requests can be handled under real-time constraints. In Section 2, we present the related work. Section 3 describes the problem we are facing and provides a solution for it. In the last section, we conclude the achievements of the paper and present possible future work.

II. RELATED WORK

In [2], a new model for organic programming is introduced. It aims to overcome limitations of the traditional programming models such as the Object Oriented Programming (OOP) [28], Model Driven Architecture (MDA) [27] or Aspect Oriented Programming (AOP) [26], where abstract classes or models are difficult to change. The idea behind the approach in [2] is to have a system that is able to grow and evolve continuously. However, it was not made for real-time systems. In our approach, we concentrate on having a system consisting of cells with defined properties that enable self-adaptability in real-time.

The approach in [3] and [4] defines different profiles with different resource requirements for each task. It enables choosing the best combination of profiles at runtime to adapt the system to certain situations. However, these profiles are developed offline, and new ones cannot be added to the system at runtime, which decreases the system adaptation ability.

Our approach applies the concept of organic programming by giving the ability to modify tasks online in a way that preserves all real-time constraints. Cells can be developed and added online to the system.

In [5], we find a summarized description for the state of the art in terms of modeling dimensions, research challenges, and requirements of self-adaptive systems. A self-adapting system has the following dimensions: (1) Goals: Evolution, Flexibility, Duration, Multiplicity, Dependency, Change, Source, Type, Frequency, Anticipation, (2) Mechanisms: Type, Autonomy, Organization, Scope, Duration, Timeliness, Triggering, and (3) Effects: Criticality, Predictability, Overhead, Resilience [5]. In our approach, system goals may change according to adaptation scenarios. Events that trigger an adaptation depend on the system where we apply the developed algorithm. The type of change that causes an adaptation could be functional, non functional, or technological. In our approach, there is no restriction on this issue; changes are foreseeable, but can change over time.

Mechanisms of adaptability summarize how the system can react to changes, in terms of space and time required. The algorithm we provide may act by decisions taken automatically or by other parties. The adaptation is done by a central component. The scope of adaptation could be local or global. The duration of the adaptation is influenced by execution time of the central component.

The set of dimensions and effects deals with results of adaptation, such as the overhead. In our approach, missing a deadline may confirm the failure of the system.

In [6], a second roadmap for state of the art is presented. Challenges of a self-adaptive system are described.

The first challenge is to understand the different alternatives that may represent designer or developer decisions. In our approach, we have developed a general strategy that applies for different kinds of real-time systems. We have an abstract implementing component, which fits as a reusable component.

The second challenge is concerned with understanding the nature, goals, and lifecycle of the system. In [6], a comparison between the basics for traditional software processes, and self-adaptive processes is described. The first one is illustrated in [7] by the traditional approach to corrective maintenance, and the second in [8] and [9] by the automatic workaround approach. The traditional approach reports the problem to the developers. The automatic workaround approach moves the corrective actions to runtime by applying alternative procedures when a failure happens. In our approach, the alternative procedure might be a new request or an update request. Analyzing causes of the failure may be assigned to a human or a subsystem. In the workaround approach, recovering methods are developed at design phase. In our approach, this can be done at runtime. In the workaround approach, if a recovering method does not exist, a report is sent to the developers, which is the same action taken in our approach.

The third challenge is concerned with decentralization of control loops. Controlling a system could be done in a centralized [10]-[12] or decentralized manner [13]-[17]. The self-adapting component is central in our approach, as network reliability in terms of time and trustworthy is a main concern in real-time systems.

The fourth challenge is the verification and validation of the system. In our approach, verification is done for requirements of real-time systems, apart from the context of the system.

In our approach, we define the optimization constraints in a multi-dimensional multiple choice knapsack problem. Most common solutions can be found in [18] and [19]. In our approach, we use a genetic algorithm inspired from [18] to solve a knapsack problem. The reason is that it can provide the whole solution (individual consisting of best variants in terms of time and cost) at once if available. This allows to use required parameters of the individual elements in order to calculate the parameters of other elements. The most important fact for our application is that it is an "Anytime Algorithm" in the sense that at any time the current valid solution of the algorithm can be used. This solution may be far away from an optimal one. However, if the initial population is a valid solution, it is guaranteed that at any time a valid solution can be provided.

III. Problem Description and Solution Concept

In our assumption, we consider periodic, aperiodic tasks or if both then evidently together. Dependability may exist between aperiodic tasks. A request can be adding a task, deleting a task, updating a task, adding a set of dependent tasks, deleting a set of dependent tasks, updating a set of dependent tasks. We assume a mixed hard-deadline periodic and aperiodic task environment. Figure 1 shows an example of request types. In case 1, the algorithm should solve the case of Task 5 not being accepted by the underlying schedulability algorithm. In case 2, the algorithm should solve the case of Task 1 update not being accepted by the underlying schedulability algorithm, and the question of how to make an update of Task 1.

In this paper, we only consider the activities on one single local node. System tasks, and tasks that are triggered have to be executed on this node. We assume that task management is carried out by a Real-Time Operating System (RTOS) with Earliest Deadline First algorithm (EDF) as the principal scheduling method. Furthermore, we assume that aperiodic tasks are handled via a Total Bandwidth Server (TBS) [20] and that the underlying RTOS runs the Stack Resource Protocol [21] to avoid unlimited blocking and deadlocks. In order to be able to run the adaptation algorithm, we come up with the concept of real-time cells. A cell is a task that is able to change its structure and behavior at runtime, to allow adaptations in real-time. The change is decided by a central cell called "Engine-Cell". Assuming that the system before update is correctly functioning, we strictly follow the concept of transactions. If a solution for an update request is found after applying the update operations, the system state is updated. If a solution is not found, the system goes back to the previous state.

The above mentioned Engine-Cell runs the adaptation algorithm using a two dimensional array as model of the underlying ecosystem. Each column stands for a class of cells which all share the same principal functionality. Each cell in the column is a variant, where these variants accomplish the same task, but with different costs and execution time demands. The Engine-Cell runs an adaptation algorithm, which intends to select over all cell classes the best combination of variants that allows to accept the newly arrived requests. The objective is to fulfill all real-time constraints and to provide a globally maximum quality of the adapted system. As this selection process takes place on the ecosystem defined by the mentioned two-dimensional array, the search space is restricted to the bounded set of cells with bounded number of variants which is present at time of adaptation.

We also assume a remote node (as model of the environment) that is dedicated to install variant updates, and newly deployed cells. An update request means updating a cell according to a provided change of parameters without altering the principal behaviour. The remote node is used for providing external storage, and also to be uploaded in an appropriate place for developers. Modelling the current state of the system and cell classes and viewing these models by developers are

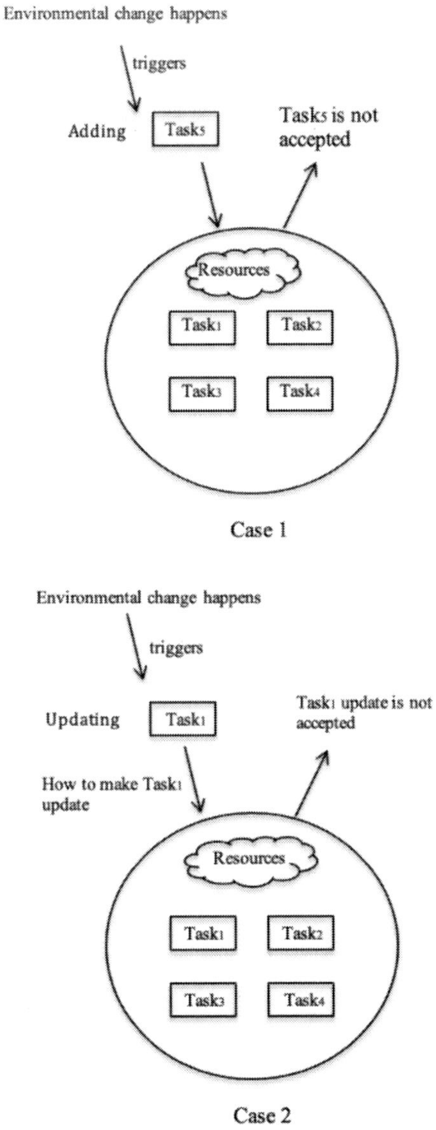

Figure 1. Request Types

not discussed in the scope of the paper. At each execution of the Engine-Cell, new requests may have arrived to the system. The adaptation algorithm is run by the Engine-Cell, trying to find a feasible solution by selecting variants over all cell types. A real-time cell becomes active when it is accepted by the system for execution. The Engine-Cell is called an Active Engine-Cell (AEC) once it is activated. Any other Real-Time Cell (RTC) is called an Active Real-Time Cell (ARTC) once it is accepted for execution. The Engine-Cell is treated here as a periodic cell and stays active as long as the system is running. We make the general assumption for all periodic cells (including AEC) that the relative deadline is equal to the period. As investigating the acceptance of newly arrived requests is part of the Engine-Cell algorithm, we ensure that the system state does not change during the execution of the Engine-Cell.

The parameters controlling the Engine-Cell are defined as follows:

1) Hyperperiod: is the hyperperiod of the currently accepted periodic ARTCs. The next point in time where a hyperperiod completes execution is abbreviated as NHP (Next Hyperperiod). Adaptation takes place only once per hyperperiod. It becomes effective not earlier than NHP.
   At the start of the system, the hyperperiod is calculated as the least common multiple of the periods of periodic ARTCs that initially might exist at the system startup. The resulting value is set as initial value for the AEC's period. We examine the total utilization (AEC and ARTCs). If it is smaller or equal to 1, we have found the shortest possible period for AEC (which at the same time by definition is the hyperperiod). If the total utilization is beyond 1 then the hyperperiod has to be extended by a harmonic multiple until the total utilization is no longer beyond 1. Calculating an initial NHP is carried out either offline or as part of the initialization when starting the system.
   Note: the response time on adaptation requests depends on the load of the system. A highly loaded system means a smaller fraction of the processing capacity to be dedicated for the AEC. At the same time, the execution time demand of the AEC tends to increase if some fixed upper bounds (such as dimensions of the RTCArray) change.
2) NumOfPARTCs: is the number of the current periodic ARTCs in the system.
3) NumOfAARTCs: is the number of the current aperiodic ARTCs in the system.
4) RTCArray: is the data structure that holds the different variants of RTCs in the system. Figure 2 shows the RTCArray consisting of different RTCs. Each column is called an RTClass. Each RTClass holds a number of variants, which are RTCs dedicated to fulfill the same task, with different cost and execution time requirements. Switching between the different variants online enables to execute tasks in the best way regarding system resources. All periodic variants, that belong to the same class, have the same period. All aperiodic variants that belong to the same class, have the same deadline. The RTCArray is a

dynamic component. RTCs can be added to it online. The upper bounds of its dimensions can grow online. Other parameters include the Worst-Case Execution Time ($WCET_{EC}$), the worst case period (WCT_{EC}), and additional properties of the EC.

Another set of properties is defined for ordinary RTCs:

1) VariantsAllowed: is a Boolean property. When it is equal to true, all variants that belong to the class of the respective RTC variant should be examined to select the best variant in the adaptation algorithm. Otherwise, the respective RTC variant is considered mandatory to be processed by the algorithm.
2) UpdatingPoints (UP): is a set of points in the code of the RTC routine. At these points, the RTC could be substituted by another variant within the same class from the RTCArray. All variants, which have the same RTClassID, have a set of updating points with the same number of points, where each point in a specific set has a counter part point in all the other considered sets. UpdatingPoints is of relevance only in case of aperiodic tasks. Instances of such tasks may have a long execution time, exceeding the current hyperperiod. Therefore, just waiting for the next instance would not be appropriate. In case of periodic tasks, we restrict updates on the natural updating point, defined as the release time of the next instance of a periodic task [22].
3) $ET_{executed}$: is the time that has been spent in executing an aperiodic RTC before the previous NHP.
4) NextUpdatingPoint: a variable that saves the next updating point which has not been yet reached by the executed code of the RTC.
5) Triggered: is a Boolean property that reflects the status of an RTC. If it is equal to true, this means that the RTC is triggered for execution.
6) TriggeringTime: is the time at which an RTC is triggered (chosen from the RTCArray).
7) TriggeringRange: is the range of time within which the arrival time of an RTC could be set. Our goal is to set the arrival time of requests greater or equal to NHP, because at this point, we assume that all accepted periodic requests are simultaneously activated (i.e., we assume all phases to be 0).
8) Deletion: a Boolean property, that is set to true if the request means deletion of a cell. It is set to false, otherwise.
9) Active: is a Boolean variable that is set to true when the cell is accepted for execution.

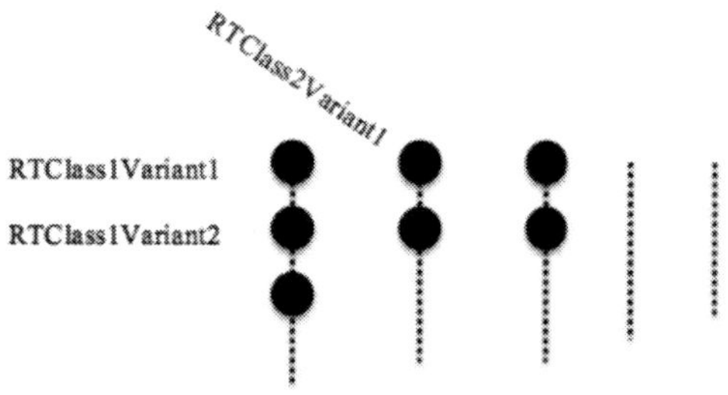

Figure 2. RTCArray

Other properties not described in the scope of this paper include the ID of the RTC (RTClassID/VariantID) inside RTCArray, the cost of an RTC, the importance factor, the factor of essentiality, the static parameters, and the updated cost, which should be calculated for an RTC, when it replaces another executing RTC.

In the following:

- We use the term ExpPARTCs to refer to the set of current periodic ARTCs excluding the RTCs, which belong to the deletion requests.

- We use the term ExpAARTCs to refer to the set of current aperiodic ARTCs excluding the RTCs, which belong to the deletion requests.

The Engine-Cell algorithm can be sketched as follows (See Figure 3):

Step 1: Gathering and filtering the newly deployed RTCs: The first step of the AEC is to collect the newly deployed RTCs, and store them in a WorkingRTCArray (a copy of RTCArray) following a procedure that ensures to keep the upper bound of the WorkingRTCArray dimensions preserved. As newly deployed RTCs enlarge the solution space RTC classes and/or variants may need to be dropped following some importance criteria.

Step 2: Triggering and handling the newly arrived requests: In this step, a TriggeredQueue is constructed from the WorkingRTCArray. Triggering a request from the WorkingRTCArray turns the Triggered property into true. Arrival times of requests are set greater or equal to NHP according to their TriggeringRange. The DeletionTime of requests that have to be deleted is set to the next updating point. If a request includes a set of dependent cells, we assume that their modified arrival times and deadlines are calculated offline following the rules of Modified Earliest Deadline First algorithm EDF* [23].

Step 3: Calculating the cost of quality factors for the system: The total cost of factors available by a node $Cost_{total}$ is calculated.

Step 4: Adaptation algorithm: In this step, we construct the lowest-cost feasible solution over the entire set of RTClasses stored in an AdaptationRTCArray which is constructed in the beginning of this step. This data structure further reduces the search space to be considered by excluding deleted cells and aperiodic cells that have their absolute deadline within the current hyperperiod. The reason for the latter exclusion is following the general assumption that adaptations become active not earlier than in the next hyperperiod.

To construct AdaptationRTCArray, we first copy variants of WorkingRTCArray into AdaptationRTCArray. We then reduce AdaptationRTCArray to contain only all classes of ExpPARTCs and such ExpAARTCs with absolute deadlines exceeding NHP. For each aperiodic ARTC that should be deleted and has an absolute deadline exceeding NHP, we add a column including the ARTC as the only variant. After that, we add a column that includes the AEC. We add the newly triggered requests, and finally the updating requests:

- Adding an aperiodic update is done (only if there exists an updating point after NHP in the aperiodic variant that is running) by adding the arrived RTClass which includes the triggered updating variant. The precise algorithm to identify the set of aperiodic ARTCs that can be updated and to calculate the time characteristics for the updates are omitted here. The number of those aperiodic ARTCs is denoted by NumOfANHP. The updated variant has been excluded when constructing ExpAARTCs.

- Adding a periodic update is done by adding the arrived RTClass, which includes the triggered updating variant to AdaptationRTCArray. The updated variant has been excluded when constructing ExpPARTCs.
- In case there is an update request for a set of aperiodic dependent RTCs the same rules as of updating a single (independent) variant are applied.

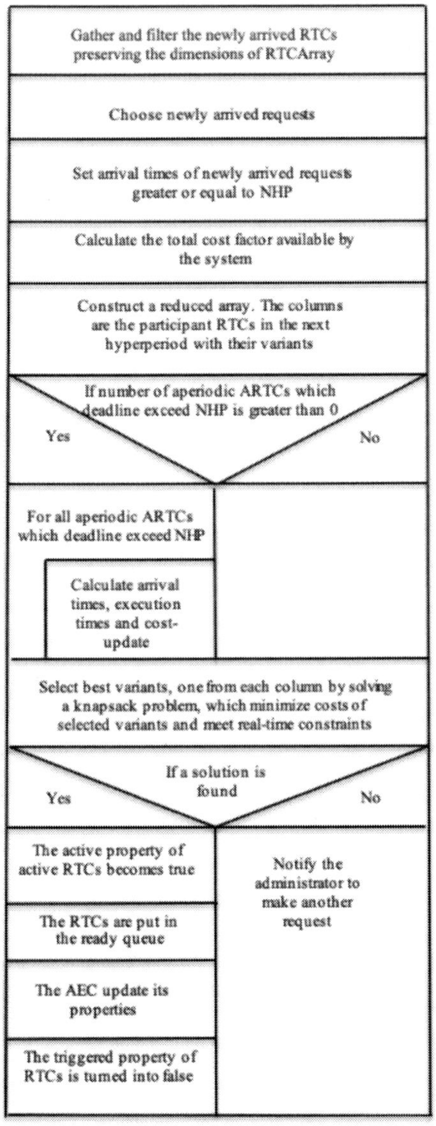

Figure 3. Nassi-Schneidermann Diagram for EC Algorithm

By the above operations, a reduced array is constructed that contains only those entries which are relevant for the adaptation algorithm. For technical reasons, the columns in the array are reordered, so that periodic columns come first, then AEC, and finally aperiodic columns.

Let us assume that the number of columns in Adaptation-RTCArray = Num. $\dot{N}$ denotes the number of columns, which represent the newly triggered aperiodic requests.

If (NumOfANHP $>$ 0) then we calculate arrival times, execution times, and Cost-Update for the running aperiodic ARTCs that are stored in AdaptationRTCArray, and deadlines exceed the NHP. The details of these calculations are omitted here.

The heart of the adaptation algorithm is to find a selection of variants for all RTC classes in the relevant ecosystem. This relevant ecosystem has been determined by the activities described above and stored in AdaptationRTCArray. The solution is a one dimensional array Solution that is assumed to contain one variant from each column in the AdaptationRTCArray. The chosen variants should pass the schedulability test of the Total Bandwidth Server (TBS) [20], and achieve the lowest possible accumulated cost.

To find the solution, we solve the following multiple choice multi dimensional knapsack problem.

$\max \sum_{i=1}^{Num} \sum_{j=1}^{n_i} -Cost_{ij} x_{ij}$

Subject to: $\sum_{i=1}^{Num} \sum_{j=1}^{n_i} W_{ij}^k x_{ij} \leq R^k$

Where:

$\sum_{j=1}^{n_i} x_{ij} = 1; i = 1..Num$ & $x_{ij} \in 0, 1$ and $j = 1..n_i$, k = 1:3

By Num is denoted the number of columns (RTC classes) in AdaptationRTCArray while by n_i is denoted the number of variants in the i_{th} column. Note that three constraints are formulated for the three values of parameter k. Constraint 1 handles periodic tasks including the AEC, constraint 2 the aperiodic ones, and constraint 3 is an optional one limiting the total cost. For these three constraints, the weights W^k and the constraining condition R^k are defined differently.

Constraint 1: $W_{ij}^1 = Factor_1 / Factor_2$

For any of the periodic RTCs: $Factor1 = C_{ij}$, $Factor2 = T_{ij}$

For the AEC, $Factor1 = WCET_{EC}$, $Factor2 = WCT_{ECTemp}$

WCT_{ECTemp} denotes the expected hyperperiod of the AEC. It is calculated the same way the initial hyperperiod is calculated. Here periodic cells are ExpPARTCs in AdaptationRTCArray, and newly triggered periodic requests in AdaptationRTCArray. Expected period of AEC is used instead of its current period. In each hyperperiod, only one execution of the AEC is assumed. For this reason, we finally update WCT_{ECTemp}, the expected period of the AEC, to be equal to the expected hyperperiod.

For any of the aperiodic RTCs: Factor1 = 0, Factor2 = 1

Constraint 2: $W_{ij}^2 = Factor1 - Factor2$

For any of the periodic RTCs and the AEC: Factor1 = 0, Factor2 = 0.

For any of the aperiodic RTCs: $Factor1 = d_{Specified,ij}$, $Factor2 = d_{Calculated,ij}$.

Where:

$d_{Specified,ij}$: The specified absolute deadline for any aperiodic variant, which belongs to an aperiodic variant in AdaptationRTCArray is equal to its arrival time + relative deadline of the variant.

By $d_{Calculated,ij}$ we denote the deadline calculated by the TBS rule.

$d_{Calculated,ij} = \max\left(d_{Calculated(i-1)j_{i-1}}, ArrivalTime_{ij}\right) + C_{ij,new}/U_s$.

$Us = 1 - Up$.

Constraint 3: Depending on the different kinds of RTCs to be considered in solving the knapsack problem, the weights W_{ij} for the optional third constraint are defined as follows:

W_{ij}^3 = Cost for periodic RTCs stored in AdaptationRTCArray

W_{ij}^3 = Cost for aperiodic RTCs that are stored in AdaptationRTCArray

After defining the weights of the different variants, we can start discussing the conditions. The constraining conditions R^k for the three constraints are defined as follows:

R^1 = 1(EDF constraint for periodic cells). R^2 = 0 (no aperiodic task missing its deadline). $R^3 = Cost_{total}$.

The limit $Cost_{total}$ is optional. If a solution is found, the newly arrived requests are accepted.

The algorithm which we are applying to solve the knapsack problem is a genetic algorithm. In the algorithm, an individual contains exactly one variant for each column in AdaptationRTCArray. In total, there exist up to f^h individuals. Each of them is a potential solution of the knapsack problem. We select smaller subsets of individuals and call them Generations. Let us assume that the number of individuals in a generation $\leq$ upper bound of number of RTCs in a class in the WorkingRTCArray. In the initial generation, the first individual is given by selecting from each RTClass the variant with the lowest respective utilization. This individual allows a simple decision whether a solution exists, as if this individual does not fulfill the constraints then there cannot exist any solution. If the knapsack constraint $\sum_{i=1}^{Num}\sum_{j=1}^{n_i} W_{ij}^k x_{ij} \leq R^k$ has a solution for a set of individuals, we choose the individual which minimizes the accumulated cost of the chosen RTCs. The lowest-cost individual of a generation is a preliminary solution of the knapsack problem. The previous operations are bounded by upper bounds of RTCArray dimensions, and the given time bound for the iteration. A generation is constructed from a previous one by applying selection and mutation. This process is iterated until no improvement can be observed or a given time limit is reached. The latter termination condition guarantees boundedness.

Step 5: Activate the accepted requests, and update the AEC: The Active property of accepted RTCs becomes true. They are put into the ready queue as managed by the underlying RTOS. The AEC updates its properties. Updating requests take place in the WorkingRTCArray. After that, AdaptationRTCArray is set to empty. Cells are still enforced when having them replaced by other variants because, by definition, updating points are designed for this reason. Values of still to be used variables are transmitted to the updating variants, and accomplishing the same functionality must be ensured by the developer.

Step 6: Turning the triggered requests into non-triggered: The Triggered Property of requests RTCs is turned into false. After that, WorkingRTCArray is copied to RTCArray if the solution is accepted, and then it is set to empty.

Step 7: Notify the system, in case the requests are not accepted. : Algorithm variables are reset to their initial values.

In [24] we modelled each of the previous steps by a Nassi-Schneidermann diagram [25]. This helps to understand the specification of code structure and points out the calculation of time complexity.

Concerning the time complexity of the developed adaptation algorithm, we can show that per single execution (i.e., once per hyperperiod) the algorithm can be solved in quadratic time in the number of RTC classes, variants and adaptation requests [24]. Parameters of time complexity are bounded. In case of solving the knapsack problem, this boundedness is enforced by setting an upper bound of execution time in the iterative genetic algorithm. Together with the fact that there are no unbounded blockings possible due to parameters not under control of the algorithm (assumption of Stack Resource Protocol included in the underlying RTOS) this implies the boundedness of the algorithm.

IV. CONCLUSION

In this paper, we have developed an approach that enhances real-time operating systems by an organic adaptability feature. This implies building an infrastructure of the system, which can change its behavior at runtime. The basic unit in this infrastructure is a cell. A cell is a task that can change its structure and behavior by selecting a variant of it at runtime. The way variants are chosen at runtime follows resource and time limitations, in order to enhance the quality of the system. The boundedness of our algorithm has been proven. Many new trends can be developed in the context of the described problem, such as distributing the central algorithm that is run by the Engine-Cell on several nodes in order to save more processor utilization on one node, obtaining fault tolerance, dealing with the boundedness of the algorithm in case of a non- deterministic network, such as in a multi-agent system, measuring the optimization output by running the algorithm on a real-time operating system and observing the results, and having several controlling cells other than the Engine-Cell or having several variants of it, etc.

REFERENCES

[1] E. A. Lee, "Cyber Physical Systems: Design Challenges," 11th IEEE Symposium on Object Oriented Real-Time Distributed Computing (ISORC), pp. 363-369, 2008.

[2] O. Imbusch, F. Langhammer, and G. von Walter, "Ercatons and Organic Programming: Say Good-Bye to Planned Economy," Dagstuhl Seminar Proceedings 2006.

[3] S. Oberthür, L. Zaremba, and H. Simon Lichte, "Flexible Resource Management for Self-X Systems: An Evaluation," in Proceedings of ISORCW2010.30, pp. 1-10, 2010.

[4] S. Oberthür, "Towards an RTOS for Self-Optimizing Mechatronic Systems, Dissertation," Paderborn, Germany, October 30, 2009.

[5] H. C. C. Betty at al. (Eds.), "Self-Adaptive Systems," LNCS 5525, pp. 1-26, Springer Verlag, Berlin Heidelberg, 2009.

[6] R. de Lemos et al. (Eds.), "Self-Adaptive Systems," LNCS 7475, pp. 1-32, Springer Verlag, Berlin Heidelberg, 2013.

[7] E. Burton Swanson, "The dimensions of maintenance," In Proceedings of the 2nd International Conference on Software Engineering (ICSE 1976), pp. 492-497. IEEE Computer Society Press, 1976.

[8] A. Carzaniga, A. Gorla, N. Perino, and M. Pezzè, "Automatic workarounds for web applications," In: FSE 2010: Proceedings of the 2010 Foundations of Software Engineering Conference, pp. 237-246. ACM, New York, 2010.

[9] A. Carzaniga, A. Gorla, and M. Pezzè, "Self-healing by means of automatic workarounds," In SEAMS 2008: Proceedings of the 2008 International Workshop on Software Engineering for Adaptive and Self-Managing Systems, pp. 17-24. ACM, New York, 2008.

[10] D. Garlan, S.W. Cheng, A.C. Huang, B. Schmerl, and P. Steenkiste, "Rainbow: Architecture-based self-adaptation with reusable infrastructure," IEEE Computer 37, pp. 46-54, 2004.

[11] IBM: "An architectural blueprint for autonomic computing," Tech. rep. IBM, January 2006.

[12] P. Oreizy et al., "An architecture- based approach to self-adaptive software," IEEE Intelligent Systems 14, pp. 54-62, 1999.

[13] Y. Brun and N. Medvidovic, "An architectural style for solving computationally intensive problems on large networks," In Proceedings of Software Engineering for Adapting and Self-Managing Systems, SEAMS 2007, Minneapolis, MN, USA, May 2007.

[14] I. Georgiadis, J. Magee, and J. Kramer, "Self-Organizing Software Architectures for Distributed Systems," In: 1st Workshop on Self-Healing Systems. ACM, New York, pp. 33-38, 2002.

[15] S. Malek, M. Mikic-Rakic, and N. Medvidovic, "A Decentralized Redeployment Algorithm for improving the Availability of Distributed Systems," In A. Dearle, R. Savani (eds.) CD 2005. LNCS, vol. 3798, pp 99-114. Springer, Heidelberg, 2005.

[16] P. Vromant, D. Weyns, S. Malek, and J. Andersson, "On interacting Control loops in self-adaptive systems," SEAMS 2011, Honolulu, Hawaii, pp. 202-207, 2011.

[17] D. Weyns, S. Malek, and J. Andersson, "On decentralized self-adaptation: lessons from the trenches and challenges for the future," In: Proceedings of the 2010 ICSE Workshop on Software Engineering for Adaptive and Self-Managing Systems, SEAMS 2010, pp. 84-93. ACM, New York, 2010.

[18] A. Duenas, C. Martinelly, and G. Tütüncü, "A Multidimensional Multiple-Choice Knapsack Model for Resource Allocation in a Construction Equipment Manufacturer Setting Using an Evolutionary Algorithm," APMS 2014, Part I, IFIP AICT 438, pp. 539-546, 2014.

[19] M. Hifi, M. Michrafy, and A. Sbihi, "Heuristic algorithms for the multiple-choice multidimensional knapsack problem," Journal of the Operational Research Society, Palgrave Macmillan, vol. 55, pp. 1323-1332, 2004.

[20] M. Spuri and G. C. Buttazzo, "Efficient Aperiodic Service under Earliest Deadline Scheduling," Real-Time Systems Symposium, pp. 2-11, 1994.

[21] T. P. Baker, "A Stack-Based Resource Allocation Policy for Realtime Processes," In: Proceedings of the IEEE Real-Time Systems Symposium (RTSS), pp. 191-200, 1990.

[22] L. Khaluf and F. Rammig, "Organic Programming of Real-Time Operating Systems," In the ninth international conference on Autonomic and Autonomous Systems (ICAS), pp. 57-60, 2013.

[23] H. Ghetto, M. Silly, and T. Bouchentouf, "Dynamic scheduling of real-time tasks under precedence constraints," Journal of Real-Time Systems, 2, pp. 181-194, 1990.

[24] L. Khaluf, "Organic Programming of Dynamic Real-Time Applications," a PhD thesis, file:///Users/lialkhaluf/Downloads/Modified%20Thesis-1%20(1).pdf, University of Paderborn, 2018.

[25] I. Nassi and B. Schneiderman, "Flowchart Techniques for Structured Programming," Technical Contributions, Sigplan Notices, pp. 12-26, 1973.

[26] G. Kiczales et al., "Aspect Oriented Programming," in ECOOP'97 — Object-Oriented Programming, pp. 220-242, 1997.

[27] R. Petrasch, O. Meimberg, "Model Driven Architecture," ISBN 3-89864-343-3, 2006.

[28] T. Benaya and E. Zur, "Understanding Object Oriented Programming Concepts in an Advanced Programming Course," in ISSEP 2008: Informatics Education - Supporting Computational Thinking pp. 161-170, 2008.

Funnel Control for a Class of High-Order Nonlinear Systems

Yong-Hua Liu and Chun-Yi Su

School of Automation
Guangdong University of Technology
Guangzhou, Guangdong 510006, China
Email: yonghua.liu@outlook.com, cysu@scut.edu.cn

***Abstract*—This paper addresses the problem of funnel output tracking control for a class of unknown high-order nonlinear systems with state feedbacks, which requires to achieve output tracking with prescribed accuracy when both the system nonlinearities and the powers of the system are unknown. Therefore, a robust funnel control algorithm, i.e., a continuous, static, universal, state-feedback controller is explicitly constructed, which ensures that the state errors evolve within the predesigned performance space. The advantages of the proposed funnel output tracking controller when compared with the current approaches lie in the fact that no *a priori* knowledge of system nonlinearities, including generally required bounding functions, is needed. Furthermore, all the powers in each high-order subsystem are not required to be known as well. A simulation example is provided to demonstrate the effectiveness of the proposed algorithm.**

Keywords–nonlinear systems; output tracking; funnel control; unstabilizable linearization.

I. INTRODUCTION

Owing to its practical significance and theoretical challenge, the control problem of high-order uncertain nonlinear systems has attracted considerable research effort. Significant progress in different directions, including adaptive regulation, output tracking control with state feedbacks, and finite-time stabilization [1]-[4], has been achieved by adding a power integrator technique and a homogeneous domination method. However, in all aforementioned developments, a priori knowledge of the system nonlinearities and the powers in each subsystem is needed.

Another important issue associated with the control design of unknown high-order nonlinear systems is the prescribed transient behaviour of the closed loop system. Recently, the work [5] introduced the concept of funnel control, which not only deals with unknown system nonlinearities, but also achieves the output tracking with prescribed performance. In particular, via the backstepping procedure, the funnel control methodology has been employed for various classes of nonlinear systems, such as Brunovsky, strict-feedback and pure-feedback systems. Working independently, an alternative approach, called Prescribed Performance Control, was proposed to achieve the same control objective [6]. Unfortunately, both schemes mentioned in [5]-[6] cannot be directly applied to high-order nonlinear systems even if the powers are precisely known, due to the singularity around the origin.

Motivated by the above discussions, this paper focuses on the output tracking problem with prescribed performance via state feedbacks for high-order nonlinear systems with unknown powers and functions. By combining the funnel control technique with barrier Lyapunov functions, the difficulty involved with the singularity problem can be avoided and a continuous, static, universal, state-feedback controller is explicitly constructed, which ensures the predesigned performance. In the proposed universal approach, the barrier Lyapunov functions are employed to enforce the unknown system nonlinearities to be bounded, making constructions of the adaptive laws or function approximators not necessary. Furthermore, the precise knowledge of all the powers in each subsystem is not needed to be known *a priori*. Thus, compared with the current state-of-the-art of the output tracking control, the proposed scheme relaxes significantly the common assumptions in the related works and represents a structurally simple and computationally inexpensive strategy. Finally, simulation results illustrate the effectiveness of the proposed theoretical findings.

The paper is organized as follows: In Section II, the problem addressed is stated. In Section III, the main result of this paper is presented without rigorous stability analysis. Further, in Section IV, a simulation example is provided to demonstrate the effectiveness of the proposed scheme. Conclusions are drawn in Section V.

II. PROBLEM FORMULATION

Notations: R denotes the set of real numbers. $R_{\geq 0}$ denotes the set of nonnegative real numbers. $R_{>0}$ denotes the set of positive real numbers. R^n denotes the real n-dimensional space. $\mathcal{W}^{1,\infty}(R_{\geq 0}, R_{>0})$ denotes the set of differential functions $\rho : R_{\geq 0} \to R_{>0}$ with ρ and $\dot{\rho}$ being essentially bounded on $R_{\geq 0}$.

Consider the following class of single-input-single-output (SISO) nonlinear systems:

$$\begin{aligned} \dot{x}_i &= d_i(t,x,u)x_{i+1}^{p_i} + \phi_i(t,x,u), \quad i = 1,...,n-1, \\ \dot{x}_n &= d_n(t,x,u)u^{p_n} + \phi_n(t,x,u), \\ y &= x_1, \end{aligned} \tag{1}$$

where $\bar{x}_i = [x_1,...,x_i]^T \in R^i$, $i = 1,...,n$; $x = \bar{x}_n = [x_1,...,x_n]^T \in R^n$ are the system states with initial condition $x^0 = [x_1^0,....,x_n^0]^T$, $u \in R$ is the control input, $y \in R$ is the output; p_i, $i = 1,...,n$ are the powers of the system; The system nonlinearities $d_i, \phi_i : R_{\geq 0} \times R^n \times R \to R$, $i = 1,...,n$ are locally Lipschitz in x and u, and piecewise continuous in t.

For simplicity of presentation, denote $x_{n+1} = u$. The following assumptions are made.

Assumption 1: The powers p_i, $i = 1,...,n$ are positive odd integers, which may be *unknown*.

Assumption 2: There exist unknown continuous and strictly positive functions $c_i : R^i \to R$ and $\bar{c}_i : R^{i+1} \to R$, $i = 1, ..., n$ such that

$$0 < c_i(\bar{x}_i) \leq d_i(t, x, u) \leq \bar{c}_i(\bar{x}_{i+1}), \ i = 1, ..., n. \quad (2)$$

Assumption 3: There exist unknown continuous non-negative functions $\bar{\phi}_{ij} : R^i \to R$, $i = 1, ..., n$, $j = 0, ..., p_i - 1$ such that

$$|\phi_i(t, x, u)| \leq \sum_{j=0}^{p_i-1} |x_{i+1}|^j \bar{\phi}_{ij}(\bar{x}_i), \quad i = 1, ..., n. \quad (3)$$

Assumption 4: The desired trajectory y_r is bounded, continuous and available, and $\dot{y}_r$ is bounded but its bound may not be available.

Remark 1: Assumptions 1-3 are sufficient conditions for global controllability of the system (1), which are extensively used in the literature [3]-[4]. It should be stressed that the developed controller in the sequel does not require the analytical expressions of system nonlinearities $d_i(t, x, u)$, $\phi_i(t, x, u)$ and their bounding functions $c_i(\bar{x}_i)$, $\bar{c}_i(\bar{x}_{i+1})$, $\bar{\phi}_{il}(\bar{x}_i)$, in contrast to some results in [3]-[4].

The *control objective* is to design a state-feedback controller

$$u = \alpha(t, x, y_r) \quad (4)$$

such that

- all signals in the closed loop system are globally bounded;
- the tracking error $e = y - y_r$ evolves within a prescribed performance funnel

$$\mathcal{F}_\rho := \Big\{(t, e) \in R_{\geq 0} \times R \Big| |e| < \rho_1 \Big\}, \quad (5)$$

  which is determined by a performance function $\rho_1 \in \mathcal{W}^{1,\infty}(R_{\geq 0}, R_{>0})$ incorporating the desired performance specifications.

III. Funnel Controller Design

In this section, we will construct a funnel controller for system (1) via barrier Lyapunov functions [7]. The design procedures of the proposed funnel controller are given as follows.

Step 1 : Preselect the first performance function $\rho_1 \in \mathcal{W}^{1,\infty}(R_{\geq 0}, R_{>0})$ that satisfies $\rho_1(0) > |x_1(0) - y_r(0)|$ and guarantees the desired performance specifications regarding the steady state error and the speed of convergence. Let $z_1 := e = x_1 - y_r$ and $\xi_1 := \frac{z_1}{\rho_1}$, then, the first virtual law is designed as

$$\alpha_1 = \frac{-k_1 \xi_1}{1 - \xi_1^2}, \quad (6)$$

where k_1 is a positive constant.

Step $i(i = 2, \cdots, n)$: Preselect the i-th performance function $\rho_i \in \mathcal{W}^{1,\infty}(R_{\geq 0}, R_{>0})$ that satisfies $\rho_i(0) > |x_i(0) - \alpha_{i-1}(0)|$. Define $z_i := x_i - \alpha_{i-1}$ and $\xi_i := \frac{z_i}{\rho_i}$, then, the i-th virtual and actual control laws are designed as

$$\alpha_i = \frac{-k_i \xi_i}{1 - \xi_i^2}, \quad (7)$$

$$u = \alpha_n, \quad (8)$$

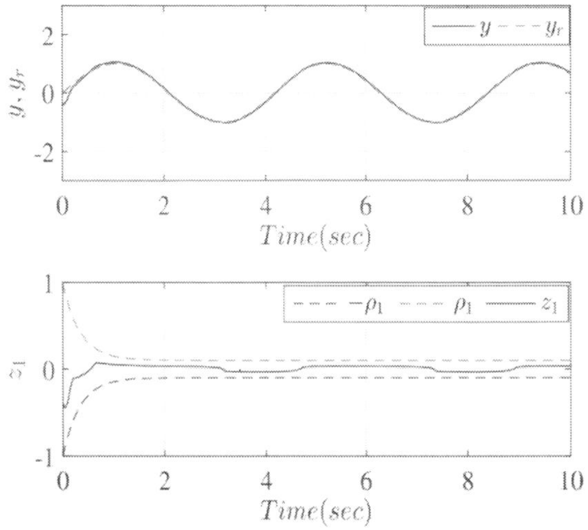

Figure 1. Output tracking performance.

where k_i is a positive constant.

Remark 2: The features of the proposed scheme lie in the fact that the exact knowledge of system nonlinearities, including generally required bounding functions, is not needed to be a priori, and all the powers in each high-order subsystem are allowed to be any unknown positive odd rational numbers. Moreover, compared with adaptive robust control approaches, no adaptive techniques are utilized in the developed controller.

Remark 3: In the proposed control design, the prescribed transient behaviour is imposed by appropriately selecting the performance function ρ_1, other controller parameters ρ_i, $i = 2, ..., n$, and k_i, $i = 1, ..., n$, are chosen flexibly according to the conditions $\rho_i(0) > |x_i(0) - \alpha_{i-1}(0)|$, $i = 2, ..., n$.

IV. A Simulation Example

To illustrate the correctness and effectiveness of the theoretical findings, we consider the following second order nonlinear system:

$$\begin{aligned} \dot{x}_1 &= (4 - \sin(x_1))x_2^3 + \sin(x_1)x_2 + x_1 e^{x_1 \cos(x_2)}, \\ \dot{x}_2 &= (3 + \sin(t))u^3 + \cos(x_1)e^{x_2 \sin(x_1)}, \\ y &= x_1, \end{aligned} \quad (9)$$

where the initial condition is $[x_1(0), x_2(0)]^T = [-0.4, 0.5]^T$. The control purpose is to force the output y to track the desired trajectory $y_r = \sin 1.5t$ with steady state error no more than 0.1 and minimum speed of convergence as obtained by the exponential e^{-3t}.

By selecting appropriately the design parameters and applying the proposed controller, the simulation result on the output tracking performance is presented in Figure 1, in which it can be observed that the prescribed performance of the tracking error is achieved.

V. Conclusion

This paper has studied the funnel output tracking problem for unknown high-order nonlinear systems. By combining the funnel control technique with barrier Lyapunov functions, we have exploited a constructive approach for designing the global universal controller, which achieves the predesigned performance of the state errors. Contrary to the current state-of-the-art of the output tracking control, the proposed funnel control does not incorporate any prior knowledge of system nonlinearities and the powers in each subsystem. Moreover, instead of utilizing adaptive laws or function approximators, the unknown system nonlinearities are guaranteed to be bounded via the barrier Lyapunov functions. Simulations performed on an illustrative example verify and clarify the theoretical findings. As a future work, we will apply the proposed method to an underactuated unstable two degree of freedom mechanical system [1].

REFERENCES

[1] C. Qian and W. Lin, "A continuous feedback approach to global strong stabilization of nonlinear systems," *IEEE Trans. Autom. Control*, vol. 46, no. 7, pp. 1061–1079, Jul. 2001.

[2] Q. Gong and C. Qian, "Global practical tracking of a class of nonlinear systems by output feedback," *Automatica*, vol. 43, no. 1, pp. 184–189, Jan. 2007.

[3] X.-J. Xie and N. Duan, "Output tracking of high-order stochastic nonlinear systems with application to benchmark mechanical system," *IEEE Trans. Autom. Control*, vol. 55, no. 5, pp. 1197-1202, May 2010.

[4] Z.-Y. Sun, L.-R. Xue, and K. Zhang, "A new approach to finite-time adaptive stabilization of high-order uncertain nonlinear system," *Automatica*, vol. 58, pp. 60–66, Aug. 2015.

[5] A. Ilchmann, E. P. Ryan, and C. J. Sangwin, "Tracking with prescribed transient behaviour," *ESAIM Control Optim. Calc. Var.*, vol. 7, pp. 471–493, 2002.

[6] C. P. Bechlioulis and G. A. Rovithakis, "A low-complexity global approximation-free control scheme with prescribed performance for unknown pure feedback systems," *Automatica*, vol. 50, no. 4, pp. 1217–1226, 2014.

[7] K. P. Tee, S. S. Ge, and E. H. Tay, "Barrier Lyapunov functions for the control of output-constrained nonlinear systems," *Automatica*, vol. 45, no. 4, pp. 918–927, 2009.

Software Architectural Style for Autonomic Cloud Computing

Zakarya A. Alzamil
Software Engineering Department
King Saud University
Riyadh, Saudi Arabia
e-mail: zakarya@ksu.edu.sa

Abstract— **Most of the autonomic cloud computing architectures are either a domain specific architecture or focus on certain properties of autonomic computing. In addition, they do not concentrate on the core issues related to the design and architectural concerns with respect to autonomic cloud computing in which the cloud can manage itself. In this paper, we propose a generic software architectural style for autonomic cloud computing systems that is based on a simplified layered approach. The proposed architectural style consists of five layers in which the bottom layer consists of cloud hardware/software resources, the second layer consists of a virtual machine that provides flexibility to service providers to utilize cloud resources, the third layer consists of an autonomic manager that manages cloud services, the fourth layer consists of a cloud service provider which provides services to cloud clients, and finally, the fifth and top layer represents the client layer that enables users to utilize the provided cloud services. This architectural style is a flexible and expandable software architecture solution for autonomic cloud computing systems, in which the service providers in the cloud can integrate their services within the architecture of the cloud computing software system. Additionally, this architecture enables the software architects to design and model their cloud computing software system in a flexible way that will maximize the reuse of existing cloud software components within their software system.**

Keywords- autonomic cloud computing; cloud computing architecture; software architecture; software architectural style; cloud computing architectural style.

I. INTRODUCTION

Cloud computing is a computing model that aims to provide services over the Internet by providing shared computing resources that are accessible by cloud service providers, as well as cloud clients. Cloud computing is defined by the National Institute of Standards and Technology (NIST) as "a model for enabling ubiquitous, convenient, on-demand network access to a shared pool of configurable computing resources (e.g., networks, servers, storage, applications, and services) that can be rapidly provisioned and released with minimal management effort or service provider interaction" [1]. A given cloud computing implementation can be viewed as a collection of interconnected computers that are presented as unified computing resources that provide services based on a certain service level agreement. Cloud computing provides different services. The most common cloud computing services are three service models: Software as a Service (SaaS), Platform as a Service (PaaS), and Infrastructure as a Service (IaaS). In addition, cloud computing may be deployed based on four deployment models: private cloud, community cloud, public cloud, or hybrid cloud [1][2]. Cloud computing relies on sharing of resources, as well as adaptation to existing technologies and paradigms without the need to know such technologies and paradigms. In addition, cloud computing adopts concepts from Service-Oriented Architecture (SOA) that can help users to breakdown the business problems into services that can be integrated to provide a solution. Cloud computing is widely used as a Web service that provides services at minimal management. The advantage of cloud computing is the flexibility of offering and delivering shared resources. Typically, the cloud service is a subscription-based service in a pay-as-you-go model. Cloud computing is a complex, large scale distributed system whose management is crucial in order to offer services in a reliable and timely manner. This requires the automation and integration of cloud service provision and management in an autonomic computing manner.

The autonomic computing model is derived from the human body autonomic nervous system [3] in which the computing system is capable of managing itself and can dynamically adjust to changes in policies without human intervention. The main property of autonomic computing is the self-management, which consists of self-configuration, self-optimization, self-healing, and self-protection [15]. Self-configuration is the system's ability to dynamically configure itself according to high-level policies, with the rest of system adjusting itself automatically and seamlessly. Self-optimization is the system's ability to automatically optimize its usage of resources and improve its performance and efficiency. Self-healing is the system's ability to automatically detect, diagnose, and repair localized software and hardware problems. Self-protection is the system's ability to automatically defend itself from malicious attacks or cascading failures, as well as from end users who accidentally make software changes, e.g., deleting an important file [3].

Software architecture deals with the design and implementation of the high-level structure of the software. It is the result of assembling a certain number of architectural elements in some well-chosen form to satisfy the major functional and non-functional requirements of a system, such as reliability, scalability, portability, and availability [4]. Software development based on common architectural idioms has its focus shifted from lines-of-code to coarser-grained architectural elements (software components and connectors) and their overall interconnection structure [5]. In order to understand the architectural style, one should understand the concept of software architecture. There are several definitions of software architecture. Perry and Wolf [6] define software architecture in terms of building blocks that are concerned with the selection of architectural elements, their interactions, and the constraints on those elements and their interactions necessary to provide a framework in which to satisfy the requirements and serve as a basis for the design. ISO/IEC/IEEE 42010 Standard [7] defines software architecture as "fundamental concepts or properties of a system in its environment embodied in its elements, relationships, and in the principles of its design and evolution". Bass et al. [8] define software architecture as the structure or structures of a system, which comprises software elements, the externally visible properties of those elements, and the relationships among them. These definitions identify the software architecture at the macro level as the software system's blueprint. The architectural style is determined by a set of element types, the topological layout of the elements indicating their interrelationships, a set of semantic constraints, and a set of interaction mechanisms that determine how the elements coordinate through the allowed topology [8]. Shaw and Clements [9] define the architectural style as a set of design rules that identify the kinds of components and connectors that may be used to compose a system or subsystem, together with local or global constraints on the way the composition is done. An architectural style determines the vocabulary of components and connectors that can be used in instances of that style, together with a set of constraints on how they can be combined. These can include topological constraints on architectural descriptions (e.g., no cycles) or some constraints on execution semantics [10].

In this paper, we propose an autonomic cloud computing architectural style for software systems that is based on a simplified layered approach. We have used the decision support system's architectural elements proposed in [11], as will be described in Section III, to support the self-management of autonomic cloud computing software systems. The proposed architectural style consists of five layers: cloud hardware/software resources layer, virtual machine layer, autonomic manager layer, cloud service providers layer, and client layer. This paper is organized as follows. In Section II, we describe the related works, and in Section III, we present our proposed approach. The conclusions are presented in Section IV.

II. RELATED WORK

Several studies have proposed architectural approaches for autonomic cloud computing. In [12], a software process based development approach for designing and building an autonomic cloud computing system is described. According to this approach, a sequence of software steps is followed for the complete design, such as control parameter identification, system model, system input identification, model identification, model update, system decision type, prediction creation, coordinator creation, data measurement, managed system control, and autonomic system control. A cluster of application servers running on top of a cloud is described as an application of autonomic management architecture to show how the development approach can be reconfigured for self-management and optimization for Web services.

A mechanism to implement autonomic cloud computing with the usage of information proxies is described in [13]. An information proxy provides useful information about a resource such as its state, works that need resources, overall resource utilization, etc. The proposed approach aims at improving the collaboration among peers in a large-scale network for the purpose of distributed resource scheduling. Results from the study showed that information proxies may improve the resource scheduling of large scale distributed systems. The information proxies help in building neighborhood nodes that contain information about the co-located nodes that share similar characteristics.

Artificial intelligence techniques such as multi agent and mobile computing are proposed in [14] for designing autonomic cloud computing. In this proposed approach, autonomous cloud agents are implemented with multi agent system which is capable of monitoring and correcting resource scheduling activities. The aim of this approach is to provide a monitoring system that facilitates autonomic clouds based on mobile agent computing. An agent enabled cloud consists of a mobile agent platform distributed on different virtual machines, and a software agent installed on the front-end to act as a proxy between the interface and agents.

An architectural blueprint for autonomic computing system is presented in [15]. The presented architecture constitutes layers that are connected using enterprise service bus patterns in which the layers collaborate using Web services. The basic building blocks of the layers include managed resources which contain system components such as hardware or software, knowledge sources such as interfaces for accessing and controlling the managed resources, autonomic managers that perform various self-management tasks to embody different intelligent control loops, and manual managers that provide a common system management interface for the informational technology professional using an integrated solutions console.

In [16], the authors explore the architectural features and requirements of cloud computing. General guidelines are presented to software architects and cloud developers for creating future architectures. The architectural requirements are classified according to the stakeholder of such software system such as cloud providers, the enterprises that use the cloud, and end-users.

A software defined cloud is proposed as an approach for automating the process of optimal cloud configuration [17]. Such optimization is obtained by extending the virtualization concept to all resources in a data center with emphasis on mobile cloud applications, in which a better quality of service can be obtained by easy reconfiguration and adaptation of physical resources in a cloud infrastructure.

In [18], a conceptual architecture of autonomic computing for cloud resources' management and provision that support SaaS applications is presented. The aim of such proposed model is to maximize efficiency and minimize the cost of services. In addition, the model aims at ensuring that the resource provisioning system is able to allocate resources only for requests from legitimate users.

An autonomic mobile cloud management framework is proposed in [21] for efficient service/resource management of mobile ad hoc cloud computing systems. The security and privacy of the proposed framework is investigated. The proposed framework uses mobile cloud application-enabling fabric to create and manage cloud applications in which a composition of autonomic cloud elements can be managed. Autonomic cloud elements can virtualize the physical resources, compose other elements, and communicate with other cloud elements using some common interface.

In [22], an elastic architecture is presented for autonomic cloud computing based on control loops and thresholds based rules. The experiment shows that cloud computing and autonomic computing may be leveraged together for elasticity provisioning. The proposed architecture enables the resources to be allocated and deallocated as needed, to adjust to the workload.

An autonomic Service Level Agreement (SLA) monitoring framework that is managed by trusted third party is proposed in [23]. The proposed framework uses calculation formulas to calculate the score of the cloud service providers and is composed of an SLA establishment module to support SLA generation and management, and a service monitoring module to monitor quality of service. The proposed framework is integrated into a real cloud based on the Apache CloudStack platform.

In [24], autonomic computing paradigm features have been used to Supervisory Control And Data Acquisition (SCADA) system's security by focusing on the self-protecting SCADA system. The proposed framework aims at leveraging autonomic computing elements to cope with cyber security threats and challenges to SCADA industrial applications. The hierarchical autonomic managers are incorporated within the framework to extract and refine inferences for decision making support.

Most of the aforementioned software architectures and frameworks are either a domain specific architecture or focus on certain properties of autonomic computing. We have observed that most of the existing studies of autonomic cloud computing did not concentrate on the core issues related to the design and architectural concerns with respect to autonomic cloud computing in which the cloud can manage itself. As stated earlier, cloud computing relies on sharing of resources, as well as adaption with existing technologies and paradigms without the need to know such technologies and paradigms which support independency of such cloud components. Therefore, we adopt a layered approach for our proposed architectural style to support independency among cloud components that support self-management in which each layer is independent from other layers. In addition, as discussed in the next Section, we have used the decision support system's architectural elements [11] that support autonomic manager to enhance the self-management of cloud resources. In the next section, we present our proposed architectural style for autonomic cloud computing software system.

III. AUTONOMIC CLOUD COMPUTING ARCHITECTURAL STYLE

The aim of the proposed software architecture is to propose a generic architectural style that serves as a software architecture foundation for autonomic cloud computing systems that are not limited to certain domain. As stated earlier, we have used the decision making subcomponents i.e., knowledge base, data mining/Online Analytical Processing (OLAP), and a judgmental heuristics of the decision support system approach that was described in [11] to propose an autonomic manager for cloud resources' self-management.

Cloud computing facilitates the accessibility to the shared computing resources by the cloud service providers. As a result, the software architectural style for such software system should be flexible and reusable to facilitate the interaction between the service providers and the computing shared resources. Therefore, the proposed architecture is based on a simplified layered approach, which supports flexibility and reusability of its components. Within the layered style, each layer is server to the layer above it and client to the layer below it.

Autonomic computing requires self-managing environments that, automatically, act and reflect the changes to cloud elements based on the observed changes, which can be achieved through employing an autonomic manager. The autonomic manager monitors and gathers required information from a system, analyzes collected information to detect whether it is necessary to take some action, creates a plan that describes the necessary changes, and executes the plan to implement these actions [19]. Monitoring cloud elements and/or services requires software or hardware sensors to capture the properties of such element or its related physical or virtual components within the environment, and an effector to adjust to the produced changes [20].

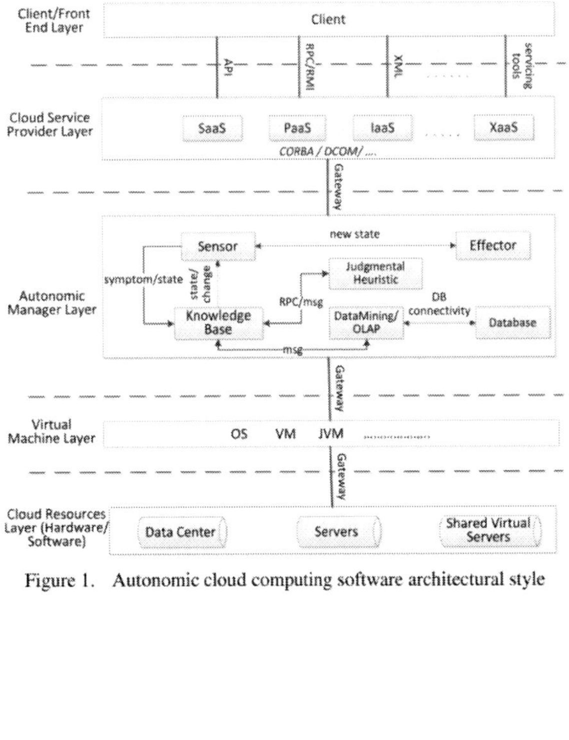

Figure 1. Autonomic cloud computing software architectural style

The proposed architectural style consists of five layers in which the bottom layer is the cloud hardware/software resources layer, the second layer is the virtual machine layer that provides flexibility to service providers to utilize cloud resources, the third layer is the autonomic manager layer which manages cloud services, the fourth layer is the cloud service provider layer that provides services to cloud clients to utilize, and the top layer is the client layer that enables the user to utilize the provided services. Figure 1 depicts the proposed software architectural style for autonomic cloud computing systems. In addition, the specification of the proposed architectural style is presented in Table I. In the following subsections, we briefly describe each layer of the proposed software architectural style for autonomic cloud computing starting from the bottom layer.

TABLE I. SPECIFICATION OF AUTONOMIC CLOUD COMPUTING ARCHITECTURAL STYLE

Item	Description
Element types	Standalone subsystems or components
Connectors	Typically procedure call Message passing
Topology layout	Hierarchical Multi-level client-server Each layer exposes an interface (API) to be used by above layers
Semantic constraints	Connectors are protocols of layer interaction Standardized layer interfaces to maintain layer independence
Interaction mechanisms	Each layer acts as a service provider to layers above and service consumer of layer below

A. *Cloud resources layer*

The cloud resources layer is the bottom layer that contains all hardware and software resources including the shared resources. It consists of data centers, servers, and other shared virtual resources. The cloud resources layer is the infrastructure of cloud computing system and it may include commercialized, as well as public domain and open source resources. This layer is interconnected with the virtual machine layer via a gateway, which can be defined as a proxy to maximize the independency among the different layers.

B. *Virtual machine layer*

The virtual machine layer contains the operating system or virtual machine that facilitates the environment to link cloud services to cloud resources. It operates as an interface between the cloud service providers and cloud resources to maximize the utilization of such resources by cloud services and, at the same time, to minimize the incompatibility among the Web services and the available cloud resources. This layer is connected to the layer above via a gateway which acts as a proxy between the two layers. It should be noticed that this layer may be skipped in the case where a service and the resource belong to the same platform and they have a well-defined connector. In such case, there is no need for a virtual machine to be in the middle.

C. *Autonomic manager layer*

This layer is the autonomic manager which is responsible for providing the self-management of cloud services. The autonomic manager is a configurable software and/or hardware component that consists of sensor, effector, and a decision making subcomponents i.e., knowledge base, data mining/OLAP, and judgmental heuristics. The autonomic manager monitors the managed resources and cloud services, in which the sensor collects data about cloud elements to monitor their states. When symptoms are discovered, the element state is identified and passed to the knowledge base to check whether an update of such state is available. The knowledge base looks for a fact or rule that is applicable for such element's state, in which a prediction of such state change is identified by the data mining or OLAP approach. OLAP is a business intelligence technique that helps in discovering some knowledge by extracting data from the database and viewing it from different points-of-view. The data mining explores data from the database and puts it into the knowledge base of the expert system to make knowledge-based reasoning for quantitative analysis to aid decision making. In other words, the data mining aims to discover new knowledge by extracting information from a database, analyzing it from different perspectives, and transforming it into an understandable structure of knowledge for further use. In some cases, there is a need for human intervention and/or interpretation to collect some information from human experts to identify the element's state change. In such cases, the system may use judgmental heuristics, which is a normative approach that aims to support the human in combing many factors into an optimal decision. Judgmental heuristics use a decision-analytic approach that applies the principles of decision theory and/or probability theory into the decision analysis. The normative system is based on graphical probabilistic models, i.e., probability distribution over model variables in terms of directed graph, also known as influence diagram. The database at this layer can be a traditional database, relational database, or multidimensional database. The database structure, e.g., the blackboard, as well as the components operating on it, are managed by a database management system (DBMS). In addition, such sub-system is controlled by the blackboard state. The autonomic manager identifies the element's new state, such as new configuration, new usage for an element, better optimization or utilization, fixing problem, or fixing security vulnerability. The new state and a request of change are passed from the sensor to the effector to execute such state change.

D. *Cloud service provider layer*

This layer consists of cloud services, such as Software as a Service (SaaS), Platform as a Service (PaaS), and Infrastructure as a Service (IaaS). In addition, it may contain any other cloud services which we describe as "X as a

Service (XaaS)". This layer provides the environment of such cloud services offered by the cloud service providers. This layer is connected to the layer above via different types of connectors such as Remote Procedure Calls (RPC), Remote Method Invocation (RMI), Application Programming Interface (API), or Extensible Markup Language (XML).

E. Client/Front end layer

This layer represents the cloud client or the front end user, which is the consumer of cloud services. This layer enables the client to request any available service using servicing tools that may utilize different technologies. Each service within this layer is defined using a specific connector, in which the client may utilize the Web services via the identified connector such as RPC, RMI, XML, API, or any other servicing tool connector.

IV. CONCLUSION

In this paper, we have introduced a software architectural style for autonomic cloud computing systems. The proposed architecture style is based on a simplified layered approach, and consists of five layers: a cloud hardware/software resources layer, a virtual machine layer, an autonomic manager layer, a cloud service provider layer, and a client layer. Within the layered style, each layer is a server to the layer above it, and a client to the layer below it.

The proposed software architectural style can accommodate most cloud computing software systems for different domains. In addition, this architectural style minimizes the dependency among its components which can enhance the reusability, integration with other software systems, and expandability. Such feature will enable software architects to design and model their cloud computing software system in a flexible way that will maximize the reuse of existing cloud software components within their software system.

The proposed architectural style is an abstract framework prototype for autonomic cloud computing software systems, and in order to understand its advantages and/or limitations, an experimental and investigation study is needed to judge the applicability of such framework on real autonomic cloud computing systems. We plan to conduct an experimental study using some commercial cloud software systems and perform a comparison study with the existing relevant architectural styles to better understand the advantages of such proposed software architecture.

REFERENCES

[1] P. Mell and T. Grance, "The NIST definition of cloud computing", Special Publication 800-145, National Institute of Standards and Technology, U.S. Department of Commerce, 2011.

[2] C.S. Yoo, "Cloud computing: architectural and policy implications", Review of Industrial Organization, Vol. 38, No. 4, June 2011, pp. 405-421.

[3] J. O. Kephart and D. M. Chess, "The vision of autonomic computing", IEEE Computer, 36(1) , Jan. 2003, pp. 41-50.

[4] P. Kruchten, "Architectural blueprints - the "4+1" view model of software architecture", IEEE Software 12 (6), November 1995, pp. 42-50.

[5] N. Medvidovic and R. Taylor, "A classification and comparison framework for software architecture description languages", IEEE Transactions on Software Engineering, Vol. 26, No. 1, January 2000, pp. 70-93.

[6] D. Perry and A. Wolf, "Foundations for the study of software architecture", ACM SIGSOFT Software Engineering Notes, Vol. 17, No. 4, October 1992, pp. 40-52.

[7] ISO/IEC/IEEE 42010:2011(E), "Systems and software engineering-Architecture description", IEEE/ISO/IEC, First edition, December 2011.

[8] L. Bass, P. Clements, and R. Kazman, Software Architecture in Practice, SEI series in Software Engineering, 2nd Edition, Addison-Wesley, 2003.

[9] M. Shaw and P. Clements, "A field guide to boxology: preliminary classification of architectural styles for software systems", IEEE Proceedings of the 21st Annual International Computer Software and Applications Conference, COMPSAC '97, 1997, pp. 6-13.

[10] D. Garlan and M. Shaw, "An introduction to software architecture", CMU Software Engineering Institute Technical Report, CMU-CS-94-166, January 1994.

[11] Z. Alzamil, "Software architectural style for decision support systems", Proceedings of the 11th International FLINS Conference on Decision Making and Soft Computing (FLINS2014), World Scientific Proceedings Series on Computer Engineering and Information Sciences, Vol. 9, August 2014, pp. 3-10.

[12] B. Solomon, D. Ionescu, M. Litoiu, and G. Iszlai, "Designing autonomic management systems for cloud computing", IEEE International Joint Conference on Computational Cybernetics and Technical Informatics (ICCC-CONTI) , 2010, pp. 631–636.

[13] D. C. Erdil, "Dependable autonomic cloud computing with information proxies",. IEEE International Symposium on Parallel and Distributed Processing Workshops and Phd Forum (IPDPSW) , 2011, pp. 1518– 1524.

[14] A. Cuomo, M. Rak, S. Venticinque, and U. Villano, "Enhancing an autonomic cloud architecture with mobile agents", Euro-Par 2011, Parallel Processing Workshops, 2012, pp. 94–103.

[15] IBM, "An architectural blueprint for autonomic computing", white paper, 3rd Edition, june 2005, http://www-03.ibm.com/autonomic/pdfs/AC%20Blueprint%20White%20Paper%20V7.pdf, [retrieved: September, 2018].

[16] B. Rimal, A. Jukan, D. Katsaros, and Y. Goeleven, "Architectural requirements for cloud computing systems: an enterprise cloud approach", Journal of Grid Computing, Vol. 9, 2011, pp. 3-26.

[17] R. Buyya, R.N. Calheiros, J. Son, A. Dastjerdi, and Y. Yoon, "Software-defined cloud computing: architectural elements and open challenges", 3rd International Conference on Advances in Computing, Communications and Informatics (ICACCI 2014), September 24-27, 2014.

[18] R. Buyya, R.N. Calheiros, and Li Xiaorong, "Autonomic cloud computing: open challenges and architectural elements," Third International Conference on Emerging Applications of Information Technology (EAIT), Nov. 30-Dec. 1 2012, pp. 3-10.

[19] M. Maurer, I. Breskovic, V. C. Emeakaroha, and I. Brandic, "Revealing the mape loop for the autonomic management of cloud infrastructures", IEEE Symposium on Computers and Communications (ISCC) , 2011, pp. 147–152.

[20] M. Huebscher and J. McCann, "A survey of autonomic computing - degrees, models and applications", ACM Computing Surveys, Vol. 40, No. 3, Article No. 7, August 2008, pp. 7-28.

[21] D. M. Shila, W. Shen, Y. Cheng, X. Tian, and X. Shen "AMCloud: Toward a secure autonomic mobile ad hoc cloud computing system", IEEE Wireless Communications, April 2017, pp. 74-81.

[22] E. F. Coutinho, P. A. Rego, D. G. Gomes, and J. Neuman de Souza "An architecture for providing elasticity based on autonomic computing

concepts", Proceedings of the 31st Annual ACM Symposium on Applied Computing, 2016, pp. 412-419.

[23] A. Maarouf, Y. Mifrah, A. Marzouk, and A. Haqiq "An autonomic SLA monitoring framework managed by trusted third party in the cloud computing", International Journal of Cloud Applications and Computing, Volume 8, Issue 2, April-June 2018, pp. 66-95.

[24] S. Nazir, S. Patel, and D. Patel "Autonomic computing architecture for SCADA cyber security", International Journal of Cognitive Informatics and Natural Intelligence, Volume 11, Issue 4, October-December 2017, pp. 66-79.